CHRIST AND CULTURE IN DIALOGUE

CHRIST AND CULTURE IN DIALOGUE

Constructive Themes and Practical Applications

Edited by

Angus J. L. Menuge, General Editor

William R. Cario
Alberto L. García
Dale E. Griffin

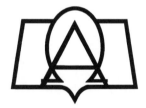

Concordia Academic Press

A Division of

Concordia Publishing House

Saint Louis, Missouri

Library of Congress Cataloging-in-Publication Data

Christ and Culture in Dialogue : constructive themes and practical applications / edited by
    Angus J. L. Menuge, general editor . . . [et al.] .].
        p.   cm.
    ISBN 0-570-04273-9
    1. Christianity and culture. 2. Two kingdoms (Lutheran theology). 3. Lutheran Church—
Doctrines.   I. Menuge, Angus, J. L.
BX8065.2.C48   1999
261—dc21   99-13295

Contents

Foreword

Carl E. Braaten

The first sentence of the introduction of Paul Tillich's *Systematic Theology* reads: "Theology is a function of the church, and must serve the needs of the church." This is a wise imperative coming from one who is generally classified—and dismissed—as a "theologian of culture." In applying his question-and-answer method, Tillich has been criticized by many, especially Barthians, as giving more weight to the questions arising out of contemporary culture than to the answers based on the Christian message. But that was not his intention. He was aware that theology always stands at the crossroads of decision, either to serve Christ and His church or succumb to the Babylonian Captivity of one's private religious experience, some fashionable philosophy, moral crusade, or political ideology. After all, Tillich personally paid the high price of exile for his opposition to the culture of German national socialism.

This brief foreword will aim to recommend and expound the unifying viewpoint that links the chapters of this book together. Various authors call this viewpoint "the paradoxical vision," which entails the doctrine of the two kingdoms, the belief that Christians are simultaneously "saints and sinners," as well as the crucial significance of making the proper distinction between Law and Gospel. It is salutary to bear in mind that Christians are called to be "in but not of" the world in which they live. Christians are admonished by Paul in Romans 12:2, "Do not be conformed to this world, but be transformed by the renewing of your minds. So that you may discern what is the will of God—which is good and acceptable and perfect." The authors of this book, *Christ and Culture in Dialogue: Constructive Themes and Practical Applications,* have jumped right into the "Christ and culture" wars going on in the contemporary academic study of religion and theology. The book recalls not only the title of H. Richard Niebuhr's classic, *Christ and Culture*, but also provides a vigorous defense of the

Lutheran model Niebuhr called "Christ and Culture in Paradox." The authors, most of them self-conscious Lutherans, have mastered the categories applicable to a constructive reappropriation of a dialectical interpretation of Luther's doctrine of the two kingdoms.

Today the Lutheran sense of the difference between the two kingdoms offers a bulwark against the cultural accommodation of theology. Much of contemporary theology is in bondage to what lies outside the circle of Christian faith, to one or another kind of cultural *ism*. Theologians are legion who promote the progressive agendas of therapeutic religion, multicultural ideology, inclusivity quotas, new age spirituality, entertainment evangelism, pantheistic eco-mysticism, radical theological feminism, gay and lesbian liberationism, and a host of other politically correct concerns. This is to do theology from the outside in rather than from the inside out.

In making a case for the Lutheran way of relating the Gospel and contemporary culture, the authors of this book are fully aware of the pitfalls that have historically accompanied a dualistic understanding of the two-kingdom model. A common failure has been to separate the two kingdoms, to seal off the kingdom on the right hand from what's going on in the kingdom on the left hand, ending up with an extreme dualism. This would mean that the kingdom of grace and love (right hand) might have a profound effect upon the inner life of an individual's faith without having anything to do with the kingdom of power and justice (left hand) at work in the realm of social and political life. Dichotomy, not dialectic, would then characterize the relations between Christ and culture.

The stress on the two kingdoms cautions against two possible dangers, that of a "Christianization of society" by ecclesiastical heteronomy, remaking the world into the image of the church, or a "secularization of the church," remaking the church into the image of the world. Both of these dangers can be avoided, without remaining impaled on the dualism of the two kingdoms, by reactivating "the paradoxical vision" as the authors of this book have done with remarkable success.

Niebuhr's treatment of Luther's view of the "Christ and culture" issue has contributed to a merciless attack on its allegedly dualistic and dichotomous character. This book demonstrates that Luther was not dualistic in this sense. For dualism involves radical separation of the doctrine of salvation from the doctrine of creation, as though it were not precisely this created world in all its dimensions that God so loved (John 3:16) and reconciled unto Himself in Christ (2 Corinthians 5:19). Dualism is wrong because it fails to recognize that the One God in Three Persons is the creator, redeemer, and consummator of the world. Dualism means that God's message in Christ would be related only to the inner-life and the after-life, surrendering the life of the body in all its present worldly entailments to other lords and powers. The problem with dualistic thinking is that it fosters dichotomies, rather than proper distinctions, between sacred and secular, spiritual and physical, private and public, religion and politics, temporal life and eternal life. Such a dichotomy prevents the salvation God has wrought in Jesus Christ from reaching the totality of life in all its dimensions. That would mean that important dimensions of the common life, many of them taken up in this book, would be declared out of bounds for the church as the community of the endtime, keeping it paralyzed, merely passive, as to what in the world to do in the meantime.

The authors capitalize on the strong points in what Robert Benne calls "the paradoxical vision." There are elements of truth that none of the other models in Niebuhr's scheme adequately embraces. In distinguishing the two kingdoms, both of which are God's, it is possible to develop a theology which sees power as the "strange work" of God's love. This is an important insight, because many an ethic of love has withered when confronted by a show of power. The two-kingdoms ethic says that Christians are not to retreat from power situations in the secular realm, because that realm is God's and He is the source of all power. Christians may thus "occupy civil offices or serve as princes and judges, render decisions and pass sentence according to imperial and other existing laws, punish evil doers with the sword, engage in just wars, serve as soldiers, buy and sell, take required oaths, possess property, be married, etc." (Augsburg Confession, Article XVI). This approach is diametrically opposed to those sectarians who withdraw from the world and eschew social and political responsibility.

The authors remind us that while there are two kingdoms, there is only one King. The lives of Christians are inescapably enmeshed in the communion of saints and the orders of creation, in the church and the world. While preserving at all costs institutional separation, say, between church and state, Christians should whenever possible work for "functional interaction," encouraging harmony, cooperation, and mutual good will. The two realms come together and overlap in the person of each individual Christian, whose faith is vertically related to God in worship as well as horizontally active in love in the service of others.

The dynamic of the Christian life in the world is the forgiveness of sins. One can joyfully be engaged in all sorts of cultural activities without having to find one's justification in them. The kingdom on the left hand of God is the realm in which the phenomena of law and justice, reason and power, threats and punishments, hold sway. The kingdom on the right hand is the realm of God's saving work in Christ, realized on earth through the church's preaching of the Gospel and the administration of the sacraments. In this realm the phenomena of faith and love, joy and peace, hope and freedom—all the gifts of the Spirit—prevail.

A non-dualistic interpretation and application of the doctrine of two kingdoms relate saving faith in God to loving action in the world, God's redemptive role in Christ to His political purposes in Caesar's realm. If dualism is inadequate, monism is equally so, for monism cannot tolerate the two-dimensional reference, first to human existence in the world as it is and, secondly, to that eschatological dimension of the life of the world to come. Two-dimensional thinking allows for the relative difference between what God is doing in the world of business, politics, and culture generally, and what the Gospel promises He has done in Christ for the final salvation of humankind in particular. Without this bifocal aspect we would join those who strive for a merger of Christianity and civilization such as we have in American civil religion.

Another strong point brought out in these chapters, especially in the chapters by Robert Kolb and Martin Marty, is the simultaneity of Christian existence in the two kingdoms. The Christian life is to be lived under the conditions of world history, permitting no premature escape into another world. The notion of simultaneity does not lead to a split in the person, the soul on an Icarian flight to another realm, and the body dragging along by ball and chain in this one. Two-dimensional thinking defined by the confession of Christ the King rather calls for the splitting of time between the qualities of life B.C. and A.D., but not the splitting of the self into body and soul.

The two-kingdoms doctrine teaches that God has more than one way of acting. God has both Law and Gospel ways of acting in the world. The authors of this book have learned that Law and Gospel are neither to be separated nor identified, but properly distinguished, as the patriarch from Missouri, C. F. W. Walther, taught with unforgettable force in his classic work, *The Proper Distinction between Law and Gospel,* a book which my first-year homiletics professor, Dr. Herman Preus of blessed memory, had every student outline chapter by chapter. Without a proper distinction we could easily slip into a one-dimensional pattern of thinking, making the Law into good news and the Gospel into bad news. The Gospel is the good news that God has acted in the exodus of Israel and the resurrection of Jesus to bring all things to their ultimate fulfillment in the kingdom of glory. And the Law is the means of the hidden God to keep people under pressure to meet the minimum demands of justice, to hold nations accountable for their actions, and to stipulate punishment to those who violate the righteous and holy will of God.

The two kingdoms are both anchored in God's will, so that what goes on in the world is as much God's concern as what goes on in the church. There is no such thing as a secular world spinning on its own axis, no such thing as autonomous social, political, and economic structures following their own laws, no such things as secular authorities who can become a law unto themselves. They are all God's agents in the drama of the world-historical process.

This "paradoxical vision" means that God has appointed some to be ministers to Christ's church and others to be administrators in the orders of creation. The authorities in this world are not to be feared as little gods, nor condemned as devils. Within limits they can perform the will of God in exerting pressure for good, for freedom, peace, and justice. Bad as it is, corrupted by sin and evil, and in thrall to the satanic powers of darkness, this world still belongs to God and He is very much in charge and at work within its structures, even apart from the ministrations of the church. God raises up servants to care for His world, whether they believe in the Gospel or not.

Therefore, on the basis of the two-kingdom paradigm we affirm with sobering realism the depth of sin and the power of the demonic in social and political life. This precludes every naive utopianism. When commitment to utopia is challenged by the grim realities of sin and the demonic, it easily turns into disillusionment and despair, and finally apathy and suicide. However, the alternative to utopianism is not pessimistic resignation in the face of sin and evil, rendering the situation so hopeless that all we could do is build dikes against their chaotic and destructive consequences.

At stake in deciding for or against a two-kingdoms model of "Christ and culture"—the paradoxical vision—is whether we as believers have confidence in the gospel-faith of the church to shape the culture of the world (examples: the history of art and music) and thereby the future well-being of humanity, and not only to secure the salvation of individuals for the hereafter.

The two-kingdoms doctrine also says: let the church be the church. If the church hankers to do what every other agency in the world is determined to do, thinking it can do it better, it may neglect doing the one thing altogether needful—preaching the Gospel to those who do not yet believe. We can be sure of one thing: if the church does not preach the Gospel of salvation in the name of Jesus, no one else will. The world needs the church to relativize the ideals, idols, and ideologies of the world, to keep them from claiming the kind of ultimate validity and supreme authority that belong solely to God and the Gospel of Jesus Christ.

Ecclesia semper reformanda is a slogan of our Reformation heritage. The church is always in need of being reformed and renewed. What shall we do in a situation when culture drives the church, when the church becomes an agency for the religious culture of today? Traditional beliefs, rituals, symbols, sacraments, and practices are set aside wholesale to appeal to the consumers of American religion; what remains is Christianity-lite.

The church will need to take much more seriously what it means to be the church, and forget about trying to be a supermarket satisfying the needs of consumers who shop around for titillating religious entertainment. The paradoxical vision of which these authors write is exactly what the church needs now, to help it to exist in a society that is at once highly secularized and still very religious. The church will need to heighten its sense of the difference between Christ and culture, between the City of God and the earthly city, its sense of being *in* but not *of* the world.

The Reverend Dr. Carl E. Braaten is Executive Director, Center for Catholic and Evangelical Theology, Northfield, Minnesota

Introduction

Angus J. L. Menuge

The Motivation and Origin of this Book

As a foreigner who has lived in America for 12 years, I have noticed a tendency toward two unhealthy extremes in the public religious imagination, two fundamentalisms, as it were. One is the familiar separatist form, characterized by Christians who blankly reject culture and who yearn for their own spiritually purified community: this is Christian fundamentalism. The other form is fueled by the relentless attempt to accommodate Christianity to whatever is "happening now" in societal praxis and (in its more intellectual form) to the pronouncements of the culture-shaping ideologues currently in vogue: this is cultural fundamentalism. There are many American Christians who strive to eschew both extremes, but the influence of these fundamentalisms is clear in the popularity of two caricatures which have helped secularizers in their attempts to exclude Christianity from public life.

One of these stereotypes portrays the Christian as the fire-breathing denizen of a ghetto, a member of the nebulous "religious right" who is possibly mentally ill, liable to intolerant ranting and sometimes violence, and certainly unable to function in civil society. This picture is used to justify the legislative removal of Christianity from the public square. The other caricature paints a Christian whose attitude to culture resembles that of a lackey to Cruella De Vil (as portrayed by Glenn Close) in the recent movie remake of *101 Dalmations*. Cruella screams, "What sort of sycophant *are* you?!" The lackey replies, "What sort of sycophant would you like?" In this image, the Christian is an intellectually dishonest quisling who curries favor with the cultured despisers of religion aiming, above all else, to be *accepted*. To be embarrassed, to be excluded, to have to take a stand, in short, to carry one's cross in the public square, these are anathema in this vision of the Christian. This picture encourages neutered Christians, safe to enter the public square because they bring nothing new to it. Tragically, there are individuals who fit these stereotypes, and more who fit the second than the first.

Of course, neither of these fundamentalisms stands up to scrutiny. But their influence reveals the need to awaken the public religious imagination from its dogmatic slumbers, to restore a living dialectic in thinking about Christ and culture. In his seminal work on the subject, *Christ and Culture*, H. Richard Niebuhr did just that. But this was almost half a century ago, and each new generation needs to re-think these issues and apply them to current cultural debates. At the same time, as Mark Noll so helpfully chided, there has not been enough publicly visible effort to elucidate "the Lutheran difference," the distinctive merits of the Lutheran account of Christ and culture. These considerations motivated the Lecture Series on Christianity and Culture which I organized at Concordia University Wisconsin in the fall of 1996. It was out of this series and subsequent presentations that the current volume grew.

As I looked around for potential contributors to the Lecture Series, Martin Marty's name was suggested as the keynote speaker. He seemed the obvious choice, but some opined that he would be unlikely to come and that there might be dire consequences (for me) if he did. This, of course, made me all the more determined to invite Dr. Marty, and, so far from unleashing an inquisition, it proved to be a valuable lesson in grace. It turned out that Dr. Marty had been wanting to visit his *alma mater*; unbeknownst to me at that time, Marty had graduated from Concordia's Milwaukee campus fifty years prior. Marty gave a superb, confessionally Lutheran address, thoughtful, sophisticated and sparkling with wit. At the end, some of the most conservative members of our church body shook Dr. Marty's hand in appreciation, and, for a brief moment, one had a glimpse of what things might have been like had there been no schism in the American Lutheran church.

Certainly it was my intention that the Lecture Series would have a strong Lutheran emphasis, particularly as the Lutheran perspective on Christ and culture is so often neglected in the public religious imagination. However, if Lutherans are to do public theology and if they are to clarify where they agree and disagree with other traditions, they must dialogue with Christians of other denominations. Furthermore, there are many issues, such as religious persecution and secularization in both society in general and education in particular, which are of general interest to all Christians, and concerning which there is valuable work by Christians of many persuasions. Finally, we lack the courage of our convictions, and a willingness to inform and be informed by those of different traditions, if we only preach to the choir or only invite our own choir members to sing. Thus in the present volume, we are privileged to include the contributions of three non-Lutherans, Wayne Martindale, Patrick Riley (note the obviously Lutheran name), and Michael Ward. Contributions from women were solicited and, indeed, one woman gave a superb presentation in the Lecture Series but declined to contribute it to this volume. While it is a shame that in the end none of the women invited were able to contribute, it is at least heartening that this was often because of prior commitments, showing how very much in demand their work is.

An Outline of the Book

The main structure of this book is straightforward. The first part, "Constructive Themes," lays out the alternative approaches to Christ and culture, and elucidates and defends a distinctively Lutheran stance. In this light, the second part, "Historical, Contemporary and International Themes," pursues the dialogue between Christ and culture as it applies to more concrete social issues of the past and present. The perspectives of both West and East are included. The third part, "The Church and Church-Based Education in Culture," is focused more narrowly on the institutions of the church, exploring the tensions between Christ and culture in worship, evangelism, and the accreditation and curriculum of Christian colleges.

Constructive Themes

The classic text for this book's topic is Niebuhr's *Christ and Culture*. My own chapter offers an introductory explanation and critical evaluation of this work and defends the Lutheran perspective. Martin Marty follows with a deeper exposition of the resources available to the Lutheran "*simul*" or paradoxical understanding of Christ and culture. He shows how the faithful Christian must simultaneously embrace "articles of war" and "articles of peace" in his or her interactions with culture. Marty does not try to sort out all of the details but clarifies the fundamentals and invites further discussion.

Alberto García presents his reflections in dialogue with the work of Latin theologians, focusing on an important area of common ground between their work and confessional Lutheran theology: a strong emphasis on the two natures in Christ. García shows that a fundamental weakness of Niebuhr's approach, which leads to distortions in his account of the paradox view, is his neglect of fundamental Christology. By returning to Chalcedon and its ramifications in Latin theology, García shows how a correct Christology steers between the Scylla of cultural relativism (Christ is God, and His Gospel is universal) and the Charybdis of ethnocentrism (Christ is man, and He welcomes the particularity of all peoples). As García argues, this creates the potential for an effective answer to the challenges of postmodernism.

Robert Kolb finds much to agree with in Niebuhr's portrait of the Lutheran stance. Yet, controversially, he challenges Niebuhr's acceptance of the widespread view that Luther's "two kingdoms" are paradoxical. Kolb does not deny the existential paradoxes in the life of Christ and the individual Christian, but he does deny that the "vertical" realm of faith and grace is itself in a paradoxical relation with the "horizontal realm" of works of love. He argues that while our relationship with God is two-dimensional, these dimensions are in themselves complementary rather than paradoxical. Kolb goes on to show the relevance of a two-dimensional approach to public theology, focusing on the issues of civic responsibility, witness, and mission.

Historical, Contemporary, and International Themes

Gene Edward Veith, an increasingly well-known cultural commentator, sets the scene for this part of the book by showing the distinct advantage of the Lutheran approach for our times and for the specific social and ethical issues that we face. He is concerned that Christianity has become culturally invisible in contemporary America, and argues that this is because Christianity has been tempted to become what it should never be, a merely cultural religion, denying transcendence by divinizing culture. Interestingly, Veith shows that not only accommodationists, but synthesists and separatists have fueled this cultural idolatry. He shows how the two kingdoms approach points the way out of this predicament by affirming both the real but penultimate value of culture and earthly vocations, and also the ultimate value of our eternal, transcultural destiny.

Statistics show that Christians have never been more persecuted than in the twentieth century. Wayne Martindale shows how acute the problem of Christ and culture is under the oppressive regime of China. Martindale endorses the Lutheran approach to the problem but shows how difficult this is for Chinese Christians to appreciate: for them, Christ and culture often seem to present a radical either-or choice. In his helpful study, Martindale gives statistics and first hand experience of the contemporary difficulties, but also analyzes and explains their historical sources in a country beset by nationalism, xenophobia, and the prevailing belief that the State, not Christ, is the final authority. On a subject where it is easy to be swamped by the negative, Martindale also emphasizes positive developments and opportunities for mission.

Christianity is neither "Western" in origin nor in its contemporary numerical concentration, yet it has come to be regarded as a Western religion and it is thought that this precludes valid communication with the Eastern worldview. Against this erroneous belief, Victor Raj emphasizes that the Gospel is a universal message which can find an incarnation in the language and concepts of any culture. He substantiates this thesis by a specific examination of Eastern metaphors for the Gospel, expressions of the Good News which are congenial to the Eastern mind. Raj explains why translation is difficult and even dangerous, yet also both possible and essential for effective missionary work.

Individualism is a problem which strikes closer to home. While individualism runs rampant in Western culture with deleterious results for Christian communities, it is less clear where this outlook originates. Cario aims to show that one popular answer—the view that individualism is entirely the outgrowth of the anti-religious sentiments of the Enlightenment—is false. In the case of America in particular, Cario shows that there were powerful religious motivations for emphasizing autonomy at the expense of community. Cario urges that Christians need to recover the balance and the paradox of St. Paul's metaphor for the Church, a body with many members, all of which contribute, yet all of which have distinctive worth in their own right. We need to value the community and the individual, yet not one at the expense of the other, and in practice this means a continuing struggle to approximate an impossible ideal.

On a more speculative note, Michael Ward pursues a narrative theology approach to the analysis of contemporary films. While Ward is not a Lutheran, he focuses on a paradox that Lutherans will likely find congenial. He starts with the observation that stories which are not officially about Christ can turn out to speak of Him all the same, a precedent set in the Bible by Old Testament stories (e.g., about Jonah) which are recontextualized by Christ to apply to Him. Pushing this further, one might suggest (to give a Lutheran cast to Ward's thesis) that just as individuals, Christian or not, can be masks of God, so stories, whether officially about the Incarnation or not, can be masks of the Great Story. Ward shows that this pattern is present not only in the Old Testament, but in paganism and the general revelation implicit in the cycles of nature. He suggests that the Great Story may speak more or less clearly through films, whether Christian or not, and that this provides one way of explaining our sense of a film's adequacy or inadequacy.

One source of the tension between Christ and culture is the conflict between different paradigms of the origins of life. Gary Locklair shows that questions of origins are not merely scientific, but that they strongly influence worldviews and the behavior which is regarded as permissible by a culture. After reviewing the arguments that favor creation over atheistic evolution, Locklair shows how the paradigms help to explain the disagreements over abortion, homosexuality, racism, and violent crimes. Locklair shows that in the end these are issues of authority: is man or God the measure of all things?

The Church and Church-Based Education in Culture

For Christians, nowhere does the tension between Christ and culture more obviously arise than in the animated debates on the proper forms of worship. Is liturgy an ancient relic or an ethnocentric and parochial stumbling block to the outsider which must give way to contemporary, non-liturgical worship styles? Or does it have more to offer? Timothy Maschke argues vigorously that it does. He shows first that while Lutheran worship is liturgical, this is not a parochial quirk, but an outgrowth of a great catholic evangelical tradition premised on a sacramental understanding of worship. The patterns of liturgy are a means of properly expressing the divine-human interaction, and, especially important for a Lutheran understanding, the centrality of the Gospel. Furthermore, liturgy mainly concerns structure and emphasis, not specific content, so it is a framework that may be fleshed out by all sorts of cultural variations. In this way there is both the universal (the Gospel) and the particular (culturally specific expressions and responses). There are however limits to this openness: liturgy must also strive to create a distinctive worship culture of its own so that the church remains a countercultural institutions: it must therefore be discriminating in what it draws from surrounding culture.

While he does not comment on liturgy specifically, Joel Heck is uneasy with approaches which mandate man-made customs and which thereby run the risk of confusing Law and Gospel. Heck insists on the importance of Biblical content, but, for the sake of evangelism, would seem to be in favor of worship styles which Maschke would view as non-liturgical. This would be an excellent issue for a classroom debate. However, the main focus of Heck's essay is not the stumbling blocks which he claims Christians lay in the path of non-Christians, but the obstacles our culture poses for evangelism. Heck analyzes and offers practical solutions to seven such obstacles: the hostility of the media to Christianity, individualism, the over-evangelization of America (poor presentation of the Gospel has inoculated the public against the real thing), relativism, secularization, materialism, and the widespread false belief that Christianity is exclusively a white man's or a Western religion.

Turning to church-based education, Patrick Riley's goal is to show that the multiculturalist agenda of accrediting bodies poses a lethal threat to the identity of Christian colleges. He argues that the multiculturalist view of the West fails to see that it is not simply one parochial voice among many, but is itself a multiculture, fashioned by a discriminating selection from a diversity of cultures, and containing certain distinctive merits which should be prized and preserved, not denigrated and undermined. Riley traces the origins of multiculturalism to Enlightenment ideology and explains why ideology, like a cuckoo's egg, is aimed at displacing the role of revelation-based religion. The brutal zeal of the ideologist is exemplified by the martyrdom of the Carmelite nuns during the French Revolution. Riley suggests that the power of accrediting bodies to control the funding of higher education institutions, coupled (in some cases) with a continuing pursuit of the Enlightenment project of a "neutral" (i.e., highly secularized, politically correct) education, poses a similar threat to the identity of authentically Christian colleges.

With an emphasis more on curriculum, Robert Benne applies the ideas he developed in his *The Paradoxical Vision* to the project of a Christian university. He aims to show the relevance of an "impossible" educational ideal—Christian humanism. Echoing Riley, Benne argues that the Enlightenment paradigm of a neutral education continues to undermine the idea of a public Christian intellectual, even among Christian faculty of Christian colleges. Despite its relativism, postmodernism ought to have helped by allowing Christianity to be one voice among many, but the postmodern culture of suspicion has allowed it to be dismissed as hegemonic. (This explains the extraordinary phenomenon that some Christian faculty think they are doing the right thing by emasculating Christianity at Christian schools with a Christian mission!) Against all this, Benne urges a dialectical Christian humanism in which Christianity and culture interact in an unresolvable, but highly fruitful exchange. Benne shows the superiority of this model to the alternatives: a separatist, biblicist model of education which ignores secular culture only uncritically to substitute its own, an aggressively transformationist "Christian education" which forces culture into dogmatic molds, an easy-going accommodationism which smothers Christianity under secular educational agendas, or a settled synthesis model which fuses Christianity to a philosophy which may later be refuted and which is inevitably incomplete. What should make Lutheran colleges (and Christian colleges sympathetic with their vision) distinctive and better than other Christian colleges is their commitment to an ongoing, always penultimate dialogue, with fragments of truth arising like sparks from the crossed swords of knights in endless combat.

I hope that these contributions are insightful and above all that they provoke debate. In a world where we are all too quick to take offense and use it as a means of censorship for views we are too lazy to think and argue about, I do not apologize for a book in which there is (to adapt a famous phrase) something to offend everyone. But my hope is that readers will not use offense as an excuse to walk away, but as a stimulus to think, and to experience in themselves the tensions and dialectic between Christ and culture.

Notes on Contributors

Robert Benne.   Dr. Benne is Jordan-Trexler Professor of Religion, chair of the Department of Religion and Philosophy, and director of the Center for Church and Society, all at Roanoke College, Salem, Virginia. He received his Ph.D. from the University of Chicago (1970), has done extensive study abroad in both Germany and England, and has lectured around the world on Christianity and culture. He is author of six books, including *Defining America—A Christian Critique of the American Dream* (1974), *The Paradoxical Vision—A Public Theology for the Twenty-first Century* (1995), and *Seeing Is Believing—Visions of Life through Film* (forthcoming). He recently spoke on the idea of Christian humanism during the inauguration activities for the new president of Concordia University Wisconsin.

William R. Cario.   Dr. Cario is associate professor of history at Concordia University Wisconsin. He received his Ph.D. in American history from New York University (1994). His research areas include colonial American history and American religious history. He was named Faculty Laureate for 1998-1999.

Alberto L. García.   Dr. García is associate professor of theology and director of the lay ministry program at Concordia University Wisconsin. He has taught as assistant professor of systematic theology at Concordia Theological Seminary, Ft. Wayne, Indiana, and as an adjunct professor of religion at Florida International University, Miami, Florida. He received his doctor of theology degree from the Lutheran School of Theology at Chicago in the area of systematic theology.

Joel D. Heck.   Dr. Heck is an Old Testament scholar and an expert in evangelism. He has authored several books, including *The Art of Sharing Your Faith*, *New Member Assimilation: Practical Prevention of Backdoor Loss through Frontdoor Care*, and *Evangelism and the Christian College*. Dr. Heck founded the journal *Evangelism*, has written many articles on religion and evangelism, and has served the church on a national level. After serving as professor of theology and assistant to the academic dean at Concordia University Wisconsin, Joel in 1998 became academic dean at Concordia University, Austin, Texas.

Robert Kolb. Dr. Kolb is director of the Institute for Mission Studies and Missions Professor of Systematic Theology at Concordia Seminary, St. Louis. He previously served as director of the Center for Reformation Research, St. Louis (1972-1977), and as instructor (1977-1993) and acting president (1990-1991) of Concordia College, St. Paul, Minnesota. He was president of the Sixteenth Century Studies Conference (1981-1982) and the Society for Reformation Research (1994-1996). Since 1993 he has served as a member of the Continuation Committee of the International Congress for Luther Research. He is author of numerous books, including *Luther's Heirs Define His Legacy: Studies on Lutheran Confessionalization* (Aldershot, Hampshire, 1996), *The Christian Faith: a Lutheran Exposition* (Saint Louis, 1993), and *Confessing the Faith: Reformers Define the Church, 1530-1580* (Saint Louis, 1991).

Gary H. Locklair. Gary Locklair is assistant professor and chair of the Computer Science Department at Concordia University Wisconsin. He holds a B.A. in chemistry, and B.S., M.S., and Ph.D. degrees in computer science. Gary worked at Hewlett-Packard for ten years before moving to academia in 1986. He is included in *Who's Who in Science and Engineering* and is a member of the Board of Directors for the Creation Research Society.

Wayne Martindale. Dr. Martindale earned his Ph.D. from the University of California, Riverside, and is currently associate professor of English at Wheaton College in Illinois. He is editor of *Journey to the Celestial City: Glimpses of Heaven from Great Literary Classics*, and co-editor with Jerry Root of *The Quotable Lewis*. Dr. Martindale was a contributor to *C. S. Lewis: Lightbearer in the Shadowlands*. He recently presented a talk on Christianity in China for Concordia University's "Christianity and Culture" lecture series from which his chapter for this book developed.

Martin E. Marty. Dr. Marty directs the Public Religion Project at the University of Chicago, where he taught for 35 years and where a new Martin Marty Center has been founded to promote public religion. Marty is Fairfax M. Cone Distinguished Service Professor Emeritus and the George B. Caldwell Senior Scholar-in-Residence at the Park Ridge Center for the Study of Health, Faith, and Ethics. He continues to edit *Context*, now in its 29th year. Marty has authored 50 books and has received numerous awards for his work, including the National Humanities Medal (1997). He has served on the Board of Regents of St. Olaf College since 1988 and is its current chairman. On the occasion of the 50th year since he graduated from Concordia's old campus in Milwaukee, he gave the keynote address for Concordia University Wisconsin's "Christianity and Culture" lecture series. Recently he hosted the educational video series on Christianity and culture, *Between Two Altars* (Seraphim Communications, 1997). Marty has done many other things, but as John says of our Lord (Jn. 21:25b), "If every one of them were written down, I suppose that even the whole world would not have room for the books that would be written."

Timothy Maschke. Dr. Maschke is chair of the Department of Theology at Concordia University Wisconsin, where he has served since 1982. Before this he served parishes in Illinois. Maschke received the master of divinity degree (1974) and a master of sacred theology degree in systematic theology (1981) from Concordia Seminary, St. Louis. Later he earned a doctor of ministry degree from Trinity Evangelical Divinity School (1984), writing a dissertation on Lutheran liturgical worship on a college campus. He holds a Ph.D. in historical theology from Marquette University (1993). Maschke has wide-ranging teaching responsibilities in theology, two of his special interests being Luther and Lutheran worship. He is the managing editor of *Luther Digest*, an annual abridgement of Luther scholarship, and continues to be a popular and dynamic speaker and preacher.

Angus J. L. Menuge. Dr. Menuge is associate professor of science and philosophy at Concordia University Wisconsin. He is the editor of *C. S. Lewis: Lightbearer in the Shadowlands* (Crossway, 1997). He organized the lecture series "Christianity and Culture" at Concordia

University Wisconsin, which was the foundation for the present volume.

A. R. Victor Raj. Dr. Raj has been Missions Professor of Exegetical Theology and assistant director of the Institute for Mission Studies at Concordia Seminary, St. Louis, since 1995. He was born in 1948 of traditional Lutheran parents in Trivandrum, Keral Sate, South India. He earned the bachelor of divinity degree from the Senate of Serampore College, Calcutta, and the master of sacred theology (1976) and the doctor of theology (1981) degrees from Concordia Seminary, St. Louis. He served in parishes and later as director of the Renewal of the Indian Evangelical Lutheran Church, and as president of Concordia Seminary, Nagercoil, India. Raj went on to become professor and chair of the theology department at Concordia University Wisconsin from 1990 to 1995. His publications include *The Hindu Connection: Roots of the New Age* (CPH, 1995); he is associate editor of *Missio Apostolica, Journal of the Lutheran Society for Missiology.*

Patrick G. D. Riley. Dr. Riley is a Roman Catholic whose education has been in political philosophy. He has numerous degrees including the Ph.L. and Ph.D. from *Pontificia Universita S. Tommaso d'Aquino.* Riley pursued a journalistic career, serving as sub-editor of Reuter, London (1955-1956), a London and Paris correspondent for United Press International (1956-1959), and a Rome-based roving correspondent and Washington-based foreign editor for the Catholic News Service (1959-1976). Later, Riley was editor of the National Catholic Register (1976-1979), an executive for De Rance, Inc. (1979-1984), and a writer for the White House (1985-1987), drafting press correspondence for former President Reagan. More recently he was a lecturer in philosophy at the Catholic University of America (1992-1993). Riley currently serves as an adjunct professor of classical antiquity at Concordia University Wisconsin.

Gene Edward Veith. Dr. Veith is professor of humanities and director of the Cranach Institute at Concordia University Wisconsin. Until the summer of 1998, he was dean of arts and sciences. He has written widely on Christianity, culture, and the arts. He is the author of eight books, including *Postmodern Times, Modern Fascism, Reading*

Between the Lines, *State of the Arts*, and *Loving God with All Your Mind*. He has written a vast number of articles, and is currently cultural editor and a regular columnist of the Christian current affairs magazine, *World*.

Michael Ward. Michael Ward read English at Oxford, England, and still lives in that city, where he works as warden of "The Kilns," the former home of C. S. Lewis, and tutors and lectures university students on Lewis's life and works. He recently assisted Walter Hooper in the preparation of *C. S. Lewis: Companion and Guide*, and was a contributor to the volume *C. S. Lewis: Lightbearer in the Shadowlands*.

Part I

Constructive Themes

1

Niebuhr's *Christ and Culture* Reexamined

Angus J. L. Menuge

Introduction

Conflict between the demands of Christ and culture is neither new nor rare. From the early Christian martyrs of Rome to the Confessing Church[1] of Nazi Germany, Christians have paid the price for rejecting the State's pretensions to supreme authority.[2] Christians indeed have often been viewed as subversive of culture precisely because of their belief in a transcultural human destiny. As C. S. Lewis put it,

> There are no *ordinary* people. You have never talked to a mere mortal. Nations, cultures, arts, civilizations—these are mortal, and their life is to ours as the life of a gnat.[3]

Contemporary America exhibits a variant of the tension as an aspect of its so-called "culture wars." Stephen L. Carter recounts the example of a Colorado public school teacher who "was ordered by his superiors, on pain of disciplinary action, to remove his personal Bible from his desk where students might see it."[4]

Such cases are typical of a disturbing general trend toward what Richard John Neuhaus memorably called "the naked public square,"[5] in which public institutions are divested of all associations with religions currently out of favor. Carter's diagnosis is that the religious views of the vast majority of Americans are being marginalized, reduced to impotent personal foibles, "like building model airplanes, just another hobby: something quiet, something private, something trivial—and not really a fit activity for intelligent, public-spirited adults."[6]

The Christian's proper response to culture is thus not only a historical, but an urgent present question. Almost half a century ago,

H. Richard Niebuhr's *Christ and Culture* laid down a useful framework of five typical answers to the question. Despite the work's deservedly great influence, critical scholarship continues to reveal flaws, both in Niebuhr's general methodology and in his treatment of specific options. In particular, Niebuhr partly endorses the frequent charges against the "paradox" answer of classical Lutheranism that it encourages antinomianism and cultural conservatism, while significant advantages of the approach are overlooked. It has to be admitted, however, that part of the blame for the continued prevalence of such misunderstandings rests with Lutherans themselves: they have not been sufficiently visible and clear in their elucidation of what Mark Noll has called the "Lutheran Difference."[7] Perhaps too, the mere fact that the Lutheran view is subtle and nuanced has prevented it from gaining a foothold in a public imagination which gravitates toward simpler answers.

The present chapter aims to evaluate the adequacy of Niebuhr's overall strategy and to provide a more compelling general picture of the Lutheran stance. I will begin with an explication of Niebuhr's *Christ and Culture*, followed by an examination of Niebuhr's methodology and presentation. A two-fold defense of what Robert Benne has called the "paradoxical vision"[8] of Lutheranism will then be offered: a negative defense against Niebuhr's objections and a positive defense emphasizing distinct advantages.

I. Niebuhr's Framework
1. Methodology

At least officially,[9] Niebuhr's approach to the problem of Christ and culture is one of methodological pluralism. That is, he thinks there is a range of typical answers to the question, but he does not claim they are exhaustive, or that they are mutually exclusive.[10] Rather, each of the answers is sometimes necessary, but also incomplete, and the final truth of the matter will elude human formulation, residing only, beyond our reach, in the providential interaction of all of the views:

> Christ as living Lord is answering the question in the totality of history and life in a fashion which transcends the wisdom of all his interpreters yet employs their partial insights and their necessary conflicts.[11]

Niebuhr claims it would be a "usurpation of the Lordship of Christ"[12] to think that one had found the one true answer, yet at the same time argues that each individual Christian has the duty of finding his or her own answers when making specific decisions.[13]

2. *Definitions*

When considering a relationship, all hinges on how we define the *relata*, so before giving his typical answers, Niebuhr provides working definitions of "Christ" and "culture." He hopes to avoid definitions which will prejudge the issue in favor of just one of the answers. Niebuhr claims that the essential character of Christ is given by His radical theocentrism, the fact that His love, hope and humility are all primarily directed to God the Father in heaven:

> As Son of God He points away from the many values of man's social life to the One who alone is good.[14]

Yet at the same time, Christ is mediator between God the Father and man:

> Because he loves the Father with the perfection of human *eros*, therefore he loves men with the perfection of divine *agape*, since God is *agape*.[15]

This duality in Christ grounds a corresponding duality in Christian response. Lutherans express this by saying that our faith has both a vertical dimension (directed toward God) and a horizontal dimension (directed toward neighbor).[16] Thus, any adequate account of the question of Christ and culture needs to emphasize both the fact that Christ draws us beyond this world so that, in the biblical sense, He hates the world (and requires us to do likewise), and the fact that He loves us and enjoins us to love others here and now in the world.

Niebuhr realizes the importance of defining "culture" in a way which has universal applicability: nothing should enter the definition that restricts it to a particular range of times or places. So his definition is very abstract.

> Culture is the "artificial, secondary environment" which man superimposes on the natural. It comprises language, habits, ideas, beliefs, customs, social organization, inherited artifacts, technical processes, and values.[17]

Niebuhr suggests that culture in this sense is what the New Testament writers meant by "the world."

3. The Options

Using these definitions, Niebuhr now explores five answers which seem to have recurred through history, suggesting great representatives of each one, though he admits that none of these people fits neatly into just one of the categories.

3.1 Christ against Culture

The most radical answer is "Christ Against Culture." On this view the Lordship of Christ does not mean that He is the highest of many authorities, but that He is the sole authority over the Christian. It thus presents Christ and culture as a radical either-or choice: if we follow Christ we must reject any loyalty to culture. Apparently the view has scriptural support. For example, John says:

> Do not love the world or anything in the world. If anyone loves the world, the love of the Father is not in him (1 John 2:15).

In a similar vein, some would argue that the prince of this world is the devil, and therefore that loyalty to worldly authority is ultimately loyalty to the devil.

According to Niebuhr, historical proponents of this sort of view have included Tertullian, Tolstoy, and the Mennonites. Tolstoy went so far as to claim that

> The Christian is independent of every human authority by the fact that he regards the divine law of love, implanted in the soul of every man, and brought before his consciousness by Christ, as the sole guide of his life and other men's also.[18]

On the basis of this radical view, Tolstoy consistently argued that

> All state obligations are against the conscience of a Christian—the oath of allegiance, taxes, law proceedings, and military service.[19]

The view encourages the separation of Christians from culture, either individually, as in Tolstoy's case, or collectively, as in the case of monasticism.

Niebuhr acknowledges the integrity of those following Christ against Culture in their courageous witness and sometimes martyrdom under evil governments, and in the social reforms they have thereby provoked. Indeed, without a continual separatist impetus,

> Christian faith quickly degenerates into a utilitarian device for the attainment of personal prosperity or public peace; and some imagined idol called by his name takes the place of Jesus Christ the Lord.[20]

However he thinks that if the view is offered as the whole answer, it is vulnerable to devastating objections.

First, the approach tends to naiveté about the nature of culture, sin, and holiness. It is impossible in practice to separate oneself from culture; as culture permeates our thinking and language, it is as much in us as it is around us.[21] We may keep out some bad influences of culture but others will remain inside. If Tolstoy, or the Amish, live apart from certain state institutions, or from mainstream technology and consumerism, they succeed only in establishing countercultures, not in becoming acultural. And although the separatist may insulate himself from some of the actual sins of prevailing culture, the original sin in his nature remains. The fact that monastic orders required so many rules and forms of discipline is a convincing testimony of the continuing presence of sin in the Christian. In the face of this, the separatist tendency to acknowledge grades of holiness can be maintained only by a works righteous ethic (for Tolstoy, for example, Christ is primarily a new Lawgiver), thus eliminating the primacy of grace. It was for this reason that Luther claimed that monasticism was not merely unnecessary but, if it was chosen as a means to greater holiness, an institution of the devil.[22]

Secondly, separatism captures only one of the two sides of Christ's nature initially noted in the working definition of Christ. The view emphasizes Christ's role in drawing us away from culture (the vertical dimension), but ignores his role in governing our continued relations with culture (the horizontal dimension). If Tolstoy were right, a Christian should pay no taxes, yet Christ himself says we must do it. Christ wants us to love our neighbors, but our neighbors are found in mainstream culture (and not merely in cloisters) and practical works of love will translate *agape* into culturally specific actions.[23] (In an undeveloped region, raising water from a well might be such an act, yet it would be inappropriate in urban America.) In fact, Christ rebukes a kind of separatism in the Parable of the Good Samaritan: the priest and the Levite keep themselves holy, separate and apart from the robbery victim, but the Samaritan, who has to cross cultural boundaries to help the man, is held up as our moral guide (Luke 10:25-37).

Yet the most devastating objection of all, Niebuhr thinks, comes from classic orthodox theology.[24] In order for culture to be radically rejected in favor of Christ, logic requires that Christ Himself is not a part of culture. This leads, however, to a purely spiritual understanding of Christ which denies His role in creation and His incarnation in history.[25] In fact, Christ affirmed the world by making it and reaffirmed the fallen world including culture by becoming one of us, a specific cultural being (Hebrews 2:14-18). Since we are to follow Christ in all things, and Christ has a cultural dimension, we must follow him in that dimension as well.

3.2 Christ of Culture

Supporters of this option, so-called cultural Christians, claim that Christ is to be understood as the highest aspiration and fulfillment of culture. In this way it is possible to affirm both Christ and culture and to deny any necessary opposition between the two.

> On the one hand they interpret culture through Christ, regarding those elements in it as most important which are most accordant with his work and person; on the other hand they understand Christ through culture, selecting from the Christian doctrine about him such points as seem to agree with what is best in civilization.[26]

The approach inevitably leads to accommodationism, the attempt to reconcile Christianity with what appear to be the greatest achievements of a culture.

Thus the early church had its Hellenizers and Judaizers of the Gospel and Gnostics who reconciled Christianity with their mystical philosophy. The medieval Abélard attempted to reduce Christianity to practical morality and Christ to a great moral teacher. During the Enlightenment, Locke, Kant, and Jefferson all tried to isolate a scientifically and philosophically reasonable Christianity, and sometimes even excised elements of the faith which could be believed only on the basis of special revelation. Contemporary manifestations of accommodationism abound in the pronouncements of mainline Protestantism and the World Council of Churches.[27]

Such views seem to have the advantage of offering more practical versions of Christianity, guiding action in the culture as it actually is. There is typically far more emphasis on concrete proposals for loving one's neighbor and less concern with what are often seen to be the abstractions of dogmatic theology. Niebuhr himself offers a substantial defense of the need for this emphasis in Christianity.[28]

One can immediately see, however, that this view tends toward an error equal, and opposite, to that committed by the separatists. In its concentration on this world, the view emphasizes the Christian's horizontal dimension to the exclusion of the vertical. Without emphasis on grace and the after-life, religion easily degenerates into a legalistic "self-reliant humanism."[29] This amounts in effect to an idolatrous worship of man or a denigration of God:

> The accommodator of Christ to the views of the time erases the distinction between God and man by divinizing man or humanizing God.[30]

The inevitable result is a theology in man's image, a danger which will always arise from the apparently innocent attempt to connect Christianity with some cultural movement one wishes to endorse, to create what C. S. Lewis called "Christianity And":

> You know—Christianity and the Crisis, Christianity and the New Psychology, Christianity and the New Order, Christianity and Faith Healing, Christianity and Psychical Research, Christianity and Vegetarianism, Christianity and Spelling Reform.[31]

The inevitable dilution of Christian orthodoxy and tendency to use a highly selective Christianity as a means to an independently conceived political end amounts to a denial that Christianity is anything more than true by occasional coincidence. This calls to mind the worst excesses of mainline Protestantism which have, as Benne says, "looked for the world to set the agenda for the church."[32] Thus for example,

> the President of the Society of Christian Ethics suggested to the assembled crowd at a recent annual conference that we must look to lesbian sexual relations to gain clues about what healthy, unoppressed sexual relations are like—never mind the millions of Christian couples

who have lived out their Christian vows of marriage throughout the ages.[33]

Much more subtle cases of deference to the ideology of political correctness abound.[34]

Thus in the end, the accommodationist posture leads to a distortion of the horizontal dimension as well as to a neglect of the vertical. By seeking the will of God in the world, Christians are apt to mistake the prevailing *Zeitgeist* for the Holy Spirit.

While there is much that is wrong about accommodationism, I think an important distinction should be made. One should not compromise the fundamental message of Christianity, but in order to communicate that message to different cultures, one can translate culture-bound ideas to their equivalents in other cultures. Christ used cultural examples drawn from agrarian Palestine to express His parables. Paul altered his delivery and style depending on whether he was trying to reach Greeks, Romans, or Jews. C. S. Lewis claimed that his task was that of a translator, turning Christian doctrine into the vernacular of unscholarly people.[35] Effective translation is incarnational, taking the Gospel message and finding culturally relevant clothing to express it.[36]

Having exposed the limitations of the two simple answers to the Christ and culture problem (rejection or affirmation of culture, for Christ), Niebuhr proceeds to three more complex answers, all of which try in some sense to acknowledge both Christ and culture, yet without reducing one to the other. The three relations considered are synthesis, paradox, and transformation.

3.3 Christ above Culture

According to this view what is needed is not blank affirmation or rejection of culture for Christ but a synthesis of Christ and culture. It is pointed out that culture cannot be all bad because it is founded on the nature created good by God, and that although nature and culture are fallen, they are still subject to God. The view emphasizes that good works are carried out in culture, yet are only made possible by grace, so that the kingdom of grace impinges on the kingdom of the world from above. Only through grace can we love our neighbor, yet only in culture can we act on that love.

On this view, "We cannot say 'Either Christ or culture,' because we are dealing with God in both cases," yet we must not say "'Both Christ and culture,' as though there were no great distinction between them."[37] For in His promises, Christ goes beyond culture, drawing us to the Father in heaven, but in His commands He directs us to act in culture and we are subject to divinely instituted representatives.

The greatest exponent of this view, Thomas Aquinas, held that the church must be viewed as simultaneously in and beyond the world, leading people to salvation in heaven yet encouraging all that is best in this world's culture. From this vision came the great ideas of general education and protective legislation for all citizens. In his Christian Aristotelianism, Aquinas held that the church must promote both people's temporal goals and their eternal goals. He distinguished the natural law and cardinal virtues (Prudence, Temperance, Justice, and Fortitude) available to all mankind from the divine law, which includes the natural law but adds the superior motivation of the theological virtues (Faith, Hope and Charity), which are available only to Christians through grace.

Above all, Aquinas wanted to achieve a stable relationship between church and state that would allow the conservation of values and authority. Since leaders are divinely instituted, the church backs up the government's authority to maintain order. There is also a continuum of authority between the earthly and heavenly realms, and a hierarchical organization in church and state offices.

There is a lot that is right about Aquinas's picture. He recognizes that there is one king over the temporal and the eternal. He offers practical solutions for living the Christian life in culture. His picture not only theoretically, but as a matter of historical fact, has enriched cultural institutions such as education and government. No academic can with good faith completely repudiate Aquinas since he is one of the principal reasons the academic vocation exists.

The approach is however beset by many problems. In its willingness to support temporal authority, the church as conceived by Aquinas will tend to be an agent of social stagnation. Synthesizing Christianity with the culture of the day may amount to cultural fossilization, and thus to "the absolutization of what is relative,"[38] or cultural idolatry. In its emphasis on conservation of values and authority the approach may perpetuate dictatorships and prevent legislative reform. Indeed the respect for temporal authority seems to be too great; there is a danger that man-made laws will undermine

God's law, after the fashion of the Pharisees who were excoriated by Christ for nullifying "Honor thy father and mother" for the sake of their tradition (Mt. 15: 3-7).

The hierarchical structure of church and state tends to create the false picture of grades of holiness.[39] And the integration of church and state creates large temptations for compromising Christian truths and for clerical abuse of temporal, political power, relying on the Sword instead of the Word to make people live by church teachings. Luther rightly attacked the church for the evil and impossible attempt to make people believe things: evil, because it produces hypocrites; impossible, because although duress changes behavior, it cannot change belief [40] (imagine, for example, being commanded to believe that someone is Napoleon on pain of torture). In all this, the fundamental weakness is the failure to realize that sin will vitiate all institutions in both church and state and that attempts at reform are liable to great corruption.

3.4 Christ and Culture in Paradox

The paradox view differs from the preceding one by maintaining that while both Christ and culture claim our loyalty, the tension between them cannot be reconciled by any lasting synthesis. The most important version of this view is Luther's doctrine of the two kingdoms or realms. (In what follows, I will use the term "realm," because "two kingdoms" makes the erroneous suggestion that there are two kings.)

Luther maintained that sin is universal and remains inside the Christian throughout his earthly life, thereby vitiating any attempt to set up a holy society on earth. There is a stark contrast between two realms: the left-hand realm of the world governed by law and the right-hand realm of God governed by grace. These two realms exist side by side in a paradoxical relation, never to be resolved in this life. To get a flavor for the paradox, we may compare the following passages from Luther. In "Temporal Authority," Luther says that Christians, who belong to God's realm, "need no temporal law or sword,"[41] for good works now flow freely without duress: "A good tree needs no instruction or law to bear good fruit."[42] Yet in his "Against the Robbing and Murdering Hordes of Peasants," Luther is an outspoken advocate of temporal law and sword: "let everyone who can, smite, slay, and stab, secretly or openly, remembering that nothing can be more poisonous, hurtful, or devilish than a rebel."[43]

Part of the explanation of this apparent contradiction is that the peasants belong to the realm of the world, and are therefore subject to the Law, including the temporal law laid down by divinely instituted human leaders, which condemns the rebellion. Such laws are needed, not because they will make the ungodly acceptable to God, but because they are a means of limiting the consequences of sin in this world. Christians, by contrast, do not need the Law or the sword as an incentive to act; this is not because temporal powers have no authority for them, but because, in normal circumstances, they freely want to follow this authority.

However, it is an oversimplification to suppose that Christians are freed from the realm of the world. In fact, a single Christian is simultaneously subject to both realms, because each Christian contains an "inner man"[44] ruled by faith and not law, and an "outer man"[45] that may stumble, ruled by the Law. Thus we are *simul justus et peccator* (simultaneously saint and sinner). What Luther insists on is that we are saved by grace, not works, yet because we also remain sinful in this life, we need the Law to curb our sin. Thus each Christian is a subject of two realms--two "kingdoms," but one king, Christ.[46]

The two realms distinction has far-reaching consequences. Since one is saved by grace, not works, there are no grades of holiness, or any need to separate oneself from culture. This means that any vocation (provided it is a true vocation, a station instituted by God) can be pursued for the glory of God. In that sense, Christians can participate fully in what is best in culture: we are "set free to serve." Our motivation for service comes from gratitude born of faith in God's love for us, but the specific techniques of service can be derived from the surrounding culture. This freedom of the Christian is balanced by a respect for temporal law and secular government (Rom. 13:1-7) as a means of curbing the consequences of sin. This balancing act will sometimes lead to paradox: as Christians under grace, we should not return harm for harm, but in time of war, we may rightly be ordered to take up arms,[47] if it is the only way of limiting greater evil. Yet if a leader is wrong, in the sense of commanding us to do something contrary to God's law, we are not bound to obey "for it is no one's duty to do wrong; we must obey God (who desires the right) rather than men [Acts 5:29]."[48]

Niebuhr correctly perceives a number of advantages in Luther's view. It is completely realistic about the extent of human sin and the continuing need of law to control it. At the same time, Luther does not fall into separatism or self-righteousness, encouraging any honorable service to culture. While the Two Realms doctrine suggests to some a compartmentalization of faith and works,[49] Niebuhr is aware that this misunderstands the interrelations between the realms:

> It is a great error to confuse the parallelistic dualism of separated spiritual and temporal life with the interactionism of Luther's gospel of faith in Christ working by love in the world of culture.[50]

On the other hand, Niebuhr thinks there is something to be said for two charges against the paradox view.[51] First, it tends toward antinomianism: if we are justified by grace, not works, and sin inevitably persists in the Christian, why should he not sin all the more? Second, it leads to cultural conservatism: if we should accept the temporal authority of existing institutions and rulers, it would seem to be unmotivated, perhaps even wrong, to call for reform. Along with this is the idea that Luther views the role of Law in a purely negative fashion (as curb and mirror, the first two uses of the Law), but does not support its positive role (as guide, the third use of the Law) in improving society.[52]

3.5 Christ the Transformer of Culture

This last option is similar to the preceding except that it is more optimistic about the ability of Christians to improve culture. It still affirms the universality of sin, but maintains that cultures can be converted. One of the fundamental theological reasons for this optimism is the view that the Fall only perverted things which were created good, that these things remain inherently good and capable of reform, even though they have been misdirected.[53]

The suggestion is not that mankind can by its own efforts create a more holy culture, but that through the action of grace, this can happen. This leads to the idea of a Holy Christian community here on earth, visibly set apart from non-Christian culture. Rather doubtfully, Niebuhr associates this idea with Augustine, though he admits that in various ways Augustine seemed to affirm all five answers.[54] Certainly, Augustine was impressed by the regeneration of Caesar-centered Rome as a Christian city, although Augustine was much more pessimistic than a typical transformationist about the fortune of any culture of this world. A better example is Calvin who emphasized the positive, third use of the Law as a guide to social reform, at least for the elect (although Calvinists have typically been more optimistic than Calvin himself, and sometimes even inclined to perfectionism), and various Christian utopians such as F. D. Maurice who championed a Christian socialist society.

Niebuhr offers no evaluation of the basic strengths and weaknesses of the transformationist view, itself a sign that he thinks it is the best. We will see, however, that it is vulnerable to serious objections.

II. An Evaluation of Niebuhr's Methodology and Presentation

Niebuhr's methodological pluralism[55] can be analyzed into several claims which Niebuhr does not clearly distinguish.

(M1) All five of the types are sometimes appropriate.

(M2) No one of the five types is simply and basically correct.

(M3) It is impossible to find one correct answer (in this or any other typology) to the Christ and culture problem.

The weakest claim, (M1), is quite plausible. Yancey, for example, confirms the intuition:

> I remember that Niebuhr's book left me feeling enlightened, but as confused as ever. All the approaches seemed to have something to contribute, and in fact, I could point to biblical examples of each one.[56]

While the claim may be true, the problem with Niebuhr's approach is that he does not provide a principle for deciding *when* one of the five types is operative, and when it is not. His injunction to individual Christians to find the answer for themselves in each decision[57] comes perilously close to a situationalist ethic. At the very least then, Niebuhr's approach is incomplete.

More troubling is the stronger claim (M2). It is clear that (M2) does not follow from (M1), since one of the five answers might subsume the others as special cases, in such a way that it agrees with them whenever they are appropriate and otherwise disagrees. Indeed, as Yoder has noted, in view of his logical strategy in presenting the five types, this seems to be exactly Niebuhr's tacit view of the transformation option.

> We see this preference in the fact that in the structure of his presentation . . . Transformation' takes into itself all the values of its predecessor types and corrects most of their shortcomings . . . a presentation following the pattern of thesis, antithesis and synthesis constitutes an implicit argument in favor of the last option reported.[58]

Thus Niebuhr's dialectic approach is at odds with his professed pluralism: he clearly does think the transformationist option is basically correct. This also conflicts with the even stronger claim (M3) of ultimate skepticism, which, as Yoder points out, is inconsistent with the widely held orthodox assumption that Christians can know the will of God.[59]

The irony is that Niebuhr offers no explicit defense (but only an explication of) the transformationist option and considers no objections. The superficial plausibility of his presentation also seems suspiciously to depend on a lack of specific proposals. Indeed,

> what H. Richard Niebuhr meant by "transformation" is so inadequately defined that its popularity with the readers seems to correlate with an assumption that it is more or less indistinguishable from our western doctrine of progress . . . .[60]

In practice, the transformationist view is vulnerable to devastating objections. It tends to a utopianism which underestimates the continuing power of sin to totter man-made Towers of Babel. Even within the church, history simply does not bear out such optimism. At the same time, such earthbound hopes tend to undermine the belief in an afterlife by seeking a heaven on earth. No one expressed the deceitfulness of such an approach better than C. S. Lewis.

> When they want to convince you that earth is your home, notice how they go about it. They begin by trying to persuade you that earth can be made into heaven, thus giving a sop to your sense of exile on earth as it is. Next, they tell you that this fortunate event is still a good way off in the future, thus giving a sop to your knowledge that the fatherland is not here and now. Finally, lest your longing for the transtemporal should awake and spoil the whole affair, they use any rhetoric that comes to hand to keep out of your mind the recollection that even if all the happiness they promised could come to man on earth, yet still each generation would lose it by death, including the last generation of all, and the story would be nothing, not even a story, for ever and ever.[61]

The emphasis on transforming culture has the danger of becoming the whole reason for the church's existence. The "social gospel" may quickly replace the true gospel of grace and promise with a works-righteous religion of Law, a danger which has been clearly realized in the strident, coercive activism of some of the main-line Protestant churches. Although Calvin's *Institutes* stressed the primacy of grace, the pervasive direct action approach of a basically Calvinist America[62] has often relied on the Law to force social reform, exchanging the Word for the Sword.

It should also be noted that some of Niebuhr's objections to the rival answers are unfair. Yoder, himself a separatist, rightly points out that some of Niebuhr's objections to the Christ against Culture view rely on a question-begging definition of culture. On Niebuhr's conception, culture is "monolithic,"[63] an all-inclusive category covering everything man does to nature. Taken literally, this automatically makes rejection of culture absurd, since the rejection itself will be carried on by human activity and hence in culture. Yet the fact is that separatists aim to be countercultural, not acultural. They reject certain aspects of mainstream culture, but not culture *in toto*. For example,

> Tolstoy was in favor of story-telling, the novel, the folk-tale, the arts, the family, the village, the schools, the restoration of peasant crafts, and heavy labor in the fields.[64]

Likewise Tertullian affirmed many aspects of Roman culture, such as the legal system and social order.

As Yoder argues, the separatist is not opposed to culture in Niebuhr's sense, but to cultural idolatry, those aspects of culture that attempt to supplant primary allegiance to the Lordship of Christ. For this reason, Niebuhr is clearly mistaken in identifying culture, monolithically conceived, with "the world":

> [W]hen the New Testament speaks of "world" it precisely does not mean . . . all of culture. It means rather culture *as self-glorifying* or culture *as autonomous* . . . .[65]

The distinction is clearly present in Jesus' reply to the question about taxes (Mt. 22:18-21). The taxes indeed belong to Caesar, but the claims to sacred status inscribed on the coin and the implied primary allegiance do not. In this sense, no Christian should deny that there can be rejection of culture, since "every morally accountable affirmation of culture discriminates."[66]

Thus the real question is not whether we should accept or reject culture *en bloc*, but what is the correct principle of discrimination. Unfortunately, even though Tertullian and Tolstoy may have been saddled with an inappropriate definition of culture, it remains quite clear that they lack such a principle. Tertullian's view does tend to a self-righteous monasticism, and Tolstoy's rejection of the state is incompatible with our duties to divinely instituted officers and leaders. We can reject the supreme authority of the state without repudiating its secondary, temporal authority. I will argue shortly, however, that the paradox view does provide a correct principle of discrimination.

III. The Lutheran Difference: A Defense of the Paradoxical Vision

1. A Negative Defense against Objections

It is odd that the paradox view is still subjected to the charge of antinomianism, since its most famous exponents, Paul and Luther, both anticipated and answered the charge in their day.[67] As Luther makes clear, since each Christian is both saint and sinner, he remains subject to Law in his sinful nature. On the other hand, the inner man of faith is not subject to Law, but does not need to be since he inevitably desires to fulfill the Law and even go further than the Law requires. Like the apple tree, the inner man produces good fruit naturally, not because a rule book requires it, and indeed even if no rule requires it.

The claim that the "paradox" view inevitably leads to a quietist cultural conservatism no doubt gains its popularity from the marginalization of Twentieth Century Lutherans.[68] However, it is a fallacy to argue that the Lutheran church's lack of influence is necessarily a consequence of its foundational theology: it could be that the dominance of rival influences (such as Calvinism) has drowned out the Lutheran voice or that the theology has not been effectively integrated with Lutheran practice. In the latter vein, for example, some would argue that Lutherans have so emphasized the importance of justification that sanctification has been neglected.

It is true that *restraint* in public involvement of the church itself is a natural consequence of Lutheran theology. Direct social action by the church is normally resisted as a contamination of the Word with the Sword. In view of the embarrassing excesses of main-line Protestantism such restraint seems wise. On the other hand, the quietism of individual lay members of the church is not justified by a proper understanding of Lutheran vocation. While direct action of the church is discouraged, the Lutheran church strongly affirms indirect influence on culture[69] via the activity of church members pursuing their secular vocations. The church prepares the laity with the Word which then shapes and transforms the way in which secular work is accomplished.

The idea that vocation and faith are to be rigidly compartmentalized is anathema to a correct understanding of vocation. As Luther said, a vocation is a cross, and the distinctive way in which a Christian carries this cross is a powerful witness and testimony to the faith.[70] Indeed, as Wingren says, Luther thought of the Christian life as a following of Christ's crucifixion and resurrection through the Two Realms.

> The Christian is crucified by the law in his vocation, under the earthly government; and he arises through the gospel, in the church under the spiritual government.[71]

Understood aright therefore, Christian vocation is anything but a timid accommodation to existing cultural institutions. In fact, as Bonhoeffer said,

> The value of the secular calling for the Christian is that it provides an opportunity of living the Christian life with the support of God's grace, and of engaging more vigorously in the assault on the world and everything that it stands for. Luther did not return to the world because he had arrived at a more positive attitude towards it . . . . He intended his action to express a radical protest against the secularization of Christianity which had taken place within monasticism. By recalling Christians into the world he called them paradoxically out of it all the more . . . . His call . . . was essentially a call to enter the visible church of the incarnate Lord.[72]

For this reason, the modern tendency noted by Neuhaus and Carter toward the "privatization" of religion is utterly at odds with a genuine Christian vocation which necessarily involves visible, public expression. Yet despite this "cost of discipleship," the paradox view does not encourage a safe quietism. Rather the individual life of each faithful Christian should constitute a protest statement against worldly corruption and idolatry. As Thielicke says,

> Woe unto you, if you, the servant of God, do *not* tell the state what it is and what it owes to God . . . . If you really give God what belongs to him, then that will not occur in your hymn-singing and church services . . . . You must bear your message into public life; you must be the salt of the earth.[73]

The most severe charge against the paradox view is that its emphasis on obedience to the rulers of the Kingdom of the World encouraged the capitulation to Fascism of the German Christians.[74] However, the action was justified by a false, compartmentalized understanding of the two realms[75] (which we saw Niebuhr himself rejects):

> Only the spiritual sphere . . . is regarded as within the competence of the divine claim and command. The secular sphere is viewed as a zone in which only economic, political, and social laws apply.[76]

But for one thing, the two realms overlap, and for another, both are subject to God, and as we saw, Luther insisted that the exigencies of one's secular vocation do not exempt one from God's law.[77]

It is true that Luther supported patient endurance of an oppressive government if indeed it was instituted by God. For in this case one of the citizen's vocations is to be a subject of that government. Luther condemned the peasant uprising precisely because it was an abandonment of this vocation, and thus a rejection of God's authority. The peasant's proper role was to influence oppressive leadership by protest within vocation, and, if that should fail, to put their trust in God's ability to raise up an enemy for the oppressor. But it is quite different in the case of a kingdom such as the Turks', which was "instituted for the purpose of dishonoring God,"[78] as it was an intentional assault on Christendom. In this case, Christians are not only permitted but required to fight the kingdom:[79] the correct vocation is one of a soldier.

A convincing case can be made that the Nazi government was not instituted by God, but by the devil, and was intent on destroying not only Christianity, but the whole monotheistic worldview, and replacing it with a culturally idolatrous nationalism.

> National socialism replaces monotheism, going so far as to assume the role of the one God of the Bible. With stunning blasphemy and idolatry,

the commandment to have no other gods is appropriated to enforce allegiance to the Nazi party.[80]

Whatever the failures of the visible church at that time, Lutheran theology is clearly opposed to such *Volkstum* ("folk," or "national spirit") worship.[81]

Again, it has been claimed that the paradox view leads to social stagnation. Although the Lutheran may witness via his vocation, there seems little incentive to call for significant reforms or indeed new vocations provided the society is genuinely ordered by those instituted by God. To a degree, a defensive reply seems appropriate. We live in an age where irresponsibility, abandonment of vocation, is widespread, particularly in that most important of vocations, parenthood. The ubiquity of day-care allows even those who can afford to raise their own children to abdicate that vocation. As Wingren argues, since a vocation is a cross and we are to take up our appointed cross, such abandonment of vocation is sin.[82] With the declining willingness of Christians to carry their own cross, rhetoric opposing "social stagnation" seems less apt than a call to restoration of institutions already seriously undermined.

On the other hand, Luther certainly believed that vocations were dynamic. Vocations are sent to us by God, and since His creative love is continuing, both the form and content of these vocations is apt to change.

> The variable element is love, which can freely go its way, since it is God. The love of the new man, which shapes his "use" of his office, is a form of God's creation in the world.[83]

As a result, "In the exercise of his vocation man becomes a mask for God."[84] Innovation and improvement in one's vocation, and flexible adaptation to changing situations and demands, are not things that need to be mandated. Indeed, more laws would merely kill a tree which is naturally able to grow and renew its fruit.

Furthermore, Luther's view supports the use of any techniques supplied by secular advances, so long as they can be applied without sin. A Christian computer scientist looks to advances in microprocessors, not Scripture, to increase his or her computational power. On the other hand, abortion, though it is a secular medical technique, should normally be eschewed by a Christian doctor[85] as a part of the protest of his or her vocation under God.

2. A Positive Defense

We agreed with Yoder that any adequate account of Christ and culture should yield a principle of discrimination, a way of telling which aspects of culture should be affirmed, and which should be rejected, for God. It should by now be clear that the Two Realms doctrine and the doctrine of vocation together accomplish just that.

The paradoxical view avoids self-righteous separatism on the one side and double-minded irresponsibility on the other, by affirming any earthly calling which is not in itself sinful. (Obviously the office-holder will continue to sin, but it is important that the office itself is not sinful.) Likewise secular techniques are affirmed so long as they do not conflict with God's Word. Temporal authority is respected and even tyranny is endured provided it is instituted by God, though not without protest from within the vocation of suffering servant. But government which in its nature directly opposes Christ must be resisted, even with force.

Reform and innovation are considered good, so long as they are the fruits of a creative *agape*. We must however test the fruits, because

> We face not only the possibility of a divine transformation of the world but a satanic transformation as well.[86]

Where the Word is preached in truth and faithfulness, God will transform the world for the better through individual laity. This hope is far more realistic than the legalistic hedges of Calvinism, for, as Lewis reminds us, "You cannot make men good by law: and without good men you cannot have a good society."[87] Indeed we see in the present state of our society considerable empirical evidence that law without inner transformation is struggling to maintain order (and even non-Christian prison governors have noted that prison evangelism reduces recidivism more than socialization attempts).

On the other hand, the paradox view will remind us of the continued presence of sin and the liability of all earthly projects to failure. This should guard us from the utopianism that would otherwise divert our gaze from our eternal goal. With its emphasis on a foundation of Word, not Sword, the Lutheran church (and those sympathetic with its paradoxical vision) can more easily avoid the temptation to corruption by the quest for temporal power. At the same time, it can equip its members with the means to effect transformation of society, through their costly witness and protest and willingness to accept their appointed cross.

Angus Menuge is Associate Professor of Science and Philosophy at Concordia University Wisconsin.

Bibliography

Benne, Robert. *The Paradoxical Vision: A Public Theology for the Twenty-first Century.* Minneapolis, MN: Fortress Press, 1995.

Bonhoeffer, Dietrich. *The Cost of Discipleship.* Revised Edition. New York, NY: Macmillan, 1963.

Carter, Stephen L. *The Culture of Disbelief: How American Law and Politics Trivialize Religious Devotion.* New York, NY: Basic Books, 1993.

Lewis, C. S. *Mere Christianity.* Revised Edition. New York: Macmillan, 1952.

_____. "Rejoinder to Dr. Pittenger." In *God in the Dock: Essays on Theology and Ethics.* Ed. Walter Hooper. Grand Rapids, MI: Eerdmans, 1996.

_____. *The Screwtape Letters.* Revised Edition. New York: Macmillan, 1982.

_____. "The Weight of Glory." In *The Weight of Glory and Other Addresses.* Revised and Expanded Edition. New York: Macmillan, 1980.

Luther, Martin. "Against the Robbing and Murdering Hordes of Peasants." In *Luther's Works*, Volume 46, The Christian in Society III. Ed. Robert C. Schultz. Philadelphia, PA: Fortress Press, 1967, pp. 45-55.

_____. "The Freedom of a Christian." In *Luther's Works*, Volume 31, Career of the Reformer I. Ed. Harold J. Grimm. Philadelphia, PA: Muhlenberg Press, 1957, pp. 327-377.

_____. "On War Against the Turk." In *Luther's Works*, Volume 46, The Christian in Society III. Ed. Robert C. Schultz. Philadelphia, PA: Fortress Press, 1967, pp. 155-205.

Luther, Martin. "Temporal Authority: To What Extent It Should be
    Obeyed." In *Luther's Works*, Volume 45, The Christian in Society
    II. Ed. Walther I. Brandt. Philadelphia, PA: Muhlenberg Press,
    1962, pp. 75-129.
_____. "Whether Soldiers, Too, Can Be Saved." In *Luther's
    Works*, Volume 46, The Christian in Society III. Ed. Robert C.
    Schultz. Philadelphia, PA: Fortress Press, 1967, pp. 87-137.
Marty, Martin E. *Righteous Empire: The Protestant Experience in
    America*. Fort Worth: Dial, 1970.
Neuhaus, Richard John. *The Naked Public Square: Religion and
    Democracy in America*. Grand Rapids, MI: Eerdmans, 1984.
Niebuhr, H. Richard. *Christ and Culture*. New York, NY: Harper and
    Row, 1951. (First Harper Torch Book, 1956.)
_____. *The Kingdom of God in America*. New York: Harper and
    Brothers, 1959.
Noll, Mark. "The Lutheran Difference." In *First Things*, February,
    1992, 31-40.
"That They May Have Life: A Statement of The Lutheran Church—
    Missouri Synod." In *First Things*, August/September 1997, 47-50.
Thielicke, Helmut. *Being Human . . . Becoming Human: An Essay in
    Christian Anthropology* (translated by Geoffrey W. Bromley).
    Garden City, New York: Doubleday and Company, Inc., 1984.
_____. *How to Believe Again*. Philadelphia: Fortress Press, 1972.
Tolstoy, Leo. *The Kingdom of God Is Within You: Christianity not
    as a Mystic Religion but as a New Theory of Life*. Trans. Constance
    Garnett. Lincoln, NE: University of Nebraska Press, 1984.
Veith Jr., Gene Edward. *Modern Fascism: Liquidating the Judeo-
    Christian Worldview*. St. Louis, MO: Concordia Publishing House,
    1993.
Wingren, Gustaf. *Luther on Vocation*. Trans. Carl C. Rasmussen.
    Philadelphia: Muhlenberg Press, 1957.
Yancey, Philip. "A State of Ungrace." *Christianity Today*, February
    3rd, 1997, 31-37.
Yoder, John Howard. "How H. Richard Niebuhr Reasoned: A Critique
    of Christ and Culture." In Glen H. Stassen, D. M. Yeager, John
    Howard Yoder (co-authors). *Authentic Transformation: A New
    Vision of Christ and Culture*. Nashville, TN: Abingdon Press,
    1996.

Notes

[1] See Veith, *Modern Fascism*, chapter 4.

[2] Of course, oppression has also gone in the opposite direction, when Christians have wrongly taken up the sword and tried to convert non-Christians by force, as will be discussed later.

[3] Lewis, "The Weight of Glory," 19.

[4] Carter, *The Culture of Disbelief*, 11.

[5] Neuhaus, *The Naked Public Square*.

[6] Carter, *The Culture of Disbelief*, 22.

[7] Noll, "The Lutheran Difference."

[8] Benne, *The Paradoxical Vision: A Public Theology for the Twenty-first Century*.

[9] Officially, because as we shall see, Niebuhr seems to regard one of the five answers as an inclusive synthesis of the other four, retaining their strengths but avoiding their weaknesses, and thus, in fact, closer to the real truth.

[10] Niebuhr, *Christ and Culture*, 231.

[11] Ibid., 2.

[12] Ibid., 232.

[13] Ibid., 233.

[14] Ibid., 28.

[15] Ibid.

[16] See Kolb's chapter in this volume for a deeper understanding of the vertical and horizontal dimensions.

[17] Ibid., 32.

[18] Tolstoy, *The Kingdom of God Is Within You*, 211.

[19] Ibid., 230-231. Also quoted in Niebuhr, *Christ and Culture*, 60-61.

[20] Niebuhr, *Christ and Culture*, 68.

[21] Ibid., 69.

[22] In other words, it is not monasticism itself, but certain self-righteous reasons for pursuing it that are objectionable.

[23] Niebuhr, *Christ and Culture*, 71.

[24] Yoder, however, casts doubt on the orthodoxy of Niebuhr's appeal to the Trinity. See especially Yoder, "How H. Richard Niebuhr Reasoned," 61-65.

[25] Niebuhr, *Christ and Culture*, 81.

[26] Ibid., 83.

[27] See Benne, *The Paradoxical Vision*, 26-44.

[28] Niebuhr, *Christ and Culture*, 101-108.

[29] Ibid., 113.

[30] Ibid., 120.

[31] Lewis, *The Screwtape Letters*, 115.

[32] Benne, *The Paradoxical Vision*, 39.

[33] Ibid., 36.

[34] See the chapter by Veith for a sustained analysis and critique of the varieties of contemporary accommodationism.

[35] Lewis, "Rejoinder to Dr. Pittenger," 183.

[36] For more on this theme, see the chapters by Alberto García and Victor Raj in this volume.

[37] Niebuhr, *Christ and Culture*, 122.

[38] Ibid., 145.

[39] Ibid., 147.

[40] See for example Luther, "Temporal Authority," 108.

[41] Ibid., 89.

[42] Ibid.

[43] Luther, "Against the Robbing and Murdering Hordes of Peasants," 50. Part of this passage is also quoted in Niebuhr, *Christ and Culture*, 170.

[44] See Luther, "The Freedom of a Christian," 344-358.

[45] Ibid., 358-371.

[46] For more on the Two Kingdoms, see Ed Veith's chapter in this volume.

[47] See Luther, "Whether Soldiers, Too, Can Be Saved."

[48] Luther, "Temporal Authority," 125.

[49] Niebuhr, *Christ and Culture*, 171.

[50] Ibid., 179.

[51] Ibid., 187.

[52] Whether or not Lutherans should endorse the Third Use of the Law is a highly debatable issue. At times Luther seems to explicitly reject it, but what he is rejecting is that the Law can somehow aid in salvation. The idea that the Law can guide Christian living without contributing to salvation is at least compatible with this.

[53] Ibid., 194.

[54] Ibid., 207.

[55] See the earlier quotation from Niebuhr (*Christ and Culture*, 231) stating his methodological pluralism at the beginning of the section on Niebuhr's framework.

[56] Yancey, "A State of Ungrace," 33.

[57] Niebuhr, *Christ and Culture*, 233.

[58] Yoder, "How H. Richard Niebuhr Reasoned," 41-42.

[59] Ibid., 72.

[60] Ibid., 53.

[61] Lewis, "The Weight of Glory," 8. To be sure, Lewis was talking of secular utopianism, but his remarks apply equally to a religious variant.

[62] That America is basically Calvinist in its outlook has been convincingly shown in H. Richard Niebuhr's *The Kingdom of God in America*, and Martin E. Marty's *Righteous Empire*. For a recent discussion, see Benne, *The Paradoxical Vision*, 26-30. See also Noll, "The Lutheran Difference."

[63] Yoder, "How H. Richard Niebuhr Reasoned," 54.

[64] Ibid., 66.

[65] Ibid., 70.

[66] Ibid., 55.

[67] See, for example, Romans 6 and Luther, "The Freedom of a Christian," 358.

[68] See Noll, "The Lutheran Difference," 31.

[69] See Benne, *The Paradoxical Vision*, ch. 6.

[70] For more on this theme, see Alberto García's chapter in this volume.

[71] Wingren, *Luther on Vocation*, 30.

[72] Bonhoeffer, *The Cost of Discipleship*, 298. For more on this theme, see Alberto García's chapter in this volume.

[73] Thielicke, *How to Believe Again*, 157.

[74] See the discussion in Veith, *Modern Fascism*, ch. 4.

[75] See also Benne, *The Paradoxical Vision*, 79.

[76] Thielicke, *Being Human . . . Becoming Human*, 256.

[77] See also Veith, *Modern Fascism*, 63.

[78] Wingren, *Luther on Vocation*, 87.

[79] See Luther, "On War Against the Turk."

[80] Veith, *Modern Fascism*, 68.

[81] See Wingren, *Luther on Vocation*, 78.

[82] Ibid., 88-89, 121. The classic biblical text is 1 Cor. 7:20.

[83] Ibid., 150.

[84] Ibid., 180.

[85] Noted exceptions include those cases where the death of the fetus is a tragically unavoidable consequence of saving the mother's life. An excellent statement on abortion is The Lutheran Church—Missouri Synod document "That They May Have Life," reprinted in *First Things*, Number 75, 1997, pp. 47-50.

[86] Wingren, *Luther on Vocation*, 149.

[87] Lewis, *Mere Christianity*, 72.

2

Articles of War, Articles of Peace: Christianity and Culture

Martin E. Marty

Christianity and Culture: Culture Defined and Inescapable

Debates rage over almost every aspect of culture, beginning with definitions of the word itself. Under the influence of a book by James Davison Hunter—or at least its title—the term "culture wars" has entered public discourse.[1] While an opinion poll might find that most citizens are unaware of this term and while it is unlikely that they would line up with militants on either side of most issues in these wars, most citizens do give every evidence of being alert to what is at stake. They may battle over obscenity and pornography in mass media of communication; the fights may have to do with concerns over morality, citizenship, civility, or public education. In either and any case, they notice that "articles of war" have been sent forth by partisans. "Articles of peace" seem to be far in the distance or brought forth by unheeded people.

In debates over culture and culture wars, it is the partisans who set up the polarities. Picture this conflict in topographical terms: A great plain or valley lies between two mesas. The artillery of opposing camps sits atop two defining bluffs from which the belligerent definers fire away at each other. Many of their shells fall on the people below, sometimes exploding and causing damage, often causing threat, and still more frequently causing those in the line of fire to huddle at distances from where the explosives go off and the shells fall.

Very few of the wounded, threatened, or huddled will put much energy into wars over the definition of culture. Instead, it is in academic circles where such debates take place. Thus one chapter of Peter Burke's *Varieties of Cultural History* surveys conventional understandings of the term culture as its history has been taught. There Burke deals with classical definitions involving formal and "high" literature, art, music, doctrine, the disciplines, and modes of thought. Eventually he even calls the roll on the great shapers of the discipline, "The History of Culture." Here we read of Francis Bacon, Voltaire, and Jacob Burckhardt.

By the end of the book, Burke is talking about partisans of the other pole among the disciplines, "Cultural Studies." These disciplines tend to be represented in radical and deconstructive approaches to both "high" and "popular" cultural evidences. Many of these approaches are in the hands of scholars on the academic left, late-stage Marxists, or articulators of cultural expression in defense of racial, ethnic, regional, "gendered," and other groups.

The first sentence of Burke's book captures its substance: "There is no agreement over what constitutes cultural history, any more than agreement over what constitutes culture." Burke refers to a forty-year-old effort by two American scholars who found more than two hundred rival definitions. "How can anyone write a history of something which lacks a fixed identity?" For present purposes, since this is not a book on history of culture or disciplinary definitions, one asks, How can one debate the culture wars involving Christianity and culture when culture lacks a fixed identity? (Many would add a similar question: What is the "fixed identity" of Christianity?)[2]

Because one may use provisional abstract definitions to introduce a work on cultural history, one serviceable approach is that of anthropologically informed historian James Axtell:

> Culture is an idealized pattern of meanings, values, and norms differentially shared by the members of a society, which can be inferred from the non-instinctive behavior of the group and from the symbolic products of their actions, including material artifacts, language, and social institutions.[3]

For present purposes, however, we can leave such formal approaches behind and get to the point. Informally: culture is the sum total of the processes and products by which humans do anything and everything to nature (divine creation). Thus: there is a river, a natural object. One can write a poem or novel about it, sing a song about "Ol' Man River" or dance to its rhythms, and thus create a cultural artifact.

Army engineers may change the course of a river, or politicians and builders may levy taxes to raise funds to dam a river, and the result will be a dam culture.

There are gang cultures, church cultures, athletic cultures, horticultures, and agricultures. Professional castes produce cultures; there is the culture of the lawyers, the physicians, and the ministers. In all of these senses, culture and cultures are simply unavoidable even among those who think that they are "above" or "apart" from culture. Thus Orthodox Jews or the Amish will say that they are repudiating the surrounding culture. They may make strenuous efforts to do so. Yet we are familiar with highly recognizable Jewish and Amish cultures (sometimes called subcultures). The Zen monks, Trappist Thomas Merton, or ascetics of any faith will describe themselves as anticultural while often indicating thereby a great awareness of and sensitivity to culture and while creating their own.

Who can escape? American evangelicals are among the more steadfast critics of the secular culture around them, and they take determined steps to reject many elements of it. Yet more than a few observers note that while the more arduous among these evangelicals work to create a culture-within-the-culture, they often replicate it. In a world overgiven, by their account, to athletics as a diversion from spiritual pursuits, they employ athletic metaphors in their sermons and have Christian athletic groups. They produce beauty queens in a culture where once they opposed them; or they promote Christian rock to prevent their youth from being overtaken by the worst in worldly rock. They negotiate with modernity by buying into many elements of it.

That the anticultural often show most awareness of culture and often do the most sophisticated accepting and rejecting of its elements is by no means new. The Old Testament is full of condemnations spoken against Canaan and Egypt, Assyria and Babylon, yet many elements of what believers see as distinctive divine revelation have counterparts in the surrounding cultures. There is a "Babylonian Genesis" that bears some similarities to biblical Genesis. The golden calf of the wandering Israelites was an idolatrous accommodation to the most offensive feature of the surrounding culture, but the Hebrew people, who were God's people, were themselves creators of elaborate cultures of sacrifice, of exodus and exile.

Culture also shows its face in the New Testament. Quite likely Jesus and the disciples were Aramaic- and Hebrew-speaking people, yet only a few Aramaic words appear in the Greek New Testament. Students of culture make much of the fact that language is one of the main bearers of culture. It is of drastic import, then, that the Gospels are in Greek, not in Hebrew. Images such as "the body of Christ" bear resemblances to Stoic terms. It is not an undercutting of the revealed and divine character of the Lord's Supper to note that it was instituted in a culture where mystery religions had confusingly similar meals. The Christian creeds make sense only in the context of Greek philosophy of a sort available in the culture of the time. Preaching today that is culturally insensitive misses connections with the "real world" of the hearers. For the preachers to claim that they are above or apart from culture is either naïve, deliberately obscuring, or an element in their strategies, never an avoidance of culture.

Jose Ortega y Gasset had as a life motto "I am I and my circumstances." The *circumstantia* is all that surrounds me. "I am I" would represent egotism and solipsism and thus seeks to avoid cultural reference. "I am my circumstances" overdoes the place of the culture and is too deterministic. Whatever Christians do to relate to the culture, they are somehow involved in this dialectic. When they work in common as Church, something similar happens. Cardinal Karol Wojtyla, before he became pope, liked to contend—and as pope did exemplify the notion—that the church has a "special interiority" and a "specific openness." We might call the former "the churchly culture" and the latter "the relation to the public culture."

Articles of War: Christianity Negates Elements of Culture

Before we launch into a general discussion of this subject, let us first frame it in a specific theological context, which we might call one version of a Pauline-Augustinian-Lutheran approach. I call it a "*simul*" understanding, using an obscure reference that needs some explaining. It bears analogical relationship to an anthropological and soteriological theme, which means it has to do with what humans are and do and what happens to them when salvation reaches them. In this understanding, the human is at one and the same time a person made righteous and a sinner, *simul justus et peccator*. The distinction depends on how one conceives the eye and mind of God regarding the person. From the aspect of God who views the baptized person "in Christ," this person is made just and regarded as righteous. From the perspective of God who views the person "in Adam," there is only sinful condition and action.

Thus we are not speaking of an "either-or" relationship to culture nor a "now and then" or "partly-partly" situation of the Christian believer in regard to culture.[4] What does that mean for the present theme? The Christian, or Christianity, regards the divine creation as good, if now fallen. Its achievements, along with nature, are *larvae dei*, masks of God, the real God. Yet, as fallen, it is also a place where the demonic pervades the dimensions of existence and will until the end-time and consummations. If that is the case, there can be no easy dismissal of the promises of culture or simple affirmation of a culture that includes blight.

Therefore, a kind of theological anthropology is involved whenever the Christian in this tradition approaches culture. Here are some samples:

- If the human is regarded as *homo economicus*, we can see that people work out the purposes of God when they labor, are productive, and make possible a material existence. Yet homo economicus can also disserve God and counter divine purposes by bad stewardship, misuse of the resources of the earth, selfishness, or falling into "consumerism" and "commodification." The choices (in H. Richard Niebuhr's terms as they inform this whole book) can then never be either "Christ above" or "Christ against" culture or "Christ of" culture.[5]

- If the human is regarded as *homo ludus*, as the playful creation of God, he or she can serve the purposes of God by observing Sabbath and taking rest; by encouraging vacation and play; by being God's "grave-merry" person who affirms in the face of realism. Or such a person may pervert the understanding and fall victim to an obsession with diversion and entertainment. Christ of culture? Christ above culture? Christ against culture? None of these options are applicable in this understanding.

- If the human is viewed in the light of her or his being *homo politicus*, the arena constituted by the *polis*, the human city, can be a place where the Lord of history is seen to rule and citizens can work out the purposes of God for justice. But such humans also can turn politics into devilish instrumentations for subjugating and terrorizing others. Since the same invention, politics, can do both and since ordinarily some expression of both is potentially or actually present, it is not in place to invoke "Christ of" or "Christ above and against" culture.

- If the human is seen as *homo religiosus*, things seem to be more complicated, but the same double perspective applies. Efforts by humans to be "spiritual" in the mode of spirituality-seekers in our present culture can often work against the purposes of God. Our human artifacts of meditation, devotion, and piety can actually keep one from seeking or recognizing the saving Gospel of God in Christ. So much for the negative dialectic. But the concept of the human as religious can be developed into enhancements, into "growth in grace," and can thus serve the purposes of God. Is this Christ above or Christ against culture? Or Christ of culture? Such options do not match the framework and perspective of the simul approach.

- If the human is seen nationalistically, for example, as *homo Americanus*, with the person defined by being in a specific nation-state's culture, he or she can be conceived of and observed as someone who serves divine order in the pursuit of justice on a communal level. But just as often the same symbols of nationhood can keep one from the God who is God, the real God, who would have humans shun idols.

But between the collapses of "Christ of culture" into mere affirmation and the negations of "Christ above" or "Christ against" culture, there are numbers of options. In H. Richard Niebuhr's terms and in most historians' understanding, the United States was shaped by Reformed-Puritan, Roman Catholic, and post-Protestant Enlightenment designs. Niebuhr saw these as "Christ transforming" culture. A kind of metaphysic of progress undergirds this view. No matter how many setbacks, how many contradictions and frustrations, overall the tendency is for people to "bring on the Kingdom of God" or utopia or the good society in processive and progressive terms.

In the face of potential allies produced in the "Christ transforming culture" school, the Pauline-Augustinian-Lutheran interpretations as here set forth (note: these may not be the only way of viewing the tradition) have their own articles of war, their own kind of culture war against the prevailing cultural ethos and ideology. Thus the Lutheran in such a culture is quite likely to confuse the "Christ transforming culture" affirmations with its own minority tradition at its most porous edges and boundaries.

So, if one may use the not fully congenial military metaphor, the Lutheran is involved in a culture war inside the culture wars. He or she is working to determine and express distinctive minority conceptions of Christ and culture and then allying with other Christians against non-, anti-, or counter-Christian interpretations. Such wars need not be violent in character. They have to do with academic, political, and esthetic distinctions that may look minor. Yet in their extensions they can lead to gross misinterpretations of how the Gospel is appropriated in the culture and how ethics, "faith active in love," is conceived. In H. Richard Niebuhr's terms, this is "Christ and culture in paradox," in dialectical relations, permitting *simul*, at the same time, affirmations and negations.

Articles of Peace: Giving Expression to the "*Simul*" Approach

John Courtney Murray liked to say that Americans could not hope to live with "articles of faith." They had to content themselves with "articles of peace," declarations and assumptions that allowed them to get on with the show of working in the culture. It is not likely that in any foreseeable generation the Pauline-Augustinian-Lutheran view, as here explicated, will prevail in—at best and at most—a culture of "Christ transforming culture." Christians who care about culture will not form a camp of people all of whom agree with each other, but they are not given the luxury of sitting out the conflicts. So it is appropriate to ask, in the face of implicit Lutheran acceptances of the "Christ against" or "Christ above" culture approaches, What makes possible even the idea of articles of peace?

Let me point to several resources.

On creedal lines, there is a distinctive understanding of creation and the Creator. In the Large Catechism, there is affirmation of God as Creator and the human as responsible agent. As already mentioned, the created order, the raw material of culture, if you will, is the *larva dei*, the mask of God. Nowhere is the Christian inhibited from creating culture, and always the creations of culture have negative and even demonic dimensions. The decisive victory over the forces that oppose the good has occurred, but evil lives on. One cannot simply affirm the culture ("Christ of") in a way that collapses creational distinctives. But one is never free either to fall into the opposite spiritualist intention and distance one's self from cultural creation ("Christ against" or "Christ above").

In respect to the Second Article of the Creed, there is in the Pauline-Augustinian-Lutheran understanding, an affirmation of the potential of the human, thanks to the incarnation. In one translation of a Christmas hymn, Lutherans used to sing (and still do affirm) the call to tell abroad God's goodness: "Who our race hath honored thus, that He deigns to dwell with us." The language of race is today confusing and not to be used in this sense. The "haths" and "deigns" are on the way to the antique shop. But vivid as always is the notion that the same person who is sinner and thus corrupter of the divine image and the relation to the Incarnate One is also "a Christ to the neighbor," which means *simul*, at the same time, capable of and called to extraordinary cultural creation. The first chapters of the Epistle to the Hebrews insist that the created and human world, not the angelic realm, is where the act of redemption and its workings out go on. Colossians 1:17 is only one of many affirmations that all things are created in and through and for Christ and in Christ all things hold together. How can that world in which God has become one of us be seen as only the devil's sphere in ways that "Christ above" or "Christ against" cultures see it? How can the world, inside whose history perfection and fulfillment are to be denied, be seen as the place where "Christ of" culture is the norm?

The Third Article of the Creed is also a part of the articles of peace for the Christian who is *simul justus et peccator* and *simul*, at the same time, someone who is at home in the culture and yet must be wary of its entanglements. The Christian confesses that, under the Holy Spirit, there is a church catholic. The word "catholic" does not only mean "universal." It also has a Greek rootage: *kata+holos*, the divine penetrates all the dimensions of being and opens them all to Christian engagement and interpretation. At the same time there is a profession that there is an "unholy" and that it exists not only in a realm away from where the Christian and the Church are active but also and often precisely near their hearts. The Church cannot be in a "Christ of" culture situation, for then its "special interiority" is eroded and exposed. It cannot be in a situation of "Christ against" or "Christ above" culture for then its "specific openness" gets closed off.

Articles of War, Articles of Peace

In the Pauline-Augustinian-Lutheran conception of culture as here interpreted, the approach is Word-centered and Christ-centered. The human is an agent, a participant. Luther liked to affirm that "the Word did it all," that while he and his colleagues sat still and drank beer, God dealt the papacy a mighty blow. But God used the activity of the reformers who had more and other to do than to sit still and drink beer.

I want to close by merely pointing to some of the Lutheran resources for dealing *simul*, at the same time, in warlike and peaceful ways with the surrounding cultures.

- *Simul justus et peccator* as already defined is a starting point for this particular set of interpretations, modalities that are not identical to those of the "Christ transforming" schools of Reformed-Puritan, Catholic, and post-Protestant Enlightenment that shaped much of the culture that is never merely secular.

- *Finitum capax infiniti*. The finite is capable of bearing the infinite. This has to do most directly with bread and wine and water of the sacraments, of lips and tongues and gestures of the preached word, or the walk of life in Christian vocation. The drama of salvation and vocation is not lived out in the angelic realm because the finite cannot bear the infinite; it is worked out in the finite realm because, under the Word, it is capable of bearing the divine.

- *Justitia civilis*. While the righteousness effected in political and other humanistic dimensions of culture is not "the righteousness that avails before God" for one's salvation, still such effects are done under the Lord of history and are God-pleasing on the civil levels. The stories of Cyrus in Isaiah and Cornelius in Acts are examples of this.

- *Extra Locum Justificationis*. The Law of God can never be the "power of God unto salvation." In this interpretation, *in loco justificationis*, when one is in the position of being justified or when one "locates" the doctrine of justification, the law only accuses and destroys, *lex semper accusat*. But in *extra locum justificationis*, the law is a power of God unto the care of the neighbor and the ordering of human affairs.

- *The exalted individual.* Here we refer not to the Man-God, the *Uebermensch* of Friedrich Nietzsche, or any one in the Promethean tradition. Instead the reference is to God-Man, God turned human in the incarnation and, derivatively, present in the workings of the made-just individual.
- *The prophetic community.* The church is a contemporary expression of the prophetic community. As a human institution, it is never perfect and is always subject to all the temptations and many of the expressions of evil. As earthen vessel bearer of the treasure of the Word, it stands against the present state of culture but never abandons it. Those who live in this realm can be allies with others who are discontented with cultural manifestations and seek to advance human purposes, but in the Lutheran interpretation, they will not thereby bring in the kingdom of God.
- *A humane-ironic view of history.* Here I collapse insights of Luther, Abraham Lincoln, and Reinhold Niebuhr. In this conspectus, the word of Psalm 2:4 depicts a laughing God who disdains human claims of perfection or high achievement: "God that sits in the heavens shall laugh" when the powers of the world take counsel together, necessarily "against the Lord's anointed." For Niebuhr this meant that things never turn out the way the well-intended want them to. There are outcomes contradictory to human purpose, and these are not the result of Fate. No, there is enough vice in human virtue (individual and collective), enough ignorance wrapped into knowledge, enough guilt contained within innocences, that things will go wrong. But the same God who laughs at human pretension also holds humans responsible, does not disdain human aspiration, and blesses effort.
- *The Church is a* Werden *and not a* Sein. This means that the Christian Church as the embodiment of the cultural construct called Christianity is not and never will be a finished product, a "being," a *Sein.* It will always be a "becoming," part of a

process that will never lead to the Kingdom or to perfection, but it is still called to faithfulness, including in culture-creation.

- *Alter Christus.* Again, as mentioned as part of the articles of peace that permit constructive but not perfecting activity, the same one who is a sinner, *peccator*, is at the same time, *simul*, the just one in Christ, and is capable of being and called to be "another Christ" to the neighbor. This insight is of great significance in culture-creation.

- *The* civitas, *the* polis *as* larva dei. The civil order, the human city, though especially prone to demonic activity because of the way power is there asserted, is precisely the sphere in which the works of God for human good are to be worked out, even if in masked creational and cultural forms.

- *Eschatology and responsibility.* I like to quote sentiments assigned to Luther but two that I've not yet found in his corpus: "God carves the rotten wood, God rides the lame horse." And "If they told me the world would end tomorrow, I would still plant my apple tree today." The "Christ transforming culture" approach pictures that one plants and builds as an element in the path to perfection. The "Christ and culture in paradox" approach calls for responsible action each day, no matter what the empirical situation or where history and the culture are going.

- *Vocation.* In this Lutheran understanding, the Gospel of forgiveness removes the burden of yesterday and care for tomorrow, freeing the baptized person for responsible action, which means culture-creation, today.

These are all and only underdeveloped clues, each of them worth a chapter, a session, a curriculum, or a life work. They are signposts along the way, suggestions of elements that provide theological interpretations of individual and collective human action.

Never do Christians find peace that will end the conflict legitimately anticipated and defined by articles of war in culture. Nor do Christians ever dare succumb to apathy, antipathy, simple irony, or false spiritualism that takes them and their company away from the scene where contention over culture occurs—which means that Christians live *simul*, at the same time, with articles of peace.

Martin E. Marty is the Fairfax M. Cone Distinguished Service Professor Emeritus at The University of Chicago and Director of the Public Religion Project.

Bibliography

Axtell, James L. *The European and the Indian: Essays in the Ethnohistory of Colonial North America*. New York: Oxford University Press, 1981.

Burke, Peter. *Varieties of Cultural History*. Ithaca, NY: Cornell University Press, 1997.

Hunter, James Davison. *Culture Wars: The Struggle to Define America*. New York: Basic Books, 1991.

Marty, Martin E. *"Simul*: A Lutheran Reclamation Project in the Humanities" in *The Cresset* (December 1981).

Notes

[1] James Davison Hunter, *Culture Wars: The Struggle to Define America* (New York: Basic Books, 1991).

[2] Peter Burke, *Varieties of Cultural History* (Ithaca, NY: Cornell University Press, 1997), chaps. 1 and 12, pp. 1-22 and 183-212 and esp. pp. 1-2. Burke's book is one of the more valuable introductions to the field of cultural history and is relatively free of "cultural studies" ideological biases.

[3] James L. Axtell, *The European and the Indian: Essays in the Ethnohistory of Colonial North America* (New York: Oxford University Press, 1981), p. 6.

[4] For an elaboration of this approach, see Martin E. Marty, *"Simul:* A Lutheran Reclamation Project in the Humanities" in *The Cresset* (December 1981), pp. 7-14.

[5] Niebuhr's types are explained in the previous chapter by Menuge, "Niebuhr's *Christ and Culture* Reexamined." The "Christ above" view holds that culture should stand in hierarchical subordination to Christ and the church. The "Christ against" view holds that Christians must separate themselves from a godless world. The "Christ of" view attempts to accommodate Christianity with what currently seems best in culture.—Ed.

3

Christological Reflections on Faith and Culture

Alberto L. García

Introduction

I received my first lesson on the relationship of Christianity and culture from Dr. Andrés Larín, my sixth grade teacher, in La Habana, Cuba. Dr. Larín narrated the following event to me from Father Bartolomé las Casas:

> A Franciscan Friar was seeking to persuade Cacique Hatuey to become a Christian before he died. The latter asked "why one must be like the Christians, who were wicked." The Father replied, "Because those who die Christian go to heaven, ever to behold the face of God, and take their ease and enjoyment." (Hatuey) inquired once more whether Christians went to heaven: the Father said yes, those who were good did. The other finally said he had no wish to go there, since they (the Christians) went there, and were there. This occurred at a moment when it had been decided to burn him alive, so then they extended him over a slow fire and burned him alive."
>
> (Las Casas, Historia de las Indias, bk. 2, ch. 25)[1]

The story narrated by Father Las Casas presents a challenge and a problem for the Christian church. It also presents a great challenge for me, a Christian missionary and theologian. Every missionary is capable of succumbing to his or her sinful pride and cultural ethnocentrism in the name of Christianity. It is important to address this problem in light of the apostolic missionary vision of the church.

I see as the primary vision of the Christian Church the missionary task of making disciples of Jesus Christ from all races and cultures (Cf. Matthew 28:18-20). The Christian church is apostolic. The apostolic adjective is derived from the verb *apostéllo*. This verb marks the

Christian church as a "sending" church with the message of the Gospel.[2] The early creeds of the Christian church were transmitted orally for the purpose of confessing Christ in a hostile world. It is in this light that the Christian church lives the vision of the early church. In the words of Leslie Newbegin: "The early church did not see itself as a private religious society; it saw itself as a movement launched into the public life of the world, challenging the *'cultus publicus'* of the empire."[3]

The early church, however, confessed her essence and work as "catholic."[4] The mission of the church has been widely misunderstood in light of this term. "Catholic" has been understood mainly as a synonym for the term "universal." Here the church is seen as exercising her universal proclamation and rule over the world in light of the Great Commission (Matthew 28:18-20). The term, however, was used by Ireneus and Ignatius of Antioch to express a more profound reality. "Catholic" *(katholikos)* means etymologically speaking "according to the whole."[5] This vision does not confess a universality where the different parts of the world and cultures are swallowed or rejected by the Gospel. Rather, as Ireneus observed, the four Gospels were necessary because they offered the four "principal" or universal (the word used by him is "catholic") winds.[6] This fourfold witness was essential to the witness of the church. Ignatius understood his witness as "catholic" because he did not conform to a single witness but rather to the witness of the "entire catholic church." The parts were important for the witness of the whole. It is in light of this reality that the church confesses her catholicity in Jesus Christ. Jesus' witness presents a contrast to the human condition and the demonic powers present in the world. His witness is "catholic" because it encompasses all the corners of God's creation in the body of Christ, the church.

The focus of this essay is, therefore, to search for a healthy relationship between faith and culture for a Christian witness in light of the church's apostolicity and catholicity. The church is apostolic in light of Christ's witness in opposition to evil in the world. It is "catholic" in light of Christ's presence encompassing the different cultures of the world. This is an essential perspective because as we will see the present postmodern situation is marked by an ethnocentrism and cultural pluralism that gives offense to Christ's testimony.

I will argue that we must return to an apostolic Christology in order to find a faithful witness and a catholic dialogue between faith and culture. This is a necessary task to confront the problems of our postmodern Western culture. This is also the greatest challenge of the Christian church as it struggles to be a "holy, catholic, and apostolic church" in the twenty-first century. I will use H. Richard Niebuhr's classic work *Christ and Culture* in this study.[7] He offers several important typologies to consider in discerning the proper relationship between Christianity and culture. It is crucial to consider these typologies in light of our Western neopaganism. We will see how an apostolic Christology incorporates Niebuhr's constructive themes for a critical witness to our contemporary culture. This constructive reflection will require, therefore: 1) a discernment of the current crisis of faith and culture; 2) an appraisal of Niebuhr's typologies in light of the contemporary situation; 3) a reconsideration of an apostolic Christology in light of the sign of the times. It is important, however, for the sake of clarity to engage in some definitions.

Definition of Terms

The terms "faith" and "Gospel" will be used interchangeably in this essay. The ground of faith in the catholic evangelical tradition is the Gospel. The term "faith," however, is sometimes used as an anthropological dimension of life. Faith as an anthropological dimension is the act of trust through which human beings find identity and meaning. This essay is directed to the ground rather than the act of our faith. We cannot separate ourselves from the act of faith. However, unless this act grounds us in God's ultimate concern for His creation, we live in idolatry. This is Luther's vision in his explanation of the First Commandment.[8]

The term "Gospel" is used in a narrower and a wider sense in the catholic evangelical tradition. "Gospel" refers in a narrower sense to the message of forgiveness in Christ. In a wider sense the term "Gospel" underscores primarily the teaching of Jesus and His apostles. I will underscore in this reflection the Gospel in the wider sense.[9] The Gospel in this context points to Christ's teachings in relationship to being the church in the world. The message of redemption is foundational. However, how we live Christ's teaching grounded in his redemption is the primary focus of this reflection.

It is important to define also the meaning of "culture" for this constructive reflection. In his address "Articles of War, Articles of Peace" [developed in the previous chapter], Martin Marty cautions the student of culture not to be hindered by so many definitions and methods in defining culture. Marty defines culture formally and informally. Culture may be defined from a descriptive phenomenological perspective. Culture is always social and bound with human life. Culture is human achievement, "a process and product of anything and everything that humans do."[10] H. Richard Niebuhr offers also a similar definition influenced by the functionalist motif in his study of culture: "Culture comprises language, habits, ideas, beliefs, customs, social organization, inherited artifacts, technical processes, and values."[11] Niebuhr identifies this "social heritage," this "reality *sui generis*" with what the New Testament writers mean by "the world."[12] The dynamic of culture is, therefore, an integral part of our created humanity.

Neopaganism in Light of Modernism and Postmodernism

In his essay "The Gospel for a Neopagan Culture," Carl Braaten describes present Western culture as a neopagan culture. He finds similarities in our contemporary paganism with "ancient beliefs of pre-Christian mystery religions."[13] Ancient pre-Christian religions prided themselves for having a secret knowledge of the sacred. They were called gnostics because they had a special inner knowledge of the divine. This special knowledge became the way of salvation or liberation of the human spirit. Today a similar situation can be discerned at the dawn of the twenty-first century. The intellectual and cultural climate of the Western worldview demonstrates an idolatrous preoccupation with the individual and her/his freedom. The important factor in the equation of the Nietzschean postmodern person is her/his ability to stand in tune with this inner identity and freedom of choice. Gnostics, however, did not retreat from culture but sought to find within culture those ideas and perspectives that were accommodating to their ideals of what they understood as best within civilization. It is in this light that they accommodated their vision of Christ. This idolatrous standing with the inner self is what Ernst Troeltsch labeled, in light of the Enlightenment's influence on Christian churches, "the secret religion of the educated classes."[14] This influence of modernism is present in the current postmodern Western worldview.[15] It is imperative to discern the influences of these intellectual movements upon out Western society in order not to give offense to the proclamation of the Gospel.

In considering the influence of the Enlightenment on the Christian church, we cannot forget that the fathers of the Enlightenment were all Christians. They viewed their work as a service to humanity. This was certainly true of Francis Bacon, René Descartes, Galileo Galilei, Isaac Newton, and Gottfried Wilhelm Leibniz. Descartes was deeply rooted for instance in the scholastic tradition.[16] It is important to summarize their key principles. They are important for our understanding of the modernist influence on postmodernism.

There are seven cardinal convictions inherited through the Enlightenment in modernism. These are:

1. The priority of the individual's ability to reason (*cogito ergo sum*, Descartes);
2. Knowledge is acquired through thinking subjects over against objects that could be analyzed and controlled;
3. All reference to purpose is dropped and every process is viewed within the Newtonian vision of cause and effect;
4. Progress, expansion, advance, and modernization is critical to the triumph of modernism;
5. There is the assumption that all knowledge is factual, value free, and neutral. Values are not objectively true. They are a matter of taste. The unhindered exercise of "universal reason" is promoted under this principle;
6. All problems are in principle solvable;
7. People are emancipated, autonomous, free thinking individuals, no longer under the tutelage of others.[17]

Enrique Dussel, a Latin American theologian and philosopher, and Lamin Sanneh, an African theologian and scholar, have shown extensively how these principles were disguised in the name of

Christianity to disdain the indigenous cultures of Latin America and Africa.[18]

In his *The Invention of the Americas*, Enrique Dussel analyses the universal, univocal use of reason in modernity. He sees in this use of reason, a biased excuse to eclipse "the Other" through the promotion of a more "cultured" Eurocentrism. This "cultured" Eurocentrism found the other non-Western cultures to be the domain of inferior, immature races. Dussel quotes Kant's answer to the question "What Is Enlightenment?" to support his answer.

> Enlightenment (*Aufklärung*) is the exit of humanity by humanity from a state of culpable immaturity (*verschuldenten Unmündigkeit*) . . . . Laziness and cowardliness are the causes which bind the great part of humanity in this frivolous state of immaturity.[19]

Dussel shows how this superior logic of universal reason was developed by Hegel and identified with Christianity.

In his lectures *Concerning the Philosophy of World History*, Hegel portrays world history (*Weltgeschichte*) as the self-realization of God, as a theodicy for the justification of reason and freedom (*Freiheit*). This self-realization of God marks the process of the Enlightenment.

In the Hegelian ontology, the concept of development (*Entwicklung*) occupies a key role. This concept of development determines the movement of a concept (*Begriff*) until it culminates in the idea. This concept unfolds in a linear dialectic. It was originally an ontological category. Today development is considered a sociological category with important consequences for world history. This concept of development was passed on to Marx, who used it primarily within economics and sociology. According to Hegel, an underdeveloped country is ontologically defined as non-modern and pre-Enlightenment.[20] Furthermore, this development has had a specific direction: "Universal history goes from East to West. Europe is absolutely the end of history. Asia is the beginning."[21] The Latin American worldview is found in the periphery of this world of influence. It has no influence in the world of European intellectual history. The same goes for the African reality. In this vision the parts have no integral contribution to make to the whole. This worldview promotes a racist view of history.

Dussel promotes, therefore, a principle of transrationality. This means that specific groups must be honored in their particular rationality. Nevertheless, this particularity must speak in an intelligible and valid manner to other cultures. This is also the aim of the African theologian Lamin Sanneh.[22]

Furthermore, the Enlightenment's absolute claim of universal reason gave way also to the demystification of religion. This outlook has led to the present crisis facing the Christian church and postmodern Western society. This crisis may be defined rephrasing the famous dictum of Lord Acton: "Individuality corrupts but absolute individuality corrupts absolutely." This consequence may be perceived in the mainline Protestant churches through their privatization of religion and uncritical agreement with contemporary human causes. It may be perceived also in the fundamentalist churches with their absolute claim to speak only of personal salvation.[23] It may be discerned also in the postmodern claim of individual choices over society. This claim comes to us through the cacophony of many imperialistic voices present in the church and society.[24] This is our inheritance from modernism.

How may we describe the present postmodern claim to maturity? We may discern clearly the modern claim to demystify religion. God is still out of the picture. Universal reason is present in an implicit manner through the contemporary idolatry of technology by society. This is quite evident in the medical, business, and educational fields. Bill Gates is the new guru.[25] We are still on the quest of mastering the world. We value above all our individual use of reason in our personal choices and in our tolerance of others. Universal reason has been elevated to an art form through the promotion of cultural relativism as a way of freedom and tolerance. Christianity is distrusted for her claim to finality. Yet postmodernism claims the finality of the right of the individual over the community.[26] There cannot be, therefore, a healthy relationship between Christianity and culture.[27] This same principle has produced a crisis in the relationship between cultures.

Today there is a crisis concerning human worth because there is a crisis concerning truth and values. We have agreed to disagree in the postmodern age. The principle of cultural relativism and the rejection of the reciprocity among cultures is central to this vision of reality.[28] The only scientific dogmatic claim possible is the fundamental claim that there are no absolutes, no universal norms. Cultural relativism claims the particularity and uniqueness of each culture. We must respect each culture for what it is. Since there are no absolute values, however, I may consider also the values of other cultures to be unimportant. These may sound like civilized claims of maturity. The problem is that the history of humanity points to the exploitation of humanity by humanity. The paradigms of scientific objectivism and cultural relativism mask our individual and collective sin of pride and self-interest. This problem may be discovered in a brief overview of the current states of affairs in the field of cultural anthropology.

Cultural anthropologists follow different methods in their studies of human culture.[29] The modern study of cultural anthropology in American universities is grounded on the work of Franz Boas (1858-1942). He was a German scientist trained in physics. Boas's premise was that "culture" refers to "customs, beliefs, and social institutions, characteristic of separate societies."[30] Each society has a culture of its own. Each society has to be studied on its own merit.

Boas's contribution is that he established the method of "ethnography" as the primary method to study cultural anthropology. Previously, the science of ethnology involved the study of people from a purely "deductive" method where "ideal types," or "dummies" were analyzed. Boas's method of study emphasized as the only proper method a direct field relationship with living cultures. Interviews are at the center of this methodology. His direct observation of cultural phenomena destroyed the myths of biological or race superiority. He observed also the importance of family lines, rather than race, as the most important mechanism of inheritance. He provided a scientific basis for individualism. He believed that each individual human being is unique, the product of her/his particular heredity, and of her/his life experience. In other words, he realized also that equality of races did not mean equality of individuals. Boas's analytic method was directed primarily to discuss the very important problems of racism, discrimination of nations, and cultures. He offered an ethical rational intentionality through his discipline.

Boas upheld the principles of universalism and particularity in his vision of humanity. Universalism spelled out the need for reciprocity, common respect and peace among all people and all human cultures. Uniformity spelled out stagnation for Boas in "keeping alive the intellectual and emotional activities of mankind."[31] This vision of maintaining a dialectical relationship between universal reciprocity and respect for particularity is imperative for any meaningful educational and missionary program. This vision suggests that a Christological reflection on faith and culture is essential to the apostolic witness. Boas's anthropological studies offer some important insights for a constructive Christological proposal.

Boas was influenced primarily by the liberal romanticism of the Enlightenment. He valued primarily the unique potentialities of each person through the use of reason. This use of reason would lead humanity to live in a sane, reasonable, and good society. He opposed the ethnocentric cultural evolution of the nineteenth century. He believed, however, in a cultural progress. This cultural progress would be demonstrated through the growth of knowledge and above all personal autonomy and human progress through the proper use of reason.[32] Boas recognized, however, the problem of power as an obstacle to his rational pursuit. Power was demonstrated primarily through imperialistic expansion. He found a key to imperialism in the vision of a fictitious common culture, and common racial language. He attributed ethnic oppositions "not to any rational cause . . . but solely to the emotional appeal of an idea that holds together the members of each group and exalts their feeling of solidarity and greatness to such an extent that compromises with any other groups become impossible . . . ."[33] He recognized, therefore, the limits of reason to overcome the real issue of power demonstrated through ideological commitments to a group.[34]

The old medieval problem of the relationship of the universal to the particular appears again in the context of this cultural crisis. Justo L. González points to the position of the radical nominalists in the Middle Ages. The universals have no correspondence to reality beyond the mind in this position. Thought has no correspondence to reality. Therefore, all statements are so particular that they become meaningless.[35] In this perspective, the rule is what a dominant group decides is important in the scheme of things. This may be done without reciprocity with other cultures. The claims made by the Enlightenment on honoring absolute reason in a cause and effect universe led to the present cultural claims of postmodernity. It has produced in effect the present anthropological crisis of honoring only the individual in their cultural world. This is evident through two case studies shared by Lamin Sanneh. How did we arrive at cultural relativism?

Cultural anthropology during World War II underscored the absolute claim of reason to cultural relativism. Each culture had to stand for their unique claim to life. Cultural relativism was established as a proper rational principle and a healthy concern to reject the destructive consequences of Western imperialism in cultural and religious concerns. This principle, however, created another form of ethnocentrism. It created the attitude of allowing each culture to be a law to itself. This freedom of the intellect created the disregard for all of God's creatures. This is evident in the U.S. War Department's efforts during World War II and in the formulation of the United Nations Chapter.

The War Department convened a group of cultural anthropologists to help fight the psychological campaign of German National Socialism. One of the anthropologists objected to the meeting on the ground that cultural anthropology was a scientific discipline that carried no ethical biases. There cannot be value judgments made. His reply was, therefore: " . . . if the Germans preferred Nazism, they were entitled to that preference, just as democratic Americans are entitled to that preference."[36]

Melvin Herskovits, a cultural anthropologist, uncovered the same problem when he was asked to draft a document on human rights for the United Nations in 1947. These were his main theses and conclusions:

   a) humanity realizes her potential only through culture;
   b) cultures are unique and therefore there are no objective
      scientific standards for their evaluation;
   c) standards of judgment are relative to each culture.

Herskovits concluded, therefore, that there are no absolute moral codes, and we cannot, therefore, impose a universal declaration of human rights on all humanity. They are in essence scientifically and morally indefensible.[37] This crisis has been aggravated in postmodernism. The claim is that reason may be used to the point of choosing her limits as to universal claims of value and meaning. We find here an important crisis for the apostolic witness in society. The denial of the worth of each human culture may lead to an ethnocentric imperialism through the misuse of power. The denial of universal values and commonality leads also to ethnocentrism and the building of walls between cultures. This is why it is important for the Christian church to reflect on the implications of an apostolic Christology for her witness. This is very important for my witness in the context of U.S. Hispanic culture.

I would like to cite here the work of the mujerista theologian Ada María Isasí-Díaz. Díaz, as well as many feminist theologians, criticizes the social sciences for their use of ideal types or "dummies" in their ethnomethodologies. The science of ethnography requires the hearing of real voices by people who are able to hear and understand these voices. Isasí-Díaz, as well as Roberto Goizueta, underscore that it is important to hear those particular voices. There is the need for a real incarnational presence of Jesus in the hearing of the human situation. The protest that follows is that while those voices may be heard, they have no universal validity to the larger dominant culture. For example, people with emotions who give priority to an aesthetic rationality vis à vis a modernistic rationality as a way of ethical commitment, are viewed as backward and inferior by the children of the Enlightenment. Fiestas, a key cultural expression to the Hispanic value system, may be considered a waste of time rather than a way of affirmation of the family, the community, and a way to live out our Christian spirituality. The point is that there cannot be an affirmation of the specific human particularity, of the specific cultures unless they have referent points in the world community.[38]

Justo L. González underscores the need for this dialogical reciprocity in his reading of Scriptures through a new metanarrative.[39] We cannot do offense to the Hatueys of this world if we proclaim the Gospel. This Gospel must also have universal validity for the world community. The reality of Jesus Christ, true God and true man, without division or confusion, can help us in this dialogical witness in the world. This is the kind of empathic witness exercised by Jesus with the Samaritan woman (John 4) and Bartimaeus (Mark 10:46-52). The incarnational listening to the human situation is as important as the universal offer of grace. This listening will also require our honoring of God's creatures within their human context. This brings us to a look at Niebuhr's *Christ and Culture* in light of the Christological question.

Christ and Culture in Postmodern Jerusalem and Athens

The purpose of this section is to show how Niebuhr's typologies help us to explain the present crisis of faith and culture. We shall see also how his analysis is not sufficient to confront the postmodern crisis of cultural relativism and ethnocentrism. This is due primarily to his approach in the matter. Niebuhr's methodology places Christ in relationship to culture in all of his typological studies. This is a mistake. There are two fallacies present in this paradigmatic vision. He assumes first of all that our knowledge of Christ may come apart from culture. This is an impossibility since none of our knowledge of Christ ever comes apart from culture. Our cultural baggage is always present in our interpretation of Christianity. Justo L. González finds this to be Niebuhr's greatest weakness in his typological framework.[40] Niebuhr also does not understand the dynamic of culture. Culture is never monolithic. Culture is like a living organism in constant change.[41] Therefore, the question of how Christ relates to culture is not the proper question. González offers some poignant critical questions to redirect Niebuhr's constructive inquiry:

> To what extent is our present understanding of Christianity determined by our culture? How does our culture limit our understanding of Christianity? How should our understanding of Christianity be corrected?[42]

I will show, therefore, how an apostolic Christology offers a more adequate model to answer these three questions in our postmodern Jerusalem. Let us first, however, consider Niebuhr's proposal.

Niebuhr's typologies are well known by North American theologians. He offers first of all two extreme positions. The first model is the one of Christ against culture exemplified by the Mennonites and Tolstoy. He calls these the radical Christians or countercultural Christians. The second model is the accommodating model of the Christ of culture exemplified by the Christian gnostics and several Christian intellectuals influenced by the Enlightenment. He discusses in particular John Locke and Albrecht Ritschl as representatives of cultural protestantism. Niebuhr finds in the outlook of these two typologies the cause for the same end result. The radical Christians create their own Christian counterculture in opposition to the world. [43] This leaves the culture a free hand to reign in her own milieu. Christians live elsewhere. The accommodating Christians leave culture unchecked also by allowing culture to dictate the way of Christianity.[44] We may say that in these two models we do not find Christ as a point of critique in relationship to culture.[45] Both positions suffer also from a certain naiveté in relationship to the human condition. In their construction of a Christian community, the radical Christians do not recognize the Trojan horse of radical sin inside their city gates. The accommodating Christians assume too much goodness within the human spirit.[46] Christ, therefore, assumes no critical function in our social existence in the world. The radical Christians also do not give much evidence of the presence of the Trinitarian God in creation. The accommodating Christians acknowledge the Creator but find very little room for Christ as Redeemer of the world.[47] It is in light of these typologies of Either/Or, that Niebuhr turns to three typologies of the church of the center. These typologies are grounded on the vision of both/and.[48] This is to say that Christ and culture must exist in a careful inclusive relationship in light of three factors. These are: 1) God is the Creator God and always exists in Trinitarian relationship with his world; 2) humans experience the reality of sin at the individual and social level; 3) Jesus the Christ and the question of Christology are key components to the dialogue with society and the transformation of society.

His main chapters in *Christ and Culture* are an attempt to construct a theological vision and method grounded in Christology to discern the proper relationship between Christ and culture. He discusses the theological traditions of Christ above culture, the Christ against culture, and Christ the transformer of culture as important contributions from the church of the center to the dialogue of the relationship of Christ to culture.[49] He finds the majority of Christianity within these movements of the center. Niebuhr finds strengths and weaknesses within each typology toward the relationship of Christ and culture.

In the relationship of Christ above culture he finds a helpful model because it provides a synthetic vision of the most important perspectives of the radical and accommodating Christians. The most important representative in this vision is St. Thomas Aquinas. This is considered a very important vision for Roman Catholic theology. In this model, God is present in Christ to bridge the gulf that exists between Him and a sinful humanity. God is also present directing humanity and creation to His final purpose. Niebuhr finds in this synthesis a proper application of the Christ of Chalcedon ("Jesus . . . is both God and man, one person, with two 'natures' that are neither to be confused or separated"[50]). Human culture is honored even though there is to be found only "imperfect happiness." This synthesis allowed Thomas to look at each culture and age anew without prejudice. In the words of Niebuhr, "Culture discerns the rules for culture, because culture is the work of God-given reason in God-given nature."[51] Each period in human history represents a time for God's creation to be valued and enjoyed. Here reason and revelation come together in a common understanding. Thomas also had a hierarchical vision. The rules of social life were directed by reason but they were finally governed by a higher purpose. For example, private property is not contrary to natural law. The use of private property, however, is indefensible for purely egotistical ends.[52]

Thomas's synthesis provides for Niebuhr some important points of departure. Thomas, Augustine, and Luther agree in the importance of civil virtues and just social institutions. Niebuhr finds, however, that Thomas exhorted the value of present institutions for the benefit of society more than Augustine or Luther.

> For the concentration on the future Kingdom of God can easily lead to the denial that God reigns now; the desire for what is not present may easily bring with it the affirmation that what is presented comes from a devil rather than from God.[53]

This is in essence an important perspective for U.S. Hispanic theologians like myself. The point being that the values inherent within each of our cultures have a place within the creative mind of God. Otherwise, we may tend to ignore the value of each specific culture. In other words, Thomas's perspective offers in my opinion a valuable model with which to look at each culture. Cultures are not monolithic. They change. They incorporate in their social life values and perspectives from other cultures and historical periods. Thomas's pre-Enlightenment picture of culture did not see his contemporary culture as superior. He found each culture as having an important place for God in the world. What is the greatest weakness of this synthetic vision? It does not deal sufficiently enough with the paradoxical realities of the world. This is due, I believe, to the tendency of medieval scholasticism to separate the person of Jesus Christ from the doctrine of the work of Christ. This Christological vision is not part of the tradition of the early church. There are always soteriological motives behind the Christological pronouncements of the early church. The person of Christ can never be separated from the work of redemption.[54] Niebuhr recognizes this important dimension in the Christology of the "dualist" typology in their vision of Christ and culture in paradox.

Niebuhr correctly describes the dualist position vis à vis Thomas and Clement. Luther and Paul are his primary examples. Niebuhr observes: ". . .[T]he dualist's . . . logical starting point in dealing with the cultural problem is the great act of reconciliation and forgiveness that has occurred in the divine-human battle—the act we call Jesus Christ."[55] The dualist understands that grace is present in God and sin is present in man. Grace is never a substance but rather God's action in relationship to human beings. While for Thomas and Clement, reason is darkened and misdirected, for dualists of Luther's type reasoning is never separable from the human condition of egotism, godlessness and perversion.[56] There is human corruption in all of man's work. Reason has been used in light of the human condition to rationalize the misuse of power in society. Our human tendency is to want to be little gods, little saviors, rather than to acknowledge the Creator God.

The dualists live, in Niebuhr's interpretation, in a dialectical relationship with God. Believers live in the tension of God's presence through grace in a sinful world. God has acted decisively in Jesus Christ for a world that is still subject to human depravity. The Creator God lives also in relationship to His world given to sin. Christians live, therefore, in a paradoxical vision in light of Paul's understanding of sin and grace. Christians are empowered through Jesus Christ to live a life of service to others in a faith active in love. They are still subject to the world and the flesh. Society may experience law and order but it is always subject to the lawlessness of the heart and the exercise of demonic power. This creates a tension that calls the Christian person to live always in relationship to Christ in her/his service to the world. Salvation and redemption bring before the individual and the Christian community the necessary vision to continue in a living relationship with Jesus the Christ through the living voice of the Gospel.

Niebuhr, however, criticizes the dualists at two important levels. First, he sees them relating to the Law only in a negative way. The Law sets the limits for the Christian and curbs evil in society. Grace under the righteousness of God given through Christ is the key to Christian living in the world. This dualistic vision is characterized as leading into antinomianism and into cultural conservatism.[57] The dualist is seen as a conservative for maintaining the status quo in culture by upholding law and order or as an antinomian for motivating others to disregard the Law since the world cannot uphold it. Niebuhr sees that this vision of Christ does not provide the most powerful vision to be critical of the current situation in culture. Nor does it provide a catalyst for social change in light of the current corruption within societies. This is why he turns to the vision of Christ as the transformer of culture. He believes that this vision of Christology is more adequate for a social ethics. Nevertheless, he praises Luther for maintaining in his vision of two "kingdoms," "the kingdom of God" and the "kingdom of the world," the reality that God rules without dividing these two realms. This dialectical vision promotes God as Creator, without neglecting the human situation, and abandoning culture to the world.[58] Niebuhr failed, however, to inquire how Luther's dynamic Christology incorporates the two natures of Christ within a soteriological vision.[59] These are two important critical elements within a Lutheran Christology that live in the paradoxical vision of the world. This vision is at the center of a Lutheran critique of Nazism.

Herman Sasse points to a compelling case study on this matter. The German Christians, the pro-Nazi group in the German churches, disregarded the affirmation of the Council of Chalcedon concerning the two natures of Christ. He points out a particular statement made by the German Christians in the Twenty-eight Theses of the Saxon Church in 1933:

> The argument whether Jesus was a Jew or an Aryan makes no contact at all with who He really was. Jesus is not the bearer of a human nature but reveals to us in His person the nature of God.[60]

This monophysitic vision of Christ permitted the Nazi group to disregard the specific humanity of the Jews. Jesus' humanity was absorbed in His divinity. The theses' writers promoted, therefore, an abstract ethical morality in their exercise of universal reason.

The Lutheran vision of Chalcedon incorporates the dynamics of the two natures of Christ with a new boldness by underscoring with a New Testament seriousness that God stands for us as a human being in the person of Jesus Christ. This soteriological vision speaks of the two natures beyond mere metaphysical identification. In fact, the Lutheran redemptive vision emphasizes the dynamic relation between God's incarnational character and our particularity.[61] This vision can address specific concerns regarding the neglect of specific cultures and people within the universal vision of God. This is evident in the catholic, evangelical vision of the Augsburg Confession in Article III concerning the Son of God. This article incorporates the Formula of Chalcedon to bring forth the universal vision that the Son of God stands in a caring manner with human beings in their human situation.[62] Niebuhr fails to make this important connection for our contemporary dialogue of Christ and culture.

We need to take a quick look at his vision of Christ as the transformer of culture. Niebuhr prefers the conversionists' model, Christ the transformer of culture, because he finds the model to be a valuable synthesis that incorporates the vision of both the "synthesists and dualists." Niebuhr sides more with the dualists in their vision of the human predicament. However, he shares with the conversionists a "more positive and hopeful attitude toward culture."[63] He grounds this model on three theological convictions in light of creation, the nature of man's fall, and the historical vision that God continues to act in history in relationship to humanity. This conversionist vision needs some careful analysis in light of Niebuhr's constructive method grounded in Christology.

Niebuhr finds in the dualist picture of creation, a prologue to the doctrine of redemption and the atonement. He sees the dualist vision promoting God's sovereign rule in culture. All Christians carry, therefore, cultural work in obedience to Christ. This vision is, however, an introduction to the more important theme of reconciliation. Niebuhr sees here an important Christological vision neglected by the dualists. He finds that the creative activity of God in Christ in the ordering of creation is overlooked. He wants to underscore the participation of the Logos not only at the dawn of time but its continuation in "the immediate origin, the logical and momentary beginning of everything."[64] Also, he wants to underscore the redemptive work of God in the incarnation rather than just under the themes of Christ's death, resurrection, and return to power. He wants to emphasize themes that are accentuated under the Johannine literature concerning Christ. However, we may say that they are not absent from the Pauline picture of Christ in Colossians (e.g., in Col. 1:15-19). Niebuhr wants to promote a Christology that holds together in one movement the themes of creation and redemption, incarnation and atonement. It is in this vision that the Word became flesh, and dwelt among us, doing the work of the Father in creation, and ordering human culture. Niebuhr, however, does not offer a clear picture of how the both/and of creation and redemption hold together in Christ's work in culture. In fact, this confusion becomes quite evident in his understanding of the relationship of the creation to the fall.

Niebuhr finds in the dualist vision of Paul and Luther a position in close proximity to Gnosticism. He finds creation being almost equated with the fall, "as if creation of finite selfhood and matter involved fall."[65] Again, Niebuhr fails to understand the Christological vision of Luther and Paul. Luther and Paul did not think, as Niebuhr suggests, that the institutions of culture had mainly a negative function in a temporal and corrupt world. This is evident in many areas of Luther's writings.[66] The paradoxical dualist vision shows how our best efforts become penultimate efforts and lead to self-idolatry. The point is to honor the Creator and not the creature in looking at the creation. It is in light of an apostolic Christology that we are to understand the problem of sin and honor the Creator. The Son in reality became a human being ["*sei Mensch geworden*" is how it is stated in Article III of the Augsburg Confession].[67] He became human in order to honor the ultimate created act of God. God created humanity, man and woman He created them, according to His image (Genesis 1:27). The *kerygma* of the early church calls Jesus "the first fruits of those who have fallen asleep" (I Corinthians 1:21). The resurrection is God's claim that He cares for His created creatures and gives them new life. This is underscored in the kerygmatic language of Christ's death and resurrection for us. God cares for each of His creatures in Jesus Christ. This is central to our apostolic confession of Jesus the Christ.

Niebuhr's view of the creatures in creation is one where creation is corrupted and misdirected. It is, however, not bad as something that ought not to exist. It is in this light that he offers the proposal that creation ought to be converted and not replaced. In this perspective, however, he fails to point out an ongoing critical method where the sinful misdirected person is kept on the goal of converting the human situation and society throughout the present life. He is not quite clear as to the human situation of sin and its consequences. He is, therefore, not emphatic as to the universal condition of sin and pride pervading our individual and social efforts even after conversion. He fails consequently to point out how the presence of Christ honors the good and criticizes the bad in culture. I believe that this is due to his failure to underscore an apostolic Christology. This weakness in his conversionist typology is demonstrated through his vision of a realized eschatology.

Niebuhr offers a platonic spatial eschatology where humanity and culture are lifted by Christ to a doxological realm and to a present and effective transformation of human life. He gives evidence of this fact in the Johannine literature where Christ is seen in the present time giving new birth, new life in "each living, existential moment."[68] He fails, however, to correlate this vision to the historical fact of universal human pride even within Christian communities. The historical proleptic vision of the Synoptic Gospels where the kingdom of God is shown to be truly present but not yet realized incorporates a more realistic vision of present cultures while taking seriously the connection between creation and redemption.[69] This proleptic vision incorporates also a Christological picture that is more faithful to the New Testament kerygma and apostolic Christology. The Gospels' narratives of the Lord's Supper portray this vision in a powerful manner for the world community.

There is a deeper question to be pursued, however, in light of the postmodern movement present within Western culture. How does Christianity demonstrate today an imperishable value for each human life and society in this age of extreme relativism? There is another important related question: how do our respective communities come together in a united voice calling for reconciliation, and a new year of

Jubilee? This has to be carried out at a time when, as Lyotard points out, there is "incredulity toward meta-narratives."[70]

During the Enlightenment the accommodating Christians abandoned the world to the project of universal human reason. Religion had to be made acceptable to its cultured despisers. Schleiermacher safeguarded theology and religion by withdrawing its influence to professionals that theologized for the sake of the believing community. Therefore, the Christian faith was relegated to the private sector. The radical and dualist Christians also privatized their faith. The Anabaptist tradition did this by failing to understand the ongoing redemptive presence of Christ for the world. The Lutheran tradition did it by turning to pessimism and not incorporating in a clear manner all the elements of an apostolic Christology, thereby creating schizophrenic Christians. In Western culture the Anabaptists and dualists lived in church by faith and in the world they lived in practice subject to a dogmatic scientific vision of the world. The synthetic Thomistic Christians, by creating two separate planes where Christ's redemption is kept apart from his creation, abandoned also the world to human work.[71]

Post-Vatican II theology, through the work of Karl Rahner and his supernatural existential vision, brought the two planes of the natural and the supernatural together, more closely in line with Thomas's synthetic vision. Gutíerrez, however, does not find this image adequate in that it does not incorporate in a dynamic manner the relationship of the world to God.[72] This modus operandi abandoned the world to Marxism, Fascism, and National Socialism.[73] Worst of all, the church did not perceive that it had brought into the gates of the city its idolatrous views of culture. These perspectives many times were baptized as genuine expressions of Gospel proclamation. Self-glorification marks this grandiose liturgical vision. Today it is the kind of theological vision that leads the church to disregard racism in its midst. It is the kind of gospel that blesses neo-capitalism and conservatism as the true expressions of faithful Christians even if the poor nations of the world suffer. It is also the kind of gospel proclaimed by socialist and Marxists nations in their rationalization of oppression.

Today in our postmodern, "post-ideological" era, we are still driven by the same shortcomings present in the Age of the

Enlightenment. Reason may seem to be dead. But it is still present to give credence to irrationality. This irrationality promotes an extremist dogmatic pluralism that blesses individuality, and particular groups over the common good of the world community. The "Grand Ideologies" may be dead but postmodernism has brought forth "Soft Ideologies" dressed in such Western garbs as "the American Way of Life," "the Free Market System," and the "New World Order."[74] All these ideologies promote universal themes and perspectives without a vision of the relation of the parts toward the whole. The point is that we have failed to show the importance of specific cultures within the global village. We have failed to show also the tendency of every world culture to worship their golden calves. We have failed, therefore, to point out the redemptive vision of God in light of the sign of the times. It is only within the vision of an apostolic Christology that we are able to write new meta-narratives for our day and time. This is the kind of narrative that takes seriously our particularity within the world community. This is the kind of narrative that welcomes the stranger as a sister or brother in our family. This narrative needs, however, a careful reflection on the important ingredients offered by an apostolic Christology for our witness in postmodern Jerusalem and Athens. Paul needs to go again to the Aeropagus. We need to hear again with astonishment the conversion of postmodern Dionysius (cf. Acts 17). This theme is powerful in the book of Acts. Peter discovered how God was speaking to Cornelius, a God-fearing man in search of Christ. Peter had to recognize this dynamic by coming to Cornelius in his context. The early church described in the book of Acts had to come to grips again and again with this word of wonder (cf., e.g., Acts 10:4, 15, 22, 34, 35, 45, 46).

An Apostolic Christology for Postmodern Times

How may we proclaim Christ in this postmodern age? The present age may be described as an age of creative ambiguity in light of the Nietzschean spirit. Particular values and communities are especially ignored by the dominant cultures. We have seen this to be the tendency even within the Age of the Enlightenment as it was observed by Franz Boas in his pioneering work on anthropology. This tendency may be described as a pluralistic "Jesuology." Jesus Christ stands only for the values we may see as important to our way of life or particular community. How may we speak, therefore, of a proper relationship between Christ and culture? Culture needs to be an integral part and a focus of our witness. Our witness cannot, however, succumb to the demonic powers present in the *cultus publicus*.

In a recent essay, Carl Braaten underscores three key elements that are essential to the proclamation of the Gospel. These elements are important foundations for an apostolic Christology: 1) "the matter of history in the Gospel"; 2) "the nature of the Gospel as kerygma"; 3) "the function of dogma for the Gospel."[75]

Jesus of Nazareth had a history. This history points to Him proclaiming the kingdom of God, living with the outcasts, listening to them, sharing His table fellowship with sinful human beings, proclaiming acceptance of the thief on the cross, having mercy toward the sick, the blind, the lepers, the mentally troubled, and the poor. He lived concretely in this manner and loved concretely other people in the world. The Gospel cannot be proclaimed in docetic terms. He who stood in close proximity to His Father, the one He called "*Abba*," stood in the name of God with every human being. The historical Jesus proclaimed also the close proximity of God, God's mighty acts in history, while calling the people to a not-yet eschatological realization of God's future. God's kingdom was fully present in Christ's mission but did not give absolute power to any human project. In fact, He died on the cross like a thief. It was necessary for Him to die before rising again. These are evident facts present in the Synoptic Gospels. The historical Jesus points to a theology of the cross. We must follow in service to others as Jesus indicates (Mark 10:45). The ones who elevate their human projects over against others follow a theology of glory. They are given up to their own vanities. In the words of the *Magnificat*: "He has filled the hungry with good things but sent the rich away empty" (Luke 1:53).

Catholic evangelicals proclaim Jesus Christ as the *viva vox evangelii*. The New Testament church proclaimed Jesus of Nazareth as the risen Christ, who sits at the right hand of the Father. Resurrection narratives unite the Jesus of history with the Jesus of faith. The proclaimed Christ of the early church is the "firstfruits of those who have fallen asleep" (1 Cor. 15:20). We know in this reality how the rest of our stories unfold as the people of God. We know this in spite of our human situation of sin, helplessness and poverty. The kerygmatic proclaimed Christ is alive for us. He is proclaimed as that *viva vox evangelii* that calls us out of our radical situation of sin into new life. The kerygma comes always as a good word *extra nos* (from outside of us) to lead us to a new life in community with others. As Dietrich Bonhoeffer observes, the very reason that this good word comes to us is because there are others willing to establish community with us through the Word.[76] This is a present need with postmodernity.

The contemporary situation needs new metanarratives that call us to God's specific word of astonishment spoken against our selfish pride and neglect of the other. In essence, we need a "metamodern" (González) or "transmodern" (Dussel) project of biblical hermeneutics in our missionary work in postmodern Jerusalem.[77] The kerygmatic Christ points to a good word that leads us to consider God's call for community beyond our preconceived notions of humanity. The kerygma leads us beyond our preconceived notions inherited through modernism and postmodernism. The other can never be seen merely as an other but should always be seen in relationship to us through the kerygma. We cannot engage in cultural relativism to neglect the other, or engage in ethnocentrism to control the other. In fact, we must accept the multicultural rainbow of people in this vision. We live interconnected, through the word of the kerygma, to new beginnings and community. We can do this in the hope of the resurrection. We need to consider also the place and function of dogma for the proclamation of a faithful apostolic and catholic witness.

The dogmatic formulations given at the Council of Chalcedon are foundational for this Christological reflection. The Fourth Ecumenical Council, held at Chalcedon in 451, is acknowledged by the Orthodox and Roman churches as a foundational dogmatic event in the history of the Christian church. It was truly an ecumenical council. It is important because it proclaimed:

> Following the holy fathers, we unanimously teach and confess one and the same Son, our Lord Jesus Christ . . . the same truly God and truly man . . . is to be acknowledged in two natures without confusion, change, division or separation. The distinction between the two natures was never abolished by the union, but rather the character proper to each was preserved as they came together in one person (*prosopon*) and one hypostasis.[78]

This is an important dogma because it reveals the wisdom of the church in confessing Christ for all generations. Chalcedon expresses for us what is the true nature of our salvation and communion in Christ in light of the two natures of Christ. They are essentially present for us "without confusion, change, division or separation." These are important relationships for an apostolic and catholic witness.

The apostolic witness of the Gospel has been hindered by the adoption of an Antiochian-Nestorianism or Alexandrian-Monophysitism throughout the history of Christianity. In the case of Protestant liberalism, the disjunctive Christology of Nestorianism was adopted by Harnack and the Ritschlian school. This Antiochian form of Christology underscored primarily the humanity of Jesus. In fact, Harnack did not want to adopt the language of the "two natures" of Christ. Therefore, he spoke only of an ethical Christ. Protestant liberalism fell prey, therefore, to a Kantian ethical Jesuology. Jesus' valuable existence was defined by Kant's standard of universal reason. Dussel has underscored for us already this Kantian ideology. Remember, Kant described those cultures living outside of the Enlightenment as living in "cultural immaturity . . . laziness and cowardliness."[79] This distorted Antiochian formulation goes contrary to the original Antiochian vision. The divorce of Christ's humanity from Christ's divinity creates an unhealthy regard for a specific human project. It destroys the value and catholicity of our respective communities. It hinders our apostolic and catholic witness.

The united vision of the Alexandrian formula has led some to adopt a monophysitic vision of Christ. This was not the vision of the early Alexandrian Christological formulations. We have seen how the swallowing of the human nature in the divine may lead also to racism and ethnocentrism. We destroy the value of other cultures for our global community. We reiterate the vision of the German Christians in 1933: "Jesus is not the bearer of a human nature but reveals to us in His person the nature of God."[80] Orlando Costas, the dean of Latino evangelical theologians, has observed how this claim of universality has relegated the minority church into fitting the mold or vision of the dominant church culture or excluded the minority church as a "heretic," or bastard child.[81] "Jews," "spiks," and "niggers" are excluded from the embracing arms of the church catholic in this posture. All minority cultures are regarded as inferior in the reality of God.

How may we speak the Gospel in an emphatic, reconciliatory manner if we do not take seriously the true human and divine natures of Christ? They must live in a genuine interrelationship. Christ's human nature points to our specific reality and culture with love and wonder. The theologian can never retreat from this reality. At the same time Christ's divine nature points in His communication of attributes to an important dialogue with our created humanity. There is God's resounding yes to the world and our specific cultures in His global proclamation. The parts become integrated in this vision within the whole of Christ's witness to every tribe and nation. This reality is important to offer a Gospel of reconciliation, unconditional love, peace, and forgiveness to the whole world. Otherwise, the reality of the Christ for us may mean "our" reality and not "your" reality. This realization underscores that the church cannot leave the world to an ethnocentric or cultural relativistic ethical agenda. In light of Chalcedon, the message of reconciliation radiates the true nature of the church. Her witness is truly apostolic and catholic in daily life. The fact is that we need this Chalcedonian vision to live in community, an essential catholic evangelical community. The two natures must exist in dialogical relationship with one another without confusion, change, division, or separation. Otherwise, we will fall into some form of "Jesuology" in our retreat from the world or affirmation of the world. We will fall prey to cultural relativism by being indifferent to others or into ethnocentrism by excluding others. Chalcedon helps us also to write new metanarratives in the proclamation of the Gospel. It may be done because as we hear the Gospel, the good word cannot be proclaimed without giving some form of rational validity to our human situation and to God's universality for us in Jesus Christ. Justo L. González has offered an important evaluation of this formula in light of the U.S. Hispanic reality.[82]

Gnostic docetism ignored the very humanity of Christ. The docetic gospel calls the overwhelmed Christian to forget the problems of our "massified" society. As González observes, this is the kind of gospel preferred by the electronic preachers. This gospel proclamation leaves the people of God abandoned to the actions of the demonic powers of the world. Peter Paris points out that the proclamation of the Gospel was preferred by the plantation and slave owners in North America.

The African American slaves had to discover the incarnational reality of the promise of God to value their cultural history.[83]

Adoptionism is another misuse of the preaching of the Gospel. This view sees Jesus as being adopted by the Father into divine sonship. It is interesting that this outlook never became a very popular vision in early Christianity. It was only a popular perspective among the privileged Protestant liberals. African Americans and Hispanic Americans doubt very seriously that within another dominant culture all people can make it. We know that only some make it to propagate the myth. The point is that it is only in the Christ who is very human and divine that our particular humanity is honored for what it truly is in God's work of redemption. God redeems the whole of humanity and does not choose the privileged ones over the poor in society.

Apollinarianism points to an Alexandrian Christology in which Christ did not assume completely the human form. Apollinarianism declares that only the body and not the mind are in need of salvation. This, again, points to the human problem as a problem of the body. Our studies on anthropology and Dussel's critique of the Enlightenment points to the danger of this position. Our minds as well as our bodies are in need of redemption. Our minds need to be redeemed from our particular idolatries.

Nestorianism has always been rejected by the Hispanic reality. This is because to deny the presence of the crucified God in our reality is to make a mockery of our human situation and suffering. The Lutheran confessional tradition is very emphatic on this reality. It is God who dies for us and stands for us in our human suffering.[84] Monophysitism ignores also the problem of suffering for our communities. If God does not stand as a truly human being "his sufferings are a sham and are not like ours."[85]

The reality of Chalcedon forces us to listen to the preaching of the kingdom of God by the historical Jesus. He is with our suffering but points beyond our suffering. He calls us beyond the present situation of sin to new life. He truly stands with us in the proclamation of the kerygmatic risen Christ. He is the "firstfruits" of the people of God. Chalcedon maintains in a dialogical vision the presence of the Gospel for us. We know what it means for us that Jesus Christ is truly human and divine without division, confusion, change, or separation for us. Chalcedon calls for the living word of God to confront our cultural relativism and ethnocentrism. It calls us to live beyond our individualism and exclusion of others. It calls us to honor the cultural community of others as a valid community. It is in this light that our particular missionary cultures do not become the carrier of the Gospel to others. Rather, the recipient culture becomes the true and final resting place of our proclamation.[86] It is in this light that we are able to offer the Gospel as a word of astonishment. It is the sweetest of miracles because through the incarnation we are able to proclaim Jesus Christ accepting the language and lives of our sisters and brothers of every tribe and nation. It is in this light that we proclaim the effective message: "Jesus our Lord . . . was delivered over to death for our sins and was raised to life for our justification" (Romans 4:24-25).

*Alberto García is Associate Professor of Theology and Director
of the Lay Ministry Program at
Concordia University Wisconsin.*

Bibliography

Althaus, Paul. *The Theology of Martin Luther*, translated by Robert C. Schultz. Philadelphia: Fortress Press, 1996.

Alvarez, Eliseo Perez. "In Memory of Me: Hispanic/Latino Christology Beyond Borders." In *Teologia en Conjunto: A Collaborative Hispanic Protestant Theology* (Louisville, KY: Westminster/ John Knox Press, 1997), 33-49.

Boas, Franz. *Anthropology and Modern Life*. New York: Dove Publications, 1962.

Bonhoeffer, Dietrich. *Life Together*, translated by John W. Doberstein. San Francisco: HarperSanFrancisco, 1992.

Bosch, David J. *Believing in the Future*: Toward a Missiology of Western Culture. Valley Forge, PA: Trinity Press, 1995.

_____. *Transforming Mission: Paradigm Shifts in Theology and Mission*. Maryknoll, NY: Orbis, 1995.

Braaten, Carl E. and Jenson, Robert W. (eds.). *Either/Or: The Gospel of Neopaganism*. Grand Rapids: William B. Eerdmans Publishing Company, 1995.

Breckenridge, James and Lillian. *What Color Is Your God?: Multicultural Education in the Church—Examining Christ and*

Culture in Light of the Changing Faces of the Church. Wheaton, IL: Victor Books, 1995.

Catechism of the Catholic Church. New York: Image Books, 1994.

Costas, Orlando. *Christ Outside the Gates: Mission Beyond Christendom.* Maryknoll, NY: Orbis Books, 1982.

Dussel, Enrique. *The Invention of the Americas: Eclipse of "The Other" and the Myth of Modernity,* translated by Michael D. Barber. New York: Continuum, 1995.

Goizueta, Roberto S. *Caminemos con Jesús: Toward a Hispanic Latino Theology of Accompaniment.* Maryknoll, NY: Orbis Books, 1995.

González, Justo L. *A History of Christian Thought.* Nashville: Abingdon, 1975.

_____. *Mañana: Christian Theology from a Hispanic Perspective.* Nashville: Abingdon Press, 1992.

_____. *Out of Every Tribe and Nation.* Nashville: Abingdon Press, 1992.

_____. "Metamodern Aliens in Postmodern Jerusalem." In *Hispano/Latino Theology: Challenge and Promise,* edited by Ada Maria Isasí-Díaz and Fernando F. Segovia. Minneapolis: Augsburg Fortress, 1996.

Gutíerrez, Gustavo. *Las Casas: In Search of the Poor in Jesus Christ,* translated by Robert R. Barr. Maryknoll, NY: Orbis Books, 1993.

_____. *A Theology of Liberation,* translated and edited by Sister Caridad Inda and John Eagleson. Maryknoll, NY: Orbis Books, 1973.

Hauerwas, Stanley. *Resident Aliens.* Nashville: Abingdon Press, 1989.

_____. *God, Medicine, and Suffering.* Grand Rapids: William B. Eerdmans Publishing Company, 1990.

Isasí-Díaz, Ada Maria. "Elements of a Mujerista Anthropology." In *In the Embrace of God: Feminist Approaches to Theological Anthropology,* edited by Ann O'Hara Graff. Maryknoll, NY: Orbis Books.

_____. "Mujerista Theology's Method." In *Mestizo Christianity: Theology from the Latino Perspective,* edited by Arturo Banuelos. Maryknoll, NY: Orbis Books.

Jeffrey Alexander, Jeffrey and Seidman, Steven (eds.). *Culture and Society: Contemporary Debates.* New York: Cambridge University Press, 1990.

Kaiser, Christopher. *Creation and the History of Science*. Grand
    Rapids: William B. Eerdmans Publishing Company, 1991.
Kasper, Walter. *Jesus the Christ*. New York: Paulist Press, 1977.
Koch, Klaus. *The Rediscovery of Apocalyptic*. Naperville, IL: A.R.
    Allenson, 1972.
Kolb, Robert. "Niebuhr's 'Christ and Culture in Paradox' Revisited."
    Lutheran Quarterly (Volume X, Number 3, Autumn 1996).
Luther Martin. *Select Works of Martin Luther*, edited and translated by
    Henry Cole. London: T. Bensley, 1924-27.
_____. *The Large Catechism, The Book of Concord*, Tappert
    edition. Philadelphia: Fortress Press, 1959.
Lyotard, J.-F. *The Postmodern Condition*. Manchester: Manchester
    University Press, 1986.
Marty, Martin E. "Articles of War, Articles of Peace," Keynote
    address, "Lecture Series on Christianity and Culture," at Concordia
    University Wisconsin, 1996.
Niebuhr, H. Richard. *Christ and Culture*. New York: Harper and Row,
    1951.
Pannenberg, Wolfhart. *The Apostle's Creed: In the Light of Today's
    Questions*, translated by Margaret Kohl. Philadelphia: The
    Westminster Press, 1976.
Paris, Peter J. "The Religious World of African Americans." In *World
    Religion in America*, edited by Jacob Neusner. Louisville:
    Westminster/John Knox Press, 1994.
Peters, Ted. "Feminist and Catholic: The Family Ethics of Lisa Sowle
    Cahill," *Dialog* (Volume 35, Number 4, 1996).
Rengstorf, Karl R. Entry for "*apostello*" in *Theological Dictionary of
    the New Testament*, edited by Gerhard Kittel. Grand Rapids:
    William B. Eerdmans Publishing Company, 1972.
Reuther, Rosemary Radford. *To Change the World: Christology and
    Cultural Criticism*. New York: Crossroad Publishing Company,
    1981.
Rodriguez, Jose David and Loida I. Martell-Otero, Loida I. (eds.).
    *Teologia en Conjunto: A Collaborative Hispanic Protestant
    Theology*. Louisville, KY: Westminster/John Knox Press, 1997.
Sanneh, Lamin. *Translating the Message: The Missionary Impact on
    Culture*. Maryknoll, NY: Orbis Books, 1989.

Sanneh, Lamin. *Religion and the Variety of Culture*. Valley Forge, PA: Trinity Press, 1996.

Sasse, Herman. *We Confess Jesus Christ* (volume 1 of three volume set, *We Confess*), translated by Norman Nagel. St. Louis: Concordia Publishing House, 1984.

Scudieri, Robert J. "The Creed of Nicea as a Paradigm for Missions," *Missio Apostolica* (Volume 2, November, 1997).

Segundo, Juan Luis. *Faith and Ideologies*, translated by John Drury. Maryknoll, NY: Orbis Books, 1984.

Tillich, Paul. *Dynamics of Faith*. New York: Harper Torchbooks, 1957.

Yoder, John Howard. "How H. Richard Niebuhr Reasoned: A Critique of Christ and Culture." In *Authentic Transformation: A New Vision of Christ and Culture*, edited by Glen H. Stassen, D. M. Yeager, and John Howard Yoder. Nashville: Abingdon Press, 1996.

Notes

[1] Gustavo Gutíerrez, *Las Casas: In Search of the Poor in Jesus Christ,* translated by Robert R. Barr (Maryknoll, NY: Orbis Books, 1993), I thank Father Gutíerrez for verifying this true narrative during the 1995 meeting of the American Academy of Religion in Chicago.

[2] Karl R. Rengstorf, "*apostello*" in *Theological Dictionary of the New Testament*, edited by Gerhard Kittel (Grand Rapids: William B. Eerdmans Publishing Company, 1972), I: 403-06. Rengstorf observes: "The missionary element is something which radically distinguishes the NT apostolate . . . " (p. 432).

[3] Quoted from Robert J. Scudieri, "The Creed of Nicea as a Paradigm for Missions," *Missio Apostolica* (Volume 2, November, 1997), 69.

[4] Justo L. González, *Out of Every Tribe and Nation* (Nashville: Abingdon Press, 1992), 19-20.

[5] Ibid., 20-21.

[6] Ibid., 20.

[7] H. Richard Niebuhr, *Christ and Culture* (New York: Harper and Row, 1951).

[8] Wolfhart Pannenberg, *The Apostle's Creed: In the Light of Today's Questions*, translated by Margaret Kohl (Philadelphia: The Westminster Press, 1976), 3-10. Cf. also Paul Tillich, *Dynamics of Faith* (New York: Harper Torchbooks, 1957). Juan Luis Segundo underscores the anthropological dimension as ideology and parts from this important dimension of faith. See Segundo's disagreement with Pannenberg in interpreting Luther in *Faith and Ideologies*, translated by John Drury (Maryknoll, NY: Orbis Books, 1984), I: 33-34, 55. Segundo's anthropological definition will place God

in the kind of box that Luther rejects and defines as idolatry. Cf. Martin Luther, *The Large Catechism*, *The Book of Concord*, Tappert edition (Philadelphia: Fortress Press, 1959), 366. However, I agree with Segundo that our neighbor's human values and concerns must be incorporated in God's vision. Otherwise, we also fall into idolatry.

[9] See *The Smalcald Articles*, Article V, and *Epitome*, Article V, 310, 478.

[10] Martin E. Marty, "Articles of War, Articles of Peace." Keynote address, "Lecture Series on Christianity and Culture," at Concordia University Wisconsin, 1996. Cf. Jeffrey Alexander and Steven Seidman, editors, *Culture and Society: Contemporary Debates* (New York: Cambridge University Press, 1990), for an excellent series of articles on the differences of opinion in defining and studying culture.

[11] Niebuhr, 32.

[12] Ibid.

[13] Carl E. Braaten and Robert W. Jenson, editors, *Either/Or: The Gospel of Neopaganism* (Grand Rapids: William B. Eerdmans Publishing Company, 1995), 7.

[14] Ibid., 8. See also Niebuhr, 83-91.

[15] Cf. Justo L. González, "Metamodern Aliens in Postmodern Jerusalem," *Hispano/Latino Theology: Challenge and Promise*, edited by Ada Maria Isasí-Díaz and Fernando F. Segovia (Minneapolis: Augsburg Fortress, 1996), 340-51. See also Roberto S. Goizueta, *Caminemos con Jesús: Toward a Hispanic Latino Theology of Accompaniment* (Maryknoll, NY: Orbis Books, 1995), 132-72.

[16] Christopher Kaiser, *Creation and the History of Science* (Grand Rapids: William B. Eerdmans Publishing Company, 1991), 161-69.

[17] Cf. David J. Bosch, *Believing in the Future: Toward a Missiology of Western Culture* (Valley Forge, PA: Trinity Press, 1995), 1-13; Lamin Sanneh, *Religion and the Variety of Culture* (Valley Forge, PA: Trinity Press, 1996). Cf. also David J. Bosch, *Transforming Mission: Paradigm Shifts in Theology and Mission* (Maryknoll, NY: Orbis Books, 1995), 262-91.

[18] Enrique Dussel, *The Invention of the Americas: Eclipse of "The Other" and the Myth of Modernity*, translated by Michael D. Barber (New York: Continuum, 1995); Sanneh, *Religion and the Variety of Culture*.

[19] Dussel, 19-20.

[20] Ibid., 20-21, 149.

[21] Ibid., 20. See Bosch, *Transforming Mission*, 291-313. Bosch shows how the Hegelian vision of the Enlightenment has been applied in the modern mission of the Western church.

[22] Sanneh, 1-25.

[23] While I recognize the importance of my personal faith in Jesus Christ for salvation, the Christian faith is always holistic (cf. Jesus' healing of Bartimaeus in

Mark 10). The faith of the Gnostics may be characterized as a very individualistic spiritual matter. See Niebuhr, 87-88.

[24] Cf. Stanley Hauerwas, *Resident Aliens* (Nashville: Abingdon Press, 1989), 32-34.

[25] A recent parody in *Saturday Night Live* portrays Gates controlling the fate of the President of the United States and other world leaders with a simple touch of his computer. Cf. Stanley Hauerwas, *God, Medicine, and Suffering* (Grand Rapids: William B. Eerdmans Publishing Company, 1990), 61-65. Technology is seen by many as making all things possible through the field of medicine. Martin Marty sees this dynamic present in "late modernism."

[26] U.S. Hispanic theologians take great pains to point to the importance of the individual within and not above the community. Roberto Goizueta has constructed an apologetics to postmodernism in light of this important vision (cf. *Caminemos con Jesús*).

[27] Bosch, 5-6; Sanneh, 41-48. Cf. Ted Peters "Feminist and Catholic: The Family Ethics of Lisa Sowle Cahill," *Dialog* (Volume 35, Number 4, 1996): 270. Peters finds two branches of thought, "holism and pluralism," in postmodernism. The two branches speak against a Cartesian dualism. Holistic postmodernism goes contrary to the pluralist postmodernists who oppose any attempts at a universal ethics. The latter is the kind of postmodernism I am rejecting. Cahill's ethical proposal to ground an ethics of marriage on a natural law in dialogue with crosscultural sensitivity and a passion for justice are important constructive themes in my Christological proposal. We cannot deny God's creative vision or our cultural particularity in the apostolic witness.

[28] Bosch, 15-25; Sanneh, 41.

[29] Cf. Alexander, *Culture and Society*; James and Lillian Breckenridge, *What Color Is Your God?: Multicultural Education in the Church—Examining Christ and Culture in Light of the Changing Faces of the Church* (Wheaton, IL: Victor Books, 1995).

[30] James and Lillian Breckenridge, *What Color Is Your God?: Examining Christ and Culture in Light of the Changing Face of the Church* (Wheaton, IL: Victor Books, 1995), 23.

[31] Franz Boas, *Anthropology and Modern Life* (New York: Dove Publications, 1962), 60. This is a reprint of his 1928 seminal work on cultural anthropology.

[32] Ibid., 8.

[33] Ibid., 102.

[34] Ibid., 104.

[35] Justo L. González, *Mañana: Christian Theology from a Hispanic Perspective* (Abingdon Press: Nashville, 1992), 51-53. Cf. also Goizueta, *Caminemos con Jesús*, 150-53.

[36] Sanneh, 45-46.

[37] Ibid., 46-47.

[38] Ada Maria Isasí-Díaz, "Mujerista Theology's Method," in *Mestizo Christianity: Theology from the Latino Perspective*, edited by Arturo Banuelos (Maryknoll, NY: Orbis Books), 178-80. Cf. also Isasí-Díaz, "Elements of a Mujerista Anthropology, "*In the Embrace of God: Feminist Approaches to Theological Anthropology*, edited by Ann O'Hara Graff (Maryknoll, NY: Orbis Books), 94-98; Jose David Rodriguez and Loida I. Martell-Otero, editors, *Teologia en Conjunto: A Collaborative Hispanic Protestant Theology* (Louisville, KY: Westminster/John Knox Press, 1997), 2-3.

[39] González, *Hispanic/Latino Theology*, 340-51.

[40] González, *Out of Every Tribe and Nation*, 40.

[41] John Howard Yoder, "How H. Richard Niebuhr Reasoned: A Critique of Christ and Culture," in *Authentic Transformation: A New Vision of Christ and Culture*, edited by Glen H. Stassen, D. M. Yeager, and John Howard Yoder (Nashville: Abingdon Press, 1996), 50-58.

[42] González, *Out of Every Tribe and Nation*, 32.

[43] Niebuhr, 48-49.

[44] Ibid., 102. Niebuhr finds the same end result achieved, therefore, by fundamentalists and accommodating Christians, i.e., cultural protestants, by allowing culture to go unchecked.

[45] Ibid., 106-17.

[46] Ibid., 112-13.

[47] Ibid., 86-87. They promote Him only as the cosmic Christ.

[48] Ibid., 120. I find, however, that the Lutheran paradoxical vision may be expressed under the paradigms of Either/Or and Both/And. This is due to the Lutheran Christological vision and understanding of grace.

[49] Ibid., 116-17, 149, 190.

[50] Ibid., 120-21.

[51] Ibid., 135.

[52] Ibid., 132-33.

[53] Ibid., 143.

[54] Walter Kasper, *Jesus the Christ* (New York: Paulist Press, 1977), 22-23.

[55] Niebuhr, 150.

[56] Ibid., 154-56.

[57] Ibid., 187. See Angus Menuge, "Niebuhr's *Christ and Culture* Reexamined" in this volume.

[58] Ibid., 171-72.

[59] Yoder found similar weaknesses with Niebuhr's Christology. He writes: "The main stream of Christian tradition has said concerning Jesus (a) that he was the Son of God incarnate, his teaching authoritative and his person unique; and (b) that his death is the atonement for human sin, following which his resurrection is a guarantee of new living power in experience. Niebuhr does not name or reject any of these themes; he never disavows the tradition they have dominated. Yet they are markedly absent from his description. The implications which would flow from them for the discipline of Christian ethics are manifold, so that their absence is significant" (Yoder, 59). I find that his silence leads to hermeneutical blindness and to a Jesuology.

[60] Herman Sasse, *We Confess Jesus Christ*, translated by Norman Nagel (St. Louis: Concordia Publishing House, 1984), 60.

[61] Paul Althaus, *The Theology of Martin Luther*, translated by Robert C. Schultz (Philadelphia: Fortress Press, 1966), 190-91. I have reached similar conclusions in my studies of Luther's theology of the cross. I would cite here as a clear example his Second Lectures of the Psalms (1519-1521). Here Luther has a clear incarnational connection to soteriology. There is here also a dialogue that is critical of a universal rationality apart from our humanity and God standing with our humanity. There is a reversal of thought in Luther that opens the divine to a serious consideration of our particular human situation, our specific culture, and context. Luther writes " . . . Christ must be apprehended as Man, before he is apprehended as God; and the cross of his humanity must be sought after and known, before we know the glory of his divinity: and when we have laid hold of Christ as Man, that soon brings with it the knowledge of him as God," *Select Works of Martin Luther*, edited and translated by Henry Cole (London: T. Bensley, 1924-27), 3: 184.

[62] *Augsburg Confession*, Article III, 30.

[63] Niebuhr, 191.

[64] Ibid., 192.

[65] Ibid., 193.

[66] See Robert Kolb, "Niebuhr's "Christ and Culture in Paradox" Revisited, *Lutheran Quarterly* (Volume X, Number 3, Autumn 1996): 262-65. This article is reprinted in this book.

[67] *Augsburgische Konfession*, Artikel III, *Bekenntis Schriften* (Göttingen: Dandehoed &Rupprecht, 1979), 54.

[68] Niebuhr, 196-202.

[69] Cf. the classic work of Klaus Koch, *The Rediscovery of Apocalyptic* (Naperville, IL: A.R. Allenson, 1972). He shows through a variety of theologians and interpreters this theme of the future and present presence of the kingdom of God as a constant theme in the gospels. See also Eliseo Perez Alvarez, "In Memory of Me: Hispanic/Latino Christology Beyond Borders," in *Teologia en Conjunto*, 33-49.

[70] J. F. Lyotard, *The Postmodern Condition* (Manchester: Manchester University Press, 1986), xxiv. Bosch points to a new missionary proposal where the creative tension between diversity and unity is applied in the missionary program. I believe we can write this type of metanarrative in light of the apostolic Christ who is proclaimed divine and human without division or confusion of natures. See Bosch, *Transforming Mission*, 366-67.

[71] Cf. Gustavo Gutiérrez, *A Theology of Liberation*, translated and edited by Sister Caridad Inda and John Eagleson (Maryknoll, NY:Orbis Books, 1973), 66-72. Gutiérrez is critical in particular of the official interpretation of Cardinal Tommaso de Vio Cajetan. Cf. Justo L. González, *A History of Christian Thought* (Nashville: Abingdon, 1975), 3:188-91 on Cajetan.

[72] Gutiérrez, 70-72.

[73] Bosch, *Believing in the Future*, 18-19.

[74] Ibid., 20-21.

[75] Braaten, *Either/Or*, 8-10.

[76] Dietrich Bonhoeffer, *Life Together*, translated by John W. Doberstein (San Francisco: HarperSanFrancisco, 1992), 21-23.

[77] Dussel, 138; González, *Hispanic/Latino Theology*, 347.

[78] *Catechism of the Catholic Church* (New York: Image Books, 1994), 131.

[79] Dussel, 19-20.

[80] Sasse, 60.

[81] González, *Teologia en Conjunto*, 88. His reference is from Orlando Costas *Christ Outside the Gates: Mission Beyond Christendom* (Maryknoll, NY: Orbis Books, 1982), 190.

[82] González, *Mañana*, 140-55. Cf. also the work of Rosemary Radford Reuther, *To Change the World: Christology and Cultural Criticism* (New York: Crossroad Publishing Company, 1981). Reuther's work uses this formula. She separates it, however, from the kerygmatic tradition of the proclamation of redemption and salvation in the forgiveness of sins.

[83] Peter J. Paris, "The Religious World of African Americans," in *World Religion in America*, edited by Jacob Neusner (Louisville: Westminster/John Knox Press, 1994), 69-77.

[84] Cf. *The Solid Declaration*, Article VIII, 599. Luther's treatise *Concerning the Councils and the Church* is quoted: "We Christians know that unless God is in the balance and throws in weight as the counterbalance, we shall sink to the bottom of the scale . . . But he could never have sat at the pan unless he had become a man like us, so it could be said: God dead, God's passion, God's blood, God's death."

[85] González, *Mañana*, 149.

[86] González, *Out of Every Tribe and Nation*, 28. González draws from the work of Lamin Sanneh, *Translating the Message: The Missionary Impact on Culture* (Maryknoll, NY: Orbis Books, 1989), 27. Please understand that I am not speaking here for a Gospel in light of a natural theology. I believe in special revelation, the canonical Scriptures, as the center and core of our message of grace. This vehicle, however, comes in a cultural garb. The cultural garb is also important in that it is a precious manifestation of God's creation. The message of salvation is not culture but there can be no communication of salvation without a cultural incarnational vision under the cross.

4

Niebuhr's "Christ and Culture in Paradox" Revisited: The Christian Life, Simultaneous in Both Dimensions[1]

Robert Kolb

Since 1951 the range of questions regarding relationships between the church and state—between religious life and society as a whole—has been discussed under the rubric "Christ and Culture," at least in North American circles. The reason for this is a book entitled *Christ and Culture* by H. Richard Niebuhr (1894-1962), professor of Christian ethics at Yale Divinity School. Influenced by Ernst Troeltsch, Karl Barth, his brother Reinhold, and the tradition of the Evangelical Synod of the West (with its roots in both Lutheran and Reformed thought), Niebuhr presented a scintillating assessment of the ways in which various Christian traditions had assessed the proper forms of interaction between church and culture.

Pressing his analysis into the "Weberian" forms in style at the time, he labeled five "types" of Christian social thought. Though appreciative of the positive aspects of each of his five types, he personally favored the "conversionist" mode of relationship between society in general and ecclesiastical life. That approach he found best expressed in Augustine and Calvin, among others.[2] For all the inevitable overgeneralization and simplification that goes into the creation of any series of analytical types like his, Niebuhr's approach has proved so helpful that it has shaped the mindset of North American theologians and Christian social analysis on this continent for two generations. Nonetheless, his analysis of Luther's "two realms" understanding of the relationship of church and society is incomplete and burdened by two significant mischoices of vocabulary.

I. "Christ and Culture in Paradox"

Niebuhr grouped the apostle Paul, the ancient heretic Marcion, Luther, and Kierkegaard together in one type which he labeled "Christ and Culture in Paradox." His description of this approach reveals his keen eye and ear, for his observations hit the mark in many ways. Nonetheless, at least when applied to Luther's understanding of the shape or structure of human life,[3] his analysis is flawed by two unfortunate choices of expression which he used to describe this position: the words "paradox" and "dualism." These choices reveal his failure to take fully into account two fundamental principles in Luther's thought which shaped his social thinking just as it shaped his entire proclamation of the biblical message: his doctrine of creation and his distinction between the two kinds of righteousness.[4]

Luther distinguished the realms of faith and the works which proceed from whatever religious commitment an individual may have. These two realms not only deal with two different relationships, with God and with other creatures. They present essentially different demands—the vertical for faith, the horizontal for works of love. Luther operated with two dimensions with different definitions of what it means to be righteous, right—properly being human—each proper for its own sphere. Thus, the one kind of righteousness defines our humanity and identifies us in the vertical sphere of human life,[5] our relationship with God. The other kind of righteousness defines our humanity and governs our activities in relationship to all other creatures of God. Luther binds together—and he sharply distinguishes—the gift of life, with the human response of trust, in the vertical sphere and the human actions in the horizontal sphere, where human creatures live out God's structures and commands for daily living. The identity of the former sphere produces the actions of the latter.

Luther's distinction of the two kinds of righteousness parallels the distinction of the two inseparable spheres of God's good giving to His human creatures. He gives the gift of the Gospel, which connects human creatures to Himself and bestows upon them their core identity, in the vertical realm. He gives the good gift of His structure for human life, which expresses the demands of human obligation to God and others in what may be called the horizontal sphere, the sphere in which human performance defines and fulfills what is right. Luther conceived of human living according to this two-dimensional design. Both realms are the spheres of God's giving and of His preserving. Both realms have been invaded by Satan's kingdom, but the source of dissonance is Satan, not the horizontal realm itself, for God still exercises His beneficent power there.

Niebuhr differentiated Luther's description of the relationship between the vertical and horizontal spheres of human life and the definition of what constitutes each from alternatives "on both sides." None of these other types, it must be observed, presupposes a distinction of two kinds of righteousness. Instead, they presuppose that obedience to all the commands of God's law determines righteousness in God's sight and in relationship to others—and that grace must assist sinners in producing this righteousness of human performance. "Radical Christians" see evil in the pagan world and insist that the Christian community separate itself from every form this evil takes. They not only distinguish church and culture but tend to separate them as fully as possible. Two other groups neither separate nor even sharply distinguish the practice of the Christian faith from societal norms. "Cultural Christians" identify the enemy with nature and place Christ on the side of the spiritual forces of culture. Synthesists believe in a "more irenic and developing world." Although the radicals focus on the dissonance produced by sin, and both cultural Christians and synthesists focus on continuity between God and culture, between church and society, all share the presumption that what makes us human before God, in the church, is that which defines our humanity in culture and society.

Niebuhr got so much right in his summary and analysis of the "Christ and Culture in Paradox" model that it seems a bit indecent to complain. To be sure, his failure to take Luther's doctrine of creation sufficiently seriously, and the absence of a clear recognition of the reformer's distinction between the "two kinds of righteousness" are understandable, for even the tradition of Lutheran Orthodoxy failed to hand down these vital elements in the conceptual framework of Luther's thought in totally clear fashion. Nonetheless, Niebuhr's failure to delineate the conceptual framework of Luther's thought has prevented many who have stood under the influence of *Christ and*

Culture from recognizing how helpful Luther's "two realms" approach to Christian living can be precisely for such a time as this.

Seven elements of Niebuhr's definition of the view he labeled "Christ and Culture in Paradox" do help crystallize for his readers much of the fundamental structure of Luther's approach to life in human society.

The Lordship of Christ

Niebuhr recognized, first of all, that this "paradoxical" type of social thought is based upon the presupposition that Christ exercises lordship over all aspects of human life. What belongs to Caesar also belongs to God. The phrase "the Lordship of Christ" may be frequently ascribed to Calvinists, but Luther's catechetical emphasis on "Jesus Christ, my Lord" permeates his whole theology.[6] "The dualist," as Niebuhr labels what is also the Lutheran position, "joins the radical Christian [the "Christ against Culture" type] in maintaining the law of Christ over all men, and in stating it in its plain literal sense, objecting to the attenuations of the Gospel precepts by cultural or synthesizing Christians [the "Christ of Culture" type]."[7] Thus, every corner of human life is subject to God's prescription and providence. "Luther does not, however, divide what he distinguishes. The life in Christ and the life in culture, in the kingdom of God and the kingdom of the world, are closely related. The Christian must affirm both in a single act of obedience to the one God of mercy and wrath, not as a divided soul with a double allegiance and duty. Luther . . . was at least equally firm [as the 'synthesist' of Niebuhr's typology] in maintaining the unity of God and the unity of the Christian life in culture."[8]

Sin and Evil

Second, Niebuhr recognized that this "dualist" or "paradoxical" approach to Christ and culture takes sin and evil very seriously. He writes, "the dualist lives in conflict, and in the presence of one great issue. That conflict is between God and man, or better—since the dualist is an existential thinker—between God and us; the issue lies between the righteousness of God and the righteousness of self." This leads to the dualist's claiming as the logical starting point for addressing culture "the great act of reconciliation and forgiveness that has occurred in the divine-human battle—the act we call Jesus Christ."[9] Luther's position takes evil seriously in two ways. First, it focuses not merely on outward human deeds but gets to the heart of the matter instead: the broken relationship with God, which destroys the human ability to lead the perfect human life. Second, it focuses not merely on outward human deeds; it soberly confronts the corruption that has so damaged human motivation that even the best of our intentions do not come to pass as we would wish. Even when we do the best we can, it falls short of the Best, as we can imagine it.

However, as right as Niebuhr is to emphasize the seriousness with which Lutherans take the permeating presence of sin and evil, his formulation of this point betrays an atrophied appreciation for the fullness of Luther's understanding of God's interaction with His human creatures and of their state in His presence even after the Fall. It is true that for Luther our "logical [or at least the theological] starting point" must be found in "my" fallenness and the fallenness and corruption of all other human creatures at the heart of our existence— our relationship to God. But Luther was never unaware of God's logical and theological starting point, His creation of the human creature and every other creature as good. Therefore, he lived in the tension between his confidence in God's restoration of the ability to do the good in the lives of His forgiven children and their continuing battle against temptation and sin. This battle rages within them, as they combat temptation; and it rages around them, as they are called within the structures of daily life to defeat evil in a host of manifestations.

Furthermore, Luther's two-dimensional view of righteousness meant that he believed that even those who do not please God with their works because of the lack of faith in Him still can do works which conform externally to divine standards and structure—and thus bring blessing to others. As important as it is to recognize how deadly seriously Luther took sin and evil, it is also important for his social thought to recognize how highly he prized "civil righteousness," the righteousness which fallen, sinful human creatures can attain in the horizontal realm of human existence even apart from the power of the Holy Spirit conveyed through faith in Christ.

Christian Realism

Third, Niebuhr's analysis does properly highlight the realism about daily life in a sinful world which Luther's view produces. Niebuhr perceived that Luther himself was a "dynamic, dialectical thinker," and that it was only his followers who often permitted his ideas to become "static and undialectical,"[10] a charge that dare not be denied. But those who catch the nuances as well as the principles of Luther's approach come to terms with "the actual struggles of the Christian who lives 'between the times,' and who in the midst of his conflict in the time of grace cannot presume to live by the ethics of that time of glory for which he ardently hopes." That means that the "dualists, however, are not only reporters of Christian experience. Far more than any of the preceding groups with which we have dealt they take into account the dynamic character of God, man, grace, and sin." [11]

At Home in God's World

Fourth, this realism means that Luther's like-minded can be at home in God's world, since it is God's creation and He is lord there and their lord. They acknowledge that they have here no abiding city, but at the same time they recognize that God has called them here to serve God's other creatures for all they are worth (and as God's creatures, we and they are worth very much!).

In speaking of Paul, Niebuhr reports what is also absolutely true for Luther. His understanding of the believer and society is not simply an eschatological escape-hatch, even though it is thoroughly eschatological in the sense that believers always know that they live in the immediate presence of God. For Paul and Luther the day of the Lord is here; the eschaton has set in with the baptismal death and resurrection of each believer. "In the cross of Christ man's work was now judged; by His resurrection the new life had now been introduced into history. Whoever had had his eyes opened to the goodness with which God is good and to His wrath upon all godlessness saw clearly that human culture [or rather the sinful abuses thereof] had been judged and condemned; . . . . The new life, moreover, was not simply a promise and a hope but a present reality . . . ."[12] Niebuhr observes in this connection, "More than any great Christian leader before him,

Luther affirmed the life in culture as the sphere in which Christ could and ought to be followed; and more than any other he discerned that the rules to be followed in the cultural life were independent of Christian or church law."[13] This insight calls attention directly to Luther's understanding of the Christian's calling to follow God in every sphere and corner of life, but it also implies the existence of the concept of civic righteousness, which was so vital to Luther's understanding of human society.

The Penultimate Nature of the Horizontal

This insight is linked with the Lutheran conviction, fifth, that all cultural institutions, at their very best, have only a penultimate goodness, to use Bonhoeffer's conceptualization.[14] It is not just that "the encounter with God in Christ had relativized for Paul all cultural institutions and distinctions, all the works of man [because] they were all included under sin; in all of them men were open to the divine ingression of the grace of the Lord," because they all stood "on the same level of a sinful humanity before the wrath of God . . . ."[15] It was even more the case, for Luther, that the activities and institutions of the horizontal sphere of human existence are by essence and definition never capable of being the human creature's "all in all." For God has created them as penultimate. He alone (and thus the vertical dimension of life) can be ultimate. However human creatures fashion the institutions and activities of the horizontal sphere, within the great freedom God has shaped for that sphere of daily life, these gifts of God (apart from their corruption through human sin) can never be more than penultimate—taking second place to the vertical relationship with the Creator Father.

Therefore, Niebuhr is correct in recognizing that for Lutherans the hope of a better culture is not the chief concern, even in the horizontal realm. Service to the neighbor is. Absolute safety and security can never be found—and should not be hoped for—in these human institutions and activities, but only in the Lord. For "living between time and eternity, between wrath and mercy, between culture and Christ, the true Lutheran finds life both tragic and joyful. There is no solution of the dilemma [and the tension] this side of death."[16] Niebuhr is correct; for "the true Lutheran"—whatever that might mean—there is the unfailing presence of the Lord and there are solutions which will serve for today. But there is no permanent solution to the persistent re-invasion of evil into daily life—apart from the resurrection of Jesus Christ and its eschatological completion. That is a matter which cannot be captured in the forms and fancies, the concepts and the capabilities, of the horizontal realm.

The Freedom of the Christian

Sixth, this penultimate nature of all human activities and institutions, along with the utterly reliable promise of God to remain our God, does create a freedom for decision-making in the horizontal sphere of daily life. "Luther understood that the self could not conquer self-love, but that it was conquered when the self found its security in God, was delivered from anxiety and thus set free to serve the neighbor self-forgetfully."[17] It should not be overlooked that when Luther first got around to composing an exposition of his doctrine of justification through faith, it was entitled "the freedom of the Christian,"[18] and it treated not only the freedom bestowed at the heart of life, in the vertical realm, before God—freedom from all that separates sinners from God. It also treated the freedom which flows from this vertical freedom in the daily life of the horizontal realm, the freedom to serve the neighbor without thought for anyone or anything else but the neighbor. (Yes, in one sense ["thought" as "worry" or "concern"], without even thought for God—since the believer knows for certain that the relationship with God requires no more human thought, concern, or worry.) Being "bound" to the neighbor's need is, in fact, being free to be human according to God's design.

The Limits of Humanity

Yet, seventh, this freedom is always exercised within the limits of our humanity which God has created. These limits, gifts of God's act of creation, define who we are, what we may be, and what we may do without fouling and forfeiting our humanity. In no way did Luther's focus upon the Gospel in the vertical realm of human existence permit him to neglect the necessity of observing the structure of God's plan and will for horizontal life. He realized that "the law of Christ was more demanding than radical Christianity believed; that it required complete, spontaneous, wholly self-forgetful love of God and neighbor, without side glances toward one's temporal or eternal profit."[19] God's providing presence makes such glances unnecessary and even unpleasant for the person of faith.

II. The Dangers Inherent in "Christ and Culture in Paradox"

In addition to these seven accurate and helpful observations regarding Luther's two-dimensional understanding of the relationship between the believer and society, between the church and the culture in which God calls it to serve, Niebuhr provides critical insight into the dangers that have beset those who follow a "Christ and Culture in Paradox" model for practicing the relationship to the culture which God has given to them as a part of His blessing.

Niebuhr notes the "great tensions" which the follower of Luther encounters in the synthesis of what he labels "technique" and "spirit."[20] He seems to mean by this the simultaneous recognition of "what I must do" as a human creature and "who I am" as a human creature, the simultaneity and inseparability of those elements of our humanity which Luther kept distinct: the "self" and "one's performance." This tension is, from Luther's point of view, inevitable if we are to avoid equating ourselves only or chiefly with our deeds (and thus fall under the crushing burden of works-righteousness). The art of living the Christian life two-dimensionally is the art of recognizing that my identity—my "self," who I am—is a gift of God the Creator, never a product of my own or other human, creaturely, hand, and at the same time—simultaneously—hearing God's voice which calls me to specific acts of obedience in response to specific calls to service. These calls come from Him through the neighbor; they are opportunities for playing out our identity in the horizontal realm.

The difficulty to which Niebuhr alludes with this point is that we may wander off from this way of life in one of two directions. First, we may fashion for ourselves a false focus on our identity as God's children which ignores the fact that God's children are to act like God's children: ignoring this leads to antinomianism or apathy and quietism. Or we may stray into a misplacement of our acts of obedience and service by removing these acts from their place between us and other creatures in order to use them to make a claim for vertical righteousness, in the place we have been given in God's sight. When we do so, we condemn ourselves to trusting our own works as sources of our identity and safety in the vertical realm, in the presence of God. The two inseparable dimensions of human life must remain distinct. Both a worldly antinomianism and a spiritualizing cultural conservatism become in fact—altogether too frequently—occasions for our repentance. Because we live always in such tensions, and experience daily the phenomenon of falling—to one side, or the other, or both— the whole life of the Christian must be a life of repentance.[21]

III. Christians and Culture in Two-Dimensional Living

In view of all that is positive about Niebuhr's summary and analysis of the "Christ and Culture in Paradox" model for the interaction of Christians and their culture, what can be said against it? First, at least in its form as expressed by Luther, the relationship between faith in Christ and the practice of life and the use of God's gifts in culture are not a genuine paradox. Second, the label "dualist," which Niebuhr admits he chose "for want of a better name,"[22] is inaccurate if the word is understood according to its normal theological usage.

In the sense in which Niebuhr uses the word, a paradox is "a statement seemingly self-contradictory or absurd, though possibly well-founded or essentially true," or "a phenomenon that exhibits some conflict with preconceived notions of what is reasonable or possible."[23] It is clear and universally recognized that Luther's theology focuses on the paradoxes of the Incarnation and of the continuance of evil in a world governed by an absolutely good and almighty God. Robert Benne has demonstrated how these paradoxes do play a most significant role in the believer's daily life in the midst of this fallen world. Benne is not wrong when he reminds us that Luther's vision of life in this world takes seriously those paradoxes and their implications in a unique way.[24] However, in Luther's view the basic structure of God's design of human life in the two dimensions which parallel his two kinds of righteousness is not paradoxical. It is not a paradox when parents discipline a child at one point and dote on him or her with expressions of love at another. Different actions and different words are proper for differing situations. This is certainly true when viewing the two dimensions of human life defined by Luther's distinction of the two kinds of righteousness.

Thus, God's Word of Gospel, which establishes the identity of His chosen people as children of God, is appropriate for that purpose and for motivating deeds of love. The Gospel is perverted when it is twisted into an antinomian principle for living in the horizontal relationship with other creatures. God's Word of Law, which prescribes the structure of human interaction with other creatures, is appropriate for governing these horizontal structures; it is inappropriate when perverted into a claim to worth before God, into a means of pleasing God and refashioning the sinner's identity into a child of God on the basis of works. God designed works for the horizontal relationship, not for the vertical. These two words are complementary when used for their proper purposes: the one to establish the identity of the children of God, the other to set in place God's structure for their acting as children of God.

Thus, there is a better term than "dualism" for this non-paradoxical structure of the relationship between Christ, His people, and their culture. It might be called "two-dimensional." Luther's view takes seriously that a different set of rules and relationships defines the Creator-creature dimension of human life than that which defines the creature-creature dimension of human life. Failure to recognize and distinguish these two inseparable dimensions of human life results in fuzzying and fogging our view of its realities. This failure can weaken, pervert, or destroy either the human relationship with God, the human relationship with fellow creatures, or both. It dare not be denied that Luther was soberly realistic about the battles which rage across both these dimensions, producing paradoxes as the kingdom of God combats the invasion of the kingdom of Satan. God has insured His triumph through the paradox of working mercy out of wrath, killing to make alive, through the justification of the sinner through baptismal death and resurrection. This justified life is lived, however, in the two distinct but inseparable dimensions into which God has fashioned human life.

Luther recognized that human life is indivisible, but he also recognized that it takes form in two distinct dimensions of faith and love, of identity and of action. These two dimensions are always with us; we live in them simultaneously. Our identity determines and shapes our deeds, and deeds do not occur apart from our identity (even though, in sin, our deeds may conflict with our true identity bestowed by God). Believers are always God's forgiven children, and they are always bound and called to serve the neighbor. Recognizing simultaneously that nothing can separate us from God's love in Christ and that we have been created and redeemed to serve the neighbor frees us for genuine service to God and His creatures.

Perceiving and practicing Luther's insight in this two-dimensional simultaneity enlightens, enriches, and energizes Christian thinking, planning, and acting in such a time as this. This may be seen in at least two areas important to the life of the church today: in Christian contributions to the discussion of societal values in this era of "the naked public square,"[25] and in Christian strategies for carrying out the mission of making disciples in cultures estranged from the God who created them.

IV. Two-Dimensional Thinking in Public Life

In the United States today people are crying out for guidance and help in determining what is right and best for this society. Luther did not teach a form of discipleship which called for defensiveness or for escape from the hard tasks of making the earthly city a better place to live. Nor did he teach that Christians may impose standards upon those outside the faith which only the Holy Spirit can make possible through faith. Luther taught that believers are called to exercise civic responsibility. He believed that the subjects of his day had no choice but to serve God through carrying out their duties as subjects and that the rulers of his day had no choice but to serve God through carrying out their duties as rulers. Modern citizens in democratic societies have some responsibilities parallel to each of these political medieval situations and callings. Christians can shape plans for their own participation within the political sphere according to the principles of the model which speaks of Christians and cultures in both dimensions of human life.

First, believers acknowledge that Caesar's sphere of competence also lies within God's sphere of lordship. What happens in society and culture is not a matter of indifference to the Christian. What happens in the public square is of concern to God and His people, for it concerns His favorite creatures, the human ones. Christians are called to serve as God's tools for making certain that life goes better rather than worse, that life conforms more closely rather than less so to God's will and structure for human living.

Second, Christians will recognize how sin and evil affect and permeate all that goes on in political life. They understand that—and why—power corrupts and absolute power corrupts absolutely, and they will try to do what can be done to limit that abuse of power. However, they will also recognize that political institutions and public life are good gifts of God. Christians are convinced that non-Christians can also exercise a civic righteousness and build a relatively good city—a city better rather than worse—with, but even without, the help of Christians. (They will also recognize that members of the church—yes, even believers—will not be immune to the temptation to abuse power and wreak evil through political institutions.)

Therefore, third, Christians will be realistic, both about the possibilities for good when human creatures conform their wisdom to God's plan for human living, and about the potential for tragic evil when human creatures try to use God's gifts for their own ends, according to their own fallen, damaged reason. Christians can be soberly realistic about aspiring and hoping for and working toward an improved social situation. They can also be soberly realistic about the difficulties which haunt such efforts and the fragility of their successes.

That this realism does not destroy Christian initiative for seeking the temporary, temporal good arises from the fact that believers are at home in God's world because it is God's—even if, in another sense, they are not at home here because God has better plans for His people ultimately. Since God is at home in His creation, however, His people are at home and at work in His presence, even as it makes itself felt through His Word.

Fifth, even at home in the earthly city, Christians perceive its penultimate nature. Therefore, they fashion systems and plans for their societies which serve the neighbor's need today and tomorrow, without the illusion that these systems and plans will or should serve forever. Christians meet human needs as they exist today and in the immediate future; for many of those outside the faith are adrift because they have lost their blueprints—but not their longing—for a tower like Babel. Believers strive to create the best they can, rather than the Best, and are content with better rather than worse, if the Best cannot be attained for the moment. For they know that the Good, the Best, will never last for more than an historical moment. Even if the best of human systems and institutions remain, the sinful world around them will twist their use for its own purposes. Thus, Christians will be deeply disappointed by and hotly indignant at the hurt of the neighbor, but not at the failure or collapse of a favorite human party or political system.

In the face of such failures and collapses, Christians are always ready to exercise imagination and freedom, sixth, in order to construct a new process for progress, and to discard it when it does not serve its purpose. For the goal of Christian political action is service to the neighbor, not the securing of the future through some human program or party. Indeed, this freedom is exercised, seventh, within God's plan for human living. It is bound to service and love as God has structured, defined, and envisioned them. But Christians recognize how many options God has given for achieving His horizontal, temporal will within the structures of humanity as He designed it.

Those who practice relating Christians to culture with a two-dimensional view of life will certainly have to heed Niebuhr's warnings against both antinomianism and cultural conservatism. That should be easy. For as children of God, His people want to please their Father and serve their brothers and sisters. Antinomianism should not be an option. It is, however. Sin's pervasive power permeates human life, to weaken faith and the resolve to love. The whole life of the Christian is a life of repentance.

As children of God His people, furthermore, place no lasting, central faith in any human institutions. They wish to conserve these institutions only for the sake of the neighbor, certainly never for God's sake, for their own sake, or for the sake of the institutions themselves. Christians are either conservative or revolutionary, not as a matter of principle, but as a matter of loving the neighbor. They are culturally conservative when it serves God's purposes; they are culturally revolutionary—downright destructive—when that serves God's purposes.

In a troubled land, in a society falling apart and crying out for a saving hand, a two-dimensional view of Christian relationships to culture has much to offer. It must be enunciated clearly by those who stand in its tradition.

V. Two-Dimensional Thinking in Christian Witness and Mission

As North American Christians seek to carry out Christ's commission to make disciples, in North American culture and in mission fields in other parts of the world, they are faced with a series of questions concerning the relationship between Christ and culture. Critical are the questions which address what cultural institutions and expressions must or should be changed if the Gospel of Jesus Christ is truly to take root. Likewise, the translation of the Gospel for effective communication always involves decisions about how the language of the culture will best express the truth of the Christian message. The seven points of analysis detailed above provoke thinking about these questions and decisions.

First, Christians begin their thinking about mission with the confession that Jesus is Lord, Lord of all. They come to those outside the church in order to serve as instruments which bring God's rule to those who do not trust in Him as Lord and Savior. They recognize, at the same time, that the fallen, the unbelievers, remain under His lordship even when they do not recognize it. That means not only that God has a claim on them which He is exercising as believers witness to their faith in order to bring people into God's family. It also means that those living outside the faith are still living with the gifts of God, bestowed within their culture and in the form of the various elements of their culture. Therefore, Christians will be respectful of these gifts of God with which they are not familiar. They will acknowledge that their own cultural tastes do not determine what is the superior or inferior gift of God, in spheres of life such as dress and architecture, art and music, political forms and institutions, economic organization, or modes of recreation and play.

Christians also recognize, as they approach another culture, that the two dimensions of human life mesh, mingle, and mix together in ways which make them difficult to distinguish practically. When God's lordship is replaced by the lordship of some kind of idol, that idol infiltrates art and sport, political, social, and economic institutions, even the use made of house, food, and shelter. Religion sets the warp and woof of culture. Its colors and designs may remain even as the Christian faith makes its presence felt in the midst of a culture. More importantly the faith will reweave the material of life as it resets the basis of human interaction in the values of the Gospel of Jesus Christ.

Second, Christians recognize that the best gifts of God are subject to the perversion of our sinfulness. All cultures and every gift which God provides through the agency of each culture are not only penultimate. They are also evil and perverted in some ways. Every culture is corruptible and conveys even in its finest elements the mark of human sinfulness. There can be no "culture of Christ" in this fallen world. There is only the call to repentance in the midst of God's good gifts in every culture.

As they assess any cultures, believers will recognize that some horizontal evils are institutionalized. The practice of power suppresses and subverts proper human relationships for the purposes and ends of the powerful of any culture. Neither progressive political institutions nor "primitive" social organization is proof against the perversions of power. All tribes turn on their neighbors to defend themselves sooner or later; sometimes, they see themselves forced to go on the offensive to secure their own borders and security. In the process, sinners will always abuse the power they hold.

Third, believers also recognize the extent to which moral but idolatrous values command cultural expressions of every kind. This means that Christian assessment of the challenges of making the Gospel understandable in another culture will be soberly realistic. This assessment will avoid the temptation to "Westernize" the other culture to which it comes (or in the case of Korean missionaries—in this happy time when mission is no longer the sole property of Western churches—the "Koreanization" of those cultures). At the same time it will be utterly realistic in recognizing the corners and crevices of the culture into which its old religions have seeped and settled. Some idolatrous cultural practices can be altered; others must be destroyed and replaced. Mission strategy must sort out the moral elements which can be preserved in Christian practice from the values which have been so tainted and entangled in the idolatry at the heart of the culture that they remain irredeemable.

Fourth, Christian missionaries will be able to do that better rather than worse to the extent that they can recognize that they can be at home in the new culture where God has called them to work. They will never be fully at home there, just as they will never fully leave the culture in which they were raised and shaped. But they will acknowledge the presence of God, the Creator who is at home throughout His creation, in the culture to which He has brought them. They will acknowledge its good points as well as its bad, embracing the former, even though these may not suit their tastes, and helping their hearers recognize and deal with the latter.

Fifth, these missionaries will recognize the penultimate nature of cultural expressions and institutions. They will not get hung up on what they like in their old culture, nor will they get romantically involved in the charms of the new. They will ask questions regarding how love and service of the neighbor may best be conducted in this particular place, how the Gospel may bring these particular people to faith and into the family of God. Other things, such as cultural forms and fancies, come second, and are penultimate forever.

Thus, sixth, the mission of God is conducted with a good deal of freedom. The message is fixed and abiding; its expressions are as innumerable as the situations in different cultures to which it must be addressed. Believers recognize that they are free to choose and reject elements of their own cultures and the cultures in which they are called to witness—not in accord with their own tastes but in accord with the purposes of God. They are freed from needing any culture elements for their sense of identity and safety. They are free to select which aspects of both cultures serve to bring the Gospel and the gift of life to the new neighbors around them.

Therefore, the forms into which cultural forms and practices flow in the church's liturgy and organization are determined not by cultural taste or tradition but by the needs of the hearers to have the Gospel of Jesus Christ enter, claim, and permeate their lives. Thus, this freedom for adapting the life of the church to the context of a new culture is always exercised within the limits imposed by God's plan and structure for human living and His gift of the life-giving Word of His Gospel.

Conversion to Christ also involves a cultural move. Believers remain in the culture of their birth when the Holy Spirit brings them into the body of Christ, but they are also initiated into another culture at the same time. This new culture extends backward and forward in time and throughout the contemporary world. It is the culture of the people of God in all times and in all places. There are inevitable tensions between the catholic Christian culture and the local, geographically restricted culture, but Christians live in both. They bear marks of both, and these marks identify them as Nigerian or Norwegian or North Dakotan Christians and as Christian Nigerians or Norwegians or North Dakotans. They recognize both sets of marks as gifts of God.

In view of this, also in pursuit of its saving mission of converting those outside God's family of the faithful, the church will avoid an antinomian spirit which spreads a Christian veneer over the idolatry of another culture. Too often Christians have brought unbelievers into the church but not into the faith. The temptation to syncretism is ever present with the church. At the same time the church will avoid a cultural conservatism which seeks to refashion people to whom God has given the gift of being Malay or Kazak or Ibo or Eskimo into folks like us from Leipzig or Los Angeles or London.

Given the urgency of the mission of salvation which God has entrusted to the church, it is incumbent upon Christians to formulate strategies for outreach which the Holy Spirit can use most readily and aptly. He effects the mission, but His human instruments should strive to place as few impediments in His path as possible. Therefore, with opportunities for witness breaking out on every side at the end of this century, the two-dimensional understanding of Christians' relationships to culture can assist in sorting out possible approaches to issues critical in the mission of the church. This understanding should be clearly enunciated by those who stand in its tradition.

* * *

H. Richard Niebuhr described the "Christ and Culture in Paradox" approach to the relationship of Christians and their cultures as "a report of experience rather than a plan of campaign."[26] It is indeed the report of the Christian experience, with sin and evil, but above all with a good and gracious God. But it is also something of a plan for something of an earthly campaign.

Politically, e.g., it is not the plan for a campaign to make the permanent improvements in the horizontal sphere of human living which will secure that realm, or which will secure the human place in the vertical sphere through activities in the horizontal dimension of life. The campaign is a somewhat more modest one, though no less important. It is exercised for the purposes of this world's affairs. It is the campaign for justice and righteousness in every relationship and institution of the human life in the horizontal realm. This, too, is God's campaign, a campaign to which he calls His children.

And Luther provides something of a plan—certainly not a prescription for every action, a regulation and rule for every circumstance. Rather, he describes life lived with a certain freedom for meeting the neighbor's need according to God's will, but under the control of no single definition of the Good as shaped by one human philosophy or another, even if it be a well-intentioned Christian philosophy. The two-dimensionally fashioned plan is a strategy; it trusts its followers to devise the tactics for today, to conserve the best of the past, and to overturn its mistakes and its outmoded blessings with a revolutionary fervor fired by the love for God, which is at the same time love for His creatures.

Also, in pursuing the mission of baptizing and teaching on which Christ sends His church, this two-dimensional understanding of Christian living gives believers general instructions for pursuing individual plans for specific times and places, as they are called to formulate the Word of God anew to make the incarnation of Jesus Christ meaningful to those outside the church in their own cultures. This campaign for eternity has the eschatological urgency which fires Christians to seek the most effective ways of being the Holy Spirit's tools for the proclamation of the Gospel. Luther's axiomatic observations about human life help direct the campaign.

For God's children, sent on Christ's saving mission and sent to seek the peace of the city, two dimensional thinking about Christians and culture is a message and a strategy for such a time as this.

*Robert Kolb is Director of the Institute for Mission Studies and
Missions Professor of Systematic Theology at
Concordia Seminary, St. Louis.*

Bibliography

Althaus, Paul. *The Ethics of Martin Luther*, trans. Robert C. Schultz. Philadelphia: Fortress, 1972.

Benne, Robert. *Ordinary Saints, an Introduction to the Christian Life.* Philadelphia: Fortress, 1988.

_____. *The Paradoxical Vision, A Public Theology for the Twenty-first Century.* Minneapolis: Fortress, 1995.

Bonhoeffer, Dietrich. *Ethics*, ed. Eberhard Bethge. New York: Macmillan, 1955.

Cargill Thompson, W. D. J. *The Political Thought of Martin Luther.* Sussex: Harvester, 1984.

Forell, George W. *Faith Active in Love, An Investigation of the Principles Underlying Luther's Social Ethics.* Minneapolis: Augsburg, 1954.

Kolb, Robert. "Niebuhr's 'Christ and Culture in Paradox' Revisited," *Lutheran Quarterly, NS* 10, 4 (1996): 259-279.

Luther, Martin. *Luther's Works (LW), Volume 6, Lectures on Galatians 1535, Chapters 1-4.* St. Louis: Concordia, 1963.

_____. *LW* 31. Philadelphia: Muhlenberg, 1957, 327-377.

Neuhaus, Richard John. *The Naked Public Square, Religion and Democracy in America.* Grand Rapids: Eerdmans, 1984.

Niebuhr, H. Richard. *Christ and Culture.* New York: Harper, 1951.

Onions, C. T. (ed.) *The Shorter Oxford English Dictionary on Historical Principles.* 3rd edition. Oxford: Clarendon Press, 1973.

Peters, Albrecht. *Kommentar zu Luthers Katechismen, Band 2: Der Glaube.* Göttingen: Vandenhoeck & Ruprecht, 1991.

Wingren, Gustaf. *Luther on Vocation*, trans. Carl C. Rasmussen. Philadelphia: Muhlenberg, 1957.

Notes

[1] This article is reprinted by permission of the author and *Lutheran Quarterly*. It first appeared as "Niebuhr's 'Christ and Culture in Paradox' Revisited," *Lutheran Quarterly, NS* 10, 4 (1996): 259-279.

[2] H. Richard Niebuhr, *Christ and Culture* (New York: Harper, 1951).

[3] See Gustaf Wingren, *Luther on Vocation*, trans. Carl C. Rasmussen (Philadelphia: Muhlenberg, 1957); George W. Forell, *Faith Active in Love, An Investigation of the Principles Underlying Luther's Social Ethics* (Minneapolis: Augsburg, 1954);

Paul Althaus, *The Ethics of Martin Luther*, trans. Robert C. Schultz (Philadelphia: Fortress, 1972); W. D. J. Cargill Thompson, *The Political Thought of Martin Luther* (Sussex: Harvester, 1984). Cf. Robert Benne, *Ordinary Saints, an Introduction to the Christian Life* (Philadelphia: Fortress, 1988) for a helpful application of Luther's views to contemporary Christian life.

⁴ *D. Martin Luthers Werke* (Weimar: Böhlau, 1883-) [henceforth *WA*], 40, I: 40-51; *Luther's Works* [henceforth *LW*], *Volume 6, Lectures on Galatians 1535, Chapters 1-4* (St. Louis: Concordia, 1963), 4-12.

⁵ It is important to note that the use of "vertical" to describe the relationship between the human creature and God dare not, in Luther's case, be understood as placing God outside the daily life and concerns of human creatures. Luther viewed the God who is above His creatures as Creator, also as the God who comes from below, from the cross, to serve and to save, and to transform the practice of daily life in relationship to the rest of creation, the horizontal sphere.

⁶ See Albrecht Peters, *Kommentar zu Luthers Katechismen, Band 2: Der Glaube* (Göttingen: Vandenhoeck & Ruprecht, 1991), 111-115.

⁷ Niebuhr, 157.

⁸ Ibid., 172.

⁹ Ibid., 150.

¹⁰ Ibid., 179.

¹¹ Ibid., 185.

¹² Ibid., 162; cf. 164-166.

¹³ Ibid., 174.

¹⁴ Dietrich Bonhoeffer, *Ethics*, ed. Eberhard Bethge (New York: Macmillan, 1955), 120-187.

¹⁵ Niebuhr, 160-161.

¹⁶ Ibid., 178.

¹⁷ Ibid., 173-174.

¹⁸ *WA* 7: 42-49; *LW* 31 (Philadelphia: Muhlenberg, 1957):327-377.

¹⁹ Niebuhr, 173.

²⁰ Ibid., 175-177.

²¹ This is the point of the first of the 95 Theses, a theme which remained important in Luther's theology throughout his life; see WA 1: 233; LW 31: 25.

²² Niebuhr, 149.

²³ *The Shorter Oxford English Dictionary on Historical Principles*, ed. C. T. Onions (3rd ed.; Oxford: Clarendon Press, 1973), II: 1508.

²⁴ Robert Benne, *The Paradoxical Vision, A Public Theology for the Twenty-first Century* (Minneapolis: Fortress, 1995), esp. 59-103. Benne's book is a most helpful and articulate representation of the insights of a Lutheran social ethic for contemporary North American society.

[25] The term is Richard John Neuhaus's, *The Naked Public Square, Religion and Democracy in America* (Grand Rapids: Eerdmans, 1984).

[26] Niebuhr, 185.

PART II

Historical, Contemporary
and
International Themes

5

Two Kingdoms under One King:
Towards a Lutheran Approach to Culture

Gene Edward Veith

Many of the most difficult issues before the church today—from in-house debates over worship styles and the best way for the church to grow, to calls for Christian activism to combat social evils, such as abortion, poverty, the decline of the family, the immorality of the media, political corruption, and the like—are actually questions about how Christians should relate to their culture.

Never have there been more professing Christians in America, and yet never has the impact of Christianity been less. Polls show that 94% of Americans believe in God, 80% claim to be Christians, 70% believe in the inerrancy of Scripture, and 43% are in church every Sunday— and yet Christianity is culturally invisible. There is almost no sign of Christianity in our culture's schools, public discourse, or works of art. Christian moral teachings seem to have little influence on our culture's entertainment media, sexual practices, or its willingness to kill the sick or the unborn. Professed Christians have about the same divorce rate as non-Christians and are otherwise virtually indistinguishable from their unbelieving neighbors. Is this because Christians are not applying their faith in their culture? Or has the culture totally swallowed up their faith?

American Christians are uncritically embracing their culture at the very time the dominant culture has become aggressively hostile against any kind of religious faith. This point is documented in the other chapters of this book. Wayne Martindale shows how official Chinese culture is opposed to Christianity—though the Gospel continues to spread like wildfire among the people, despite (and indeed partly as a result of) overt persecution. Ironically, the cultural obstacles to evangelism in China may be less severe than those in contemporary

America which Joel Heck explores later in this book. Our individualism, relativism, and materialism are utterly opposed to biblical truth. Patrick Riley argues that the secular spirit of the Enlightenment has persecuted Christians just as ruthlessly as have the Communist Chinese and continues an aggressive agenda to silence Christian ideas. Secularism, as Gary Locklair shows, has its own religious worldview, an evolutionary naturalism that shapes not only science, but ethical ideas and cultural behavior, a worldview that is philosophically opposed on every level to Christian truth. How can Christians function—much less participate in—such a hostile cultural environment?

To try to sort out these very practical concerns, I will take a page from Alberto García, who shows how cultural questions can be illuminated by our rich theological heritage. He focuses on the natures of Christ. Lutheran theology is Christocentric, committed to justification by grace through faith, and can be recognized by its distinction between Law and Gospel. A corollary of these convictions is the doctrine of the two kingdoms. I will be following Martin Marty in applying this doctrine, which has tended to be applied merely to political issues, to culture as a whole.

My thesis is that Christianity must never be turned into simply a cultural religion. And yet, Christianity has cultural implications. All Christians have both a spiritual vocation and a cultural vocation, requiring them to be both separate from the world and yet actively engaged in that world. God is sovereign over the culture as well as the church, but He operates in different ways in each sphere. The church and the culture are not to be confused with each other; but God is King over them both.

Religion and Culture

Most of the world's faiths are cultural religions. Hinduism, with its caste system and social rituals, is inextricably tied to the culture of India. Islam seeks to apply the Koranic law to every detail of society and so creates a specific culture, as evident throughout the Middle East. Tribal religions mythologize the tribe's customs, history, and social organization. Secular sociologists go so far as to define religion as a means of sanctioning the social order. According to this line of thought, religion invests cultural institutions with a spiritual, divine significance, so that people will more obediently go along with them.

Christianity, on the other hand, is not supposed to be merely a cultural religion. To be sure, the laws of sociology and the tendencies of our fallen nature give us a penchant for human-made or culture-made faiths that often hijack the church. The Bible, though, outlines a much more complex approach to culture, one that offers a radical critique of culture while encouraging believers to engage their culture in positive ways.

In the Old Testament, God elects the tribes of Israel, giving them a law and a covenant that turns them into something like a holy culture. But, far from having their social practices sanctioned by their God, the Hebrews are constantly being chastised for their failures to obey God's transcendent demands. Their kings, for example, are constantly being condemned for their unrighteousness by the prophets and the inspired writers of the historical books, something literally unthinkable by Israel's Canaanite neighbors, for whom the king was an avatar of a god. The people of God were strictly forbidden to follow after the religions and cultural practices of their pagan neighbors. When the Israelites nevertheless adopted the easygoing sexual and ethical mores of their neighbors and developed a syncretic theology that allowed the God of Abraham to be worshipped in the same culture-friendly terms as in the pagan religions, they experienced the full measure of God's wrath.

The coming of Christ complicates the believer's relationship to culture even further. Christianity is to be a faith for all cultures, "for every nation, tribe, people and language" (Rev. 7:9). Victor Raj, in his chapter, shows how the Gospel is comprehensible in terms of the vastly different conceptual framework that characterizes the culture of India. Timothy Maschke shows how liturgical worship, in its origins and in its nature, is transcultural. And in fact Christianity has become a world religion. There are more Lutherans in Africa, Asia, and Latin America than there are in the United States. It has been said that the only true multicultural institution is the Christian church.

The New Testament emphasizes how cultural differences are not to stand in the way of Christian unity, as the controversies in Acts and the Epistles over the status of gentile believers demonstrates. The New Testament also describes the sometimes precarious relationship that

Christians will have with their surrounding cultures. Though Jesus tells His followers to be salt, light, and leaven in the world, He also warns that the world will hate them (Matthew 5). Christian freedom and service extend to every dimension of life, yet Christians are warned about the temptation of worldliness. Christians are told to obey the secular authorities (Romans 13:1-7), and yet to obey God rather than men (Acts 5:29).

Then we have the curious counsel of St. Paul: "I have written you in my letter not to associate with sexually immoral people—not at all meaning the people of this world who are immoral, or the greedy and swindlers, or idolaters. In that case you would have to leave this world. But now I am writing you that you must not associate with anyone who calls himself a brother but is sexually immoral or greedy, an idolater or a slanderer, a drunkard or a swindler. With such a man do not even eat" (1 Cor. 5:9-11). Apparently, we should not associate with immoral Christians, but we *should* associate with immoral unbelievers.

Jesus, in His prayer in Gethsemane, sets forth the principle that His followers are to be "in the world," but not "of the world": "I have given them your word and the world has hated them, for they are not of the world any more than I am of the world. My prayer is not that you take them out of the world but that you protect them from the evil one. . . . As you sent Me into the world, I have sent them into the world" (John 17:14-18). Christians are somehow to be separated from the world, while still being involved, redemptively, in the world.

Theological Alternatives

Earlier in this book, Angus Menuge surveyed the different ways theologians have approached the relationship between Christianity and culture. He drew on Richard Niebuhr's classic little book *Christ and Culture,* which outlines the different possible relationships between the two, each of which has been advocated in the history of the Church.

One option is to put culture above Christ. In this view, Christianity serves culture, or, in the words of the National Council of Churches slogan, the world sets the agenda for the Church. When the culture changes, Christianity must also change to maintain its relevance. This is the path of *liberal theology.*

There have been many different kinds of theological liberalism in church history. During the Age of Reason of the eighteenth century Enlightenment, many theologians jettisoned the supernatural teachings of Scripture in an effort to turn Christianity into a "rational" religion. When the rationalistic vogue gave way to the emotional focus of nineteenth century Romanticism, the liberal theologians changed their tune and taught that Christianity is a matter of religious *feelings*. After Darwin, Romanticism gave way to a trust in utopian social progress, and the liberal theologians said *that's* what Christianity is all about. The twentieth century has seen a plethora of intellectual fashions and social movements—existentialism, socialism, the peace movement, gay rights, feminism—and each has had its liberal theologians revising Christianity accordingly.

Today, in our postmodern era, belief in the supernatural is once again socially acceptable, though the relativism now in vogue makes doctrine and absolute standards of morality highly suspect. Mostly, people in our contemporary American culture want to have a good time, have their consumer needs met, and be left alone to their own values, beliefs, and vices. These new cultural attitudes have given rise, as always, to another form of liberal theology.

Churches that were once evangelical, boldly standing up for the Gospel and the authority of the Bible against modernist culture and its liberal theologians, are now changing their teachings and their practices to keep up with the culture. They do market surveys to find what the religious consumers of their culture want, then they respond like any other successful business. They throw out time-tested modes of worship in favor of whatever styles are most popular. Told that people do not want to hear about how sinful they are, they switch to more positive messages of self-esteem, combing the Bible for principles for successful living rather than preaching that Christ died for sinners. Though these Christians are sometimes with the best of motives trying to reach their culture, they often fail to see that instead their culture has reached them. Though they often call themselves evangelical, those who uncritically follow the dictates of the culture are not evangelicals at all but simply the latest version of an old theology: They are *liberals*.

The problem with liberal theology in all of its manifestations is that it turns Christianity into what it must never merely be, a cultural religion. Passively agreeing with a godless world, the church, in trying so hard to be relevant, actually loses its relevance. Why should anyone go to church if it offers nothing more than what the culture has already provided? Disabled from criticizing or influencing the culture and having surrendered its transcendent moorings, religion is reduced to the role that sociologists have assigned it—making people feel good about their society by peddling the illusion that their culture is the ultimate reality.

The danger of any kind of divinized culture is that religious devotion is displaced away from the transcendent God onto human institutions. To worship one's culture is, in the strictest meaning of the word, idolatry. This is the phenomenon behind the most vicious forms of ethnocentrism, what Dr. García describes as cultural idolatry. On the social level, divinized cultures are nearly always oppressive, since God's transcendent Law, which holds even the state to moral standards, is replaced by the dictates of the state. The ruler thus blasphemously assumes the role of God and demands the devotion due to God alone. Divinized cultures also tend to be brutal and warlike, suppressing cultural enemies with the merciless self-righteousness of any bad religion. To invest one's culture with divine status and Godlike authority was the mistake of Fascism. Its results today can also be seen in debacles such as the crisis in Bosnia. It has been observed that the Bosnian Christians do not actually go to church very much; nor do the Bosnian Moslems much frequent their mosques. Their faith is little more than their cultural identity, but they kill each other with religious zeal.

Instead of placing culture above Christ, as the liberals do, other Christians have, more nobly, placed Christ above culture. According to this view, Christianity offers standards according to which the culture should be made to conform. Those who place Christ above culture will attempt to develop and promote distinctly Christian approaches to art, music, economics, science, and every other sphere of life. Society should be reformed until it approximates a Christian civilization.

This option has also been found throughout the history of the church. The Lordship of Christ over the earthly kingdoms has been emphasized by medieval popes, Reformation commonwealths, nineteenth century social reformers, twentieth century liberation theologians, and some contemporary Christian political activists.

Christians with this stance towards culture have boldly stood up against social evils and in many cases have exerted a powerful influence for good. Many Calvinists have adopted this approach, from Puritan revolutionaries in seventeenth century England and eighteenth century America to today's Reconstruc-tionists who seek to make the Bible the Law of the land.

While I cannot find anything about theological liberalism to respect, I do admire those Christian reformers and revolutionaries who defy their cultures and attempt to make them conform to God's Law. And yet, there are problems with this position. In the first place, it often underestimates the effect of the Fall and the scope of human sinfulness. No human being, much less a culture, can in fact keep God's Law. No earthly kingdom, even one ruled by or consisting of Christians, can be a utopian paradise this side of Eden. All are transient and will prove disappointing, corrupted by injustice or pride, until Christ rules directly in the kingdom of heaven.

There can be no such thing as a Christian culture as such, because Christianity comes from faith in the Gospel, not the works of the Law. God saves individuals, not nations. Not every member of a culture is going to be a Christian. Since conversion is the work of the Holy Spirit, it is impossible to coerce or manipulate or require anyone to become a Christian. The unregenerate *cannot* obey biblical principles so as to be part of a Christian culture. Neither, while they are in their fallen flesh, can Christians.

A culture ruled completely by Christ *is* a reality in heaven and *will* be realized on earth at His return, but attempts on the part of human beings to establish heaven on earth prematurely by their own efforts and on their own terms, are doomed. At the worst, they result in the divinization of culture. Christianity becomes reduced, once again, to a cultural religion.

Another option cited by Niebuhr is Christ against culture. This view recognizes the sinfulness of human institutions and calls Christians to separate from the corrupt culture, withdrawing into distinct Christian communities. The church becomes an *alternative* to the mainline culture, and Christians refuse to take part in the culture as a whole.

This has been the approach of the early monastic movement, the anabaptist subcultures, fundamentalist separatism, and the various experiments in Christian communal living of the last few decades. The Amish are a continual example of a group of Christians who refuse to compromise with the worldly culture, rejecting military service, contemporary dress, and modern technology as being unworthy of their commitment to radical discipleship.

Again, this kind of integrity and radical commitment commands respect. But it too is problematic. Besides denying God's sovereignty over the rest of the world, it violates the words of Jesus: "My prayer is not that you take them out of the world. . . . As you sent Me into the world, I have sent them into the world" (John 17:15, 18). Jesus directs us not into the protection of a fortified bunker; rather, He sends us *into* the world in service and evangelism.

Furthermore, the option of separatism, in forming a Christian sub-culture, has the effect of, again, reducing Christianity to a cultural religion. The "church," far from being a universal, transcultural institution, becomes just another culture. The Amish end up defining themselves by their beards and buggies, rather than by a transcendent Gospel. Evangelical ghettos set up parallel institutions to the secular world they reject, but those institutions end up being little different from secularist counterparts. Purposeful ghettoization does not usually result in the purification of Christianity, but rather its corruption. Christianity, once again, becomes a cultural religion.

Two Kingdoms under One King

Niebuhr also proposes Christ and culture in synthesis, but if the divinization of culture is so much to be avoided, this would seem to be the worst possibility of them all, combining the dangers of both theocracy and secularism. The possibility for the relationship between Christ and culture that seems to best account for the scriptural injunctions Niebuhr calls "Christ and culture in paradox"; Luther calls it the doctrine of the two kingdoms. This view accounts for the insights of the other positions, acknowledging that we are cultural creatures, that God is sovereign over every sphere of life, and that Christians must both be separate from the world and actively involved in it.

The doctrine of the two kingdoms has been explored not only by Lutheran theologians but by Augustine in his great work *The City of God* (see, for example, James Boice's *Two Cities, Two Loves*) and probably describes the way most faithful Christians have always carried out their fidelity to Christ in their secular callings.

According to this view, God is sovereign in both the Church and in the culture—but He rules the two in different ways. In the Church, God reigns through the work of Christ and the giving of the Holy Spirit, expressing His love and grace through the forgiveness of sins and the life of faith. God also exercises His authority and providential control through all of creation—upholding the very universe, so that the laws of physics, the processes of chemistry, and other natural laws are part of what He has ordained. Similarly, God rules the nations—even those who do not acknowledge Him—making human beings to be social creatures, in need of governments, laws, and cultures to mitigate the self-destructive tendencies of sin and to enable human beings to survive.

Thus, God has a spiritual rule in the hearts and lives of Christians; He also has a secular rule that extends throughout His creation and in every culture. God reigns in the Church through the Gospel, the proclamation of forgiveness in the Cross of Jesus Christ, a message which kindles faith and an inward transformation in the believer. He reigns in the world through His Law, which calls human societies to justice and righteousness.

Notice that, according to this view, morality is *not* a matter of religion. Contrary to those who would silence Christian objections to abortion, for instance, on the grounds that moral issues are inappropriate intrusions of private religious belief, the doctrine of the two kingdoms insists that God's Law is universal in its scope and authority. As C. S. Lewis has shown in *The Abolition of Man*, it is simply not true that every culture and every religion has its own morality. Principles of justice, honesty, courage, and responsibility to one's neighbor are universal. Though revealed most fully in Scripture, God's Law is written on the hearts even of the unbelieving Gentiles (Romans 2:14-16).

Human beings and cultures are, however, in a state of rebellion against Him. No individual can keep God's Law and entire cultures are subject to corruption, injustice, sexual depravity, and every kind of evil. While the world is condemned and all human institutions will pass away, God saves some in the ark of His Church. Christians, strictly speaking, are no longer under the Law at all—their new life of faith will make them spontaneously do what God requires, though because of their fallen nature full perfection will be found only in heaven.

In the meantime, Christians have a vocation in the world. They are called to evangelize, serve others, and do good works in the unbelieving world. Moreover, according to the Lutheran doctrine of vocation which is integral to the doctrine of the two kingdoms, Christians are called to actively play their part in their cultures, serving God in His secular kingdom in secular ways. A Christian farmer is expressing his love for God and neighbor by growing food for everyone, not just fellow believers; a Christian CEO serves God and neighbor by selling useful products, giving a livelihood to employees, making money for stockholders, and contributing to the good of the economy.

A Christian is thus a citizen of two kingdoms—the kingdom of heaven and the kingdom of this world. These spheres have different demands and operate in different ways. But God is the King of both. This doctrine has sometimes been misunderstood to mean that the secular government has absolute authority as an agent of God. This is the farthest from the truth. God is the King. His Law judges the kingdoms of the earth. A governmental system, such as that of Nazi Germany, which is in stark violation of that Law is in a state of rebellion and can demand no allegiance. A nation, however, need not be ruled by a Christian to exercise legitimate authority. The ruler's personal faith is a matter of the spiritual kingdom and a function of the Gospel; even an unbelieving ruler, however, can be held accountable to God's Law and to its corollaries in the secular requirements of good government.

This doctrine does affirm culture in a very powerful way. God is at work through human cultures, even those that are oblivious to Him. All cultures have families, moral laws, governmental structures, and economic relationships—these all involve divinely-ordained vocations, given to believer and unbeliever alike, which serve, in Luther's words, as "masks of God." As Gustaf Wingren explores in his classic book *Luther on Vocation*, God could create the new generations from the dust, but instead He ordained families and the vocation of parenthood through which children are born, raised, and taught. We pray that God give us our daily bread, which He does—through the vocation of farmers, bakers, transportation workers, retailers, and every other cog of the economic order. God is "hidden" in the office of parents and the work of farmers and secular rulers, through whom He accomplishes His will on earth despite human sin. A human culture is thus already part of God's kingdom—the kingdom of the left hand—even when on the surface it is pagan or tyrannical or secularist. To be sure, particular human cultures may have institutionalized sinful practices—such as infanticide, abortion, or human sacrifice—and these violations of God's Law demand reform. But even systems based on an ideology that denies private property have a way of still locking up those who violate the Seventh Commandment. The doctrine of the two kingdoms is thus radically affirmative of the diverse cultures of the world. Since culture is not religious as such, but human institutions through which God works, it is transient and cannot be absolutized. This actually allows for cultural diversity, which exists both globally and through time.

While both kingdoms have legitimate claims, they are not to be confused with each other. The secular values of the culture are not to be imposed upon the church. Nor may the spiritual realm be imposed upon the secular culture. Saving faith is a gift of the Holy Spirit and cannot be a matter of coercion. Nor can the freedom created by the Gospel be applied to unbelievers, who are still in their sins.

People today who oppose the death penalty, for example, because we should *forgive,* would be confusing the two kingdoms, as would pacifists who oppose all war because we are told to love our enemies. I recently came across a book that addressed the problem of crime by advocating that all criminals be released from prison. Jesus said that He came to proclaim release to the captives, the author argued. Therefore, we should do as He said, trusting that the gesture would transform the criminals' hearts. Christians must certainly express the love and forgiveness of Christ in their relationship with others, both inside and outside of the Church. But God's secular kingdom operates in terms of power, coercion, punishment, and the sometimes harsh demands of justice. The lawful magistrate is "God's servant, an agent of wrath to bring punishment on the wrongdoer" and "does not bear the sword for nothing" (Romans 13:4).

As a citizen in both kingdoms, a Christian may thus operate in different ways in the two spheres. No Christian should take private revenge, but a Christian soldier, judge, police officer, or juror may well have to "bear the sword."

If the government bears the sword, the church bears only the Word. Though the local church is also an earthly institution and so must be concerned with committees, by-laws, and even politics, the church is not to be run like a business, a nation, or the surrounding culture. It should be a haven of love and mutual forgiveness in the midst of a fallen, sin-sick world.

Christians exercising their vocations in the secular culture must assess their activity in secular terms, which are also under God's sovereignty. Christian artists may well express their faith in their work, but the quality of the art lies primarily not in its theological message but in its aesthetic excellence, since the laws of aesthetics have been ordained by God in His creation. There is no need for a distinctly Christian approach to music, plumbing, computer science, physics, or wood-carving, because all of these things, no matter how secular or non-religious they appear, already fall under God's sovereignty.

Conversely, the Church must never uncritically capitulate to the culture. Money-making, marketing techniques, entertainment ventures, power politics, sociological developments, and intellectual fashions must never set the church's agenda, which must be governed instead solely by the Word of God.

The Two Kingdoms and the Culture Wars

The doctrine of the two kingdoms is most often applied to the Christian's obligations to the state, but it also illuminates the cultural controversies which are causing so much confusion in today's church.

Should Christians get involved in politics? Yes, as part of our vocation in God's secular kingdom. The goal should not be necessarily the election of Christian rulers, nor to make America a "Christian nation." Rather, it should be to apply God's Law in our social relationships and to establish justice and righteousness in our land. Abortion, for example, is a monstrous crime against the weakest and most defenseless in our society, and Christians are right to work against this evil, as against many others. Christians in politics must play by political rules, whether hardball power plays or the arts of compromise and consensus building. The church should be gentle and loving, while never compromising its doctrines; the rough-and-tumble of the political process, however, means that Christian politicians should not be prevented from exercising power or from making a tactical compromise by the charge that to do so is "not Christian." That confuses the kingdoms. Christian politicians, however, like all politicians, must exercise their power justly and in accord with God's Law.

Can a Christian take part in the expressions of the surrounding culture? Yes. Christians are still part of their culture and can be expected to share the tastes of their neighbors. A Christian may enjoy, perform, and get involved in secular art forms. These art forms need not be religious. As with the rest of God's secular kingdom, of course, they remain subject to God's Law. Christians need to draw the line at music or any other form of entertainment that violates God's canons of morality by tempting us to sin.

Can a Christian, then, like rock music? Yes, for the most part. This does not mean, however, that Christians should demand rock music in church. The secular kingdom, again, must be kept separate from the spiritual kingdom. Churches must keep themselves distinct from the surrounding culture. Churches must be, to some degree, countercultural.

To return to our earlier categories, a liberal would have no trouble accepting any brand of currently popular music and would even import it into the church. By this way of thinking, the church must always give in and conform itself to whatever the culture is doing. A Christian who believes in Christ above culture would reject secular music and try to devise a completely distinct Christian style, to which every subsequent piece of music should conform. A Christian who believes in Christ against culture would allow the world its own music but never listen to it, developing instead a separate Christian musical style.

A two kingdoms approach would allow the Christian to enjoy secular music, even, for those with the God-given talent, to pursue a musical vocation. The Christian's standards for this music would be God's moral Law, but also God's aesthetic laws, which were built into the created order and human nature by God Himself. The Christian musician might express his or her faith artistically, but the work would be assessed not primarily by its theology but by its aesthetic merits, which also come under God's dominion. The music, though, would not have to be explicitly religious at all—it is part of God's dominion even in its secularity.

This same Christian musician, whether a rock 'n' roller or a concert violinist, may very well object to electric guitars or chamber music in church. Art designed to please and to gratify the senses has its place, but worship belongs to the Word of God. Here, theological truth must take priority. The purpose is not to entertain the congregation but to convict them of sin and convert them to Christ. The audience is not the culture but God, whom the entire congregation is seeking to glorify—in His terms, not ours.

Kenneth Myers has said in his brilliant book *All God's Children and Blue Suede Shoes* that the contemporary church has reversed Christ's injunction to be in the world, but not of the world. Instead, he says, we are not *in* the world, but we are *of* the world. Contemporary Christians tend to have separate schools, bookstores, music companies, and other cultural institutions, so that we seldom interact with non-believers. This places us out of the world. Nevertheless, we are of the world. Our music, stores, schools, and corporate structures, however separated, are exactly like their secular counterparts, with the very same emphasis on entertainment, material success, mass commercial appeal, and other worldly values. In contrast, we need to be *in* the world—engaged in our culture in its own terms—while not being *of* the world, having our values and our motivations grounded in our spiritual identity as redeemed children of God.

Myers makes the further distinction between the folk culture, consisting of the traditions and values of a particular people, the high culture, consisting of the creative contributions of a civilization, and today's popular culture, which is mass produced as an entertainment commodity. He argues that Christianity can interact with folk cultures and high culture. The pop culture, however, is more of an anti-culture, displacing both the traditional values of folk communities and the standards of excellence of high civilization. In their place, pop culture offers a purposefully shallow promise of instant gratification, anti-intellectual, antimoral, and self-centered.

Immigrants to America tend to come with strong ethnic—that is, folk—cultures, which tend to value strong families and other "traditional" values. One of their major problems is what happens to their children as they become enculturated into American pop culture.

Their children no longer respect the authority of their parents, they reject the traditional sexual taboos, and often fall in with peers who lead them astray. This is happening globally as the mass produced commodities of the pop culture—commercial TV, R-rated movies, rebellious rock 'n' roll music, and the like—undermine the traditional ways and in some cases create a literal social breakdown. In two kingdoms terms, folk cultures tend to establish some sort of social order, which can function as a mask of God. The high culture too rests on possibilities, standards, and raw material that are functions of God's creation, which is the foundation and model of human creativity. Pop culture tends to reject authority, truth, and the social good of others in favor of a purely selfish orientation. To that extent, it is rebelling against God's reign.

The point is, the doctrine of the two kingdoms can account for such contemporary concerns as multiculturalism and globalism. It also provides a framework for cultural criticism and moral activism.

Recognizing God's double sovereignty over all of life can enable Christians to be engaged with their culture in a positive, transforming way, without succumbing to the deadly, spirit-quenching sin of worldliness. Christians are called to be both faithful and relevant; active in service to the world, yet having their minds fixed "on things that are above" (Colossians 3:2); open to culture—and secular education and to the secular world in general—yet looking at culture and the secular realm with critical eyes. As Martin Marty pointed out, Christians will always be both at war and at peace with their cultures. Christians must be citizens of two qualitatively different kingdoms at the very same time; but their loyalties, while sometimes conflicting, are not necessarily divided, insofar as both kingdoms have the same King.

Gene Edward Veith is Professor of English and Director of the Cranach Institute at Concordia University Wisconsin.

Bibliography

Augustine of Hippo. *The City of God*. Trans. Marcus Dods. New York: Modern Library, 1950.

Boice, James Montgomery. *Two Cities, Two Loves: Christian Responsibility in a Crumbling Culture*. Downers Grove, IL: Intervarsity Press, 1996.

Lewis, C. S. *The Abolition of Man*. New York: Macmillan, 1947.

Myers, Kenneth. *All God's Children and Blue Suede Shoes: Christians and Popular Culture*. Westchester, IL: Crossway Books, 1989.

Niebuhr, H. Richard. *Christ and Culture*. New York: Harper, 1951.

Wingren, Gustaf. *Luther on Vocation*. Trans. Carl Rasmussen. Philadelphia, PA: Muhlenberg Press, 1957.

6

Christianity and Culture: The China Challenge

Wayne Martindale

Setting Boundaries

After positioning myself philosophically in the discussion, I want to address five main issues in the broader area of Christ and culture in China, organized under the following headings: (I) Culture against Christ in China; (II) Why Is the Chinese Government So Hostile toward Christianity? (III) Why Should We Care? (IV) On the Bright Side; and (V) What Can We Do about It?

The issue of Christ and culture is prickly enough in countries that have a long and deeply rooted history of Christian influence. In the case of China, with its recent history of systematic assault on Christianity, the problems loom even larger. The first hurdle is defining "culture." In the narrow sense it may mean the arts, or, as Matthew Arnold suggested, "the best that is thought and said." Instead of Arnold's notion of "high culture," I will use the distinctions common to social scientists: the state (the political and governmental apparatus), society (the visible institutions like economic entities and families), and culture (all that is left, though at times including the other two as "the totality of a people's communal life in all its manifestations").[1] Culture especially denotes the invisible attitudes and values toward everything from persons to immortality.

In the debate on Christ and culture, I line up with Martin Marty in his paradoxical "War and Peace" approach, which is to say I agree with Martin Luther. We may also add C. S. Lewis to this noble band, who reminds us in his stunning sermon on Christianity and culture called "Learning in War-Time" that it is impossible to live without culture.

If you attempted . . . to suspend your whole intellectual and aesthetic activity, you would only succeed in substituting a worse cultural life for a better. You are not, in fact, going to read nothing: . . . if you don't read good books, you will read bad ones. If you don't go on thinking rationally, you will think irrationally. If you reject aesthetic satisfactions, you will fall into sensual satisfactions.

. . . There is no question of a compromise between the claims of God and the claims of culture. . . . God's claim is infinite and inexorable. Yet . . . it is clear that Christianity does not exclude any other ordinary human activities. St. Paul tells people to get on with their jobs. . . . The solution of this paradox is . . . "Whether ye eat or drink or whatsoever ye do, do all to the glory of God."

All our merely natural activities will be accepted, if they are offered to God, even the humblest, and all of them, even the noblest, will be sinful if they are not. Christianity does not simply replace our natural life and substitute a new one; it is rather a new organization which exploits, to its own supernatural ends, these natural materials.[2]

This same view is expressed in one of the most public and popular of Christian forums, the back page of *Christianity Today*. Using terms from historian of the Victorian period Gertrude Himmelfarb, Philip Yancey reminds us that

> . . . we can 'Christianize' people, but not institutions. We can baptize, teach, and hold accountable individuals, but not a government, school, or court system. Thus, we have no mandate to 'Christianize' the United States—an impossible goal in any case. Yet Christians can work simultaneously toward a different goal, the 'moralization' of society. We can help tether the values and even the laws of a society to some basis in transcendence.[3]

I line up with Yancey, Lewis, Luther, and Marty because they line up with Scripture: Jesus said, "be in the world but not of it." In Niebuhr's terms, this position is called "Christ beside Culture." While I believe this is the best model for China, or anyplace else, I'm afraid that many Chinese would think that Americans have the luxury of thinking in these terms, while they do not. I am fairly certain that the only model making any sense for the many Chinese Christians in China now or in most of their history is Niebuhr's model #1: "Christ against Culture."

I. Culture against Christ in China.

For most of the world, this tension of being citizens of heaven and citizens of an earthly kingdom strains body, mind, and spirit. Worldwide, 160,000 people will die this year for no other reason than their embrace of Christ. An equally large number have died for their faith throughout the last decade in this the bloodiest century in world history, both in general and with respect to martyrdom.[4] Jim Jacobson, president of Christian Solidarity International, says, "More people today are being tortured, imprisoned, maimed and killed for their faith than ever before in history."[5] And though the situation is worse in many Muslim-dominated cultures, Chinese Christians are still among the most persecuted in the world.

According to the *Wall Street Journal* (September 26, 1996), since March 1996, China has been in what they have called a "Strike Hard" campaign, in large part against religious people, which, in just the first five months, has resulted in "at least 1,000 executions and more than 160,000 arrests. . . . Authorities have destroyed 15,000 unregistered temples, churches and other religious sites in Zhejiang province alone. The most recent stage of the crackdown seems to have coincided with a June Ministry of Public Security document urging a renewed struggle against religion, particularly Christianity." So intense is the pressure that persecution is worse now than any time in the last twenty years. In March 1998, Focus on the Family aired a hard-hitting indictment of both the Chinese government and of American Christians for their lack of outrage and inaction. Their "Information" sheet on "International Persecution of Christians" claims that "Christians today are the most persecuted religious group in the world, and persecution has intensified during the past few years."[6] Perhaps because of the number involved, China appears first on their list of eleven countries where persecution is "most fierce." U.S. lawmakers have begun to grasp the gravity of the situation. As *World* magazine reports, in March 1998 the U.S. House "unanimously passed a resolution urging the White House to condemn China's human-rights record at the annual UN Commission on Human Rights then convening in Geneva."[7]

Diane Knippers, president of the Institute on Religion and Democracy, Washington, D.C., makes a similarly grave assessment: "Persecution of Chinese Christians has expanded during the past five years. Underground Protestant church leaders report continuing church closings, sentences to 'reeducation through labor' camps, and torture." On being forced to choose between human rights and evangelism, Knippers says, "that sounds like the tired, old debates between evangelism and social action. It is a false choice, especially when the freedom to share one's faith is the right being denied." She is not hopeful that a laissez-faire policy on the part of Christians will bring relief:

> Some also argue that if Christians simply keep a low profile, things will ease for the Chinese Christians. It is true that virtually all Chinese Christians are markedly apolitical. They simply want to be left alone to preach and teach and worship.
>
> But what the Chinese government's leaders are most distressed about is what they saw happen in Eastern Europe where the Christian church played an integral part in the largely peaceful overthrow of communism. In this respect, the paranoid leaders of China may understand the nature of the Christian faith far better than we recognize—that the Christian's ultimate loyalty is a threat to any authoritarian regime. No matter how peaceful and loyal individual Christians are, their faith is, by its very nature, a threat to Chinese communism."[8]

Jonathan Chao of China Ministries International agrees that the purpose of the present repressive campaign "as stated in some of the official notices, is to split the spiritual strength of house churches, destroy their leadership, and reduce the influence of the Christian faith in Chinese society to make sure that what happened in Eastern Europe and the former USSR will not happen in China."[9] The Chinese government issued regulations detailing even more restrictions effective March 1, 1998, including fines the equivalent of several years' wages.[10]

Let me try to put a human face on the problem. Wang—not his real name—lived in a large Chinese city in Institute "housing" in a converted rest room with his wife and in-laws. Though construction goes on apace, this situation is not uncommon. Wang was led to faith in Christ over eight years ago by an American English teacher. Wang would finish his assigned work for the institute early in the week. Part of the remaining week went to teaching the Bible to 200 people packed in a single small room in the countryside. The rest he spent working with several dozen Christian university students.

One fall, he led an outreach that attracted 250 participants; many came to Christ. In our last meeting before leaving China, he asked for prayer, not for protection, but a spirit of boldness instead—"like Paul." The following summer, we learned that Wang had been imprisoned for two months. He was released in hopes that he would lead authorities to other converts and with the very real threat of re-arrest. American friends tried to help, but to no avail. Both Wang and his wife were released from their jobs, which meant they would be blacklisted with little possibility of finding other jobs, even if he stayed out of jail. Since receiving housing is a condition of employment, they were turned out of their meager lodging. They were homeless and without personal resources; in short, beggars. The couple fled to the countryside; the wife was pregnant, but could not go to the state-controlled clinics or hospitals. Such was their condition for some time, until they escaped to Hong Kong, thence to the U.S. Though this story has a happy ending, many do not. Examples, even within my own experience, could be multiplied.

From the perspective of many Chinese Christians, the government, which has been by intention the dominant shaper of culture in this century, is out to destroy them. Will I obey Jiang Zemin and Li Peng and stop preaching or obey God and proclaim Him? Will I obey government policies and register my house group so it can be controlled by the government or remain secretive and evangelize as led by the Spirit? Will I report this pregnancy and submit to an abortion or hide to protect the baby? In China, one must count the cost. A visiting scholar recently told me, "If I were going to live in America I would become a Christian, but in China, I can't. I would lose my job, and my family would disown me."

II. Why Is the Chinese Government So Hostile toward Christianity?

History may not seem terribly important to many in the "now" generation of America, but it is supremely important to the Chinese. Mao, for example, was constantly culling the history of China for a model that would keep him in power. Knowing the importance of history to the Chinese people, the twentieth-century party revisionists have been busy reshaping the past to suit the utopian dreams of the present. To the Chinese, history matters a great deal, even enough to falsify it. History is also important for us if we want to understand why the government is so ruthless in its persecution today.

Christianity has had its chances in China's history. Readers of Coleridge will immediately recognize the name Kublai Khan. In the mid-thirteenth century, he was the most powerful man on earth. In 1266, he asked father Marco Polo to take an official request to the Pope in Rome for a hundred Christian teachers. If persuaded that Christianity is best, he and the nation would embrace it. Polo could find only two willing to attempt the mission, and they were turned back by the rigors of the journey.

In his quest to found a new religion in his country, the Khan turned to Tibetan Buddhism, which spread for nearly seven hundred years until, at the turn of the twentieth century, Mongolia (all that remained of the empire) was the most religious country on earth with over seven thousand temples.[11] Later attempts to introduce Christianity into China found hard sledding and met with persecution, largely because it became associated with turbulent and unpopular movements. I will list and comment briefly on the six most important of these in the last 150 years.

First, there were the Opium Wars, fought between 1839 and 1842, deeply wounding China's pride as she was forced to cede five ports which would operate under foreign, not Chinese, law. As part of the port treaties, the Chinese were forced to allow Christian missionaries the right to propagate their faith. In the Chinese mind, foreign sovereignty, opium, and Christianity were shoved down their throat together.

The second gets superb scholarly treatment from Yale's Professor Jonathan Spence's recent historical look at the mid-nineteenth century in *God's Chinese Son: The Taiping Heavenly Kingdom of Hong Xiuquan.* Hong Xiuquan claimed to have had visions of a divine being while he was seriously ill in 1837. He did nothing about these visions until he read some Christian tracts in 1843 and concluded that the person who appeared to him was God. In time, Hong declared himself a second "Son of Heaven," a second Christ. He hadn't read Niebuhr, but if he had, he would have no trouble positioning himself in model

#1, Christ against Culture. Hong took it upon himself and his followers to forcefully bring in the kingdom of God. He set up his capital in Nanjing, proclaimed the advent of Taiping Tianquo—"Heavenly Kingdom of Great Peace"—and battled the forces of the Qing dynasty for nearly fifteen years, very nearly toppling it.

In the end, Hong, the self-proclaimed second Christ who published his own edited version of the Bible, lost. The casualties? An unimaginable twenty million people. In 1916, Baptist writer Timothy Richard observed that the thirteen years of Taiping rule resulted in a "legacy of hatred against Christianity, a hatred which has scarcely yet melted away." The editor of a Missions Handbook agrees: "Christianity still suffers from the travesty."[12] To the worldly-minded politicos uninterested in the fine distinction between a born-again believer and a usurper of the name, the Taiping Rebellion is proof that Christian propaganda is politically dangerous.

Third, at the turn of the century, there were the Boxer Rebellions in which Christians were cast as the "foreign devils." The movement was not mainly anti-Christian in origin; it was anti-foreign and was strongest in the north, where the humiliation from the Japanese was the strongest. But Christians were often isolated and in vulnerable positions, so they were easy targets: 200 missionaries were killed along with more than 30,000 Christians, the bulk of them Catholic. The action was part of the Empress Dowager's attempt to regain control and oust foreigners. She was defeated, but even this defeat was a source of continued national humiliation.

Next came the May Fourth Movement of 1919, which marked the beginning of the Chinese intellectual revolution. One of its tenets was the embrace of science and the rejection of all religions as superstition. Where did these intellectuals get their anti-religious ideas? From universities abroad, where they had been trained in Enlightenment thinking, which, ironically, often viewed the Confucian conception of social organization with its humanistic assumptions about the innate goodness and educability of humanity as ideal.

Fifth, Mao embraced the Marxist notion that religion was the handmaiden of economic repression. Nothing was allowed to take precedence over the revolutionary struggle of the working class. From 1949 to 1976, the Communists did their level best to eradicate religion of all kinds—except the cult of Mao. Finally, 1989 saw both the collapse of the Berlin Wall and the Chinese student-led, pro-democracy movement, brutally crushed in the June 4th Tiananmen Massacre. In the years immediately following, the USSR came apart, followed closely by the Communist regimes of Romania and Albania. As the Chinese clearly saw, each of these revolutions had significant linkage with Christianity, something that could also be said of the American Revolution. As the last major Communist country in the world with an economy not yet out of the woods, there was due cause for anxiety.

These examples of China's hostility to religion are relatively modern and, for the most part, specifically Christian. The roots of this branch of xenophobia go rather deep and embrace all religions. Brian Palmer reports that "China's leaders have long feared religion's capacity to erode political power. 'No emperor would tolerate an organized group that he did not control,' says Deng Zhaoming, a Hong Kong-based church watcher. Nor will China's Communist rulers yield control. 'In China,' says Deng, 'Caesar is above Christ, no question. Christ can never be head of the church. It's the state that's the head of the church.'"[13] This attitude is especially true of the Catholic church in China. "Members of the unsanctioned house churches recognize papal authority. Members of the state-approved churches, a RAB [Religious Affairs Bureau] official says, 'may pray for the pope but they must accept that the Vatican cannot interfere with our internal affairs, including religious affairs.'"[14] Brian Palmer concludes: "Nearly everyone in China understands that Beijing's primary aims are social stability and party supremacy. But not everyone is in step with the government's goals."[15]

James Hitchcock summarizes the view of renowned historian Christopher Dawson on the reason for the state's antagonism toward religion. "Among other things, religion teaches that there is a divine purpose to history, that man owes God collective as well as individual worship, and that the human race must be obedient to a law higher than that of the state, all of which make the relationship between religion and the state problematical and, to the degree that religion inspires the culture and is part of it, makes culture also a danger to the authority of the state. The Roman Empire persecuted Christianity not because Christians held different beliefs from the Romans but because the state could not control the church."[16] Kenneth Lieberthal, in his recent book

Governing China, concurs: "The imperial tradition nurtured the idea of basing the state system on ideological commitment, strong personal leadership at the apex, and impressive nationwide governing bureaucracies; the assumption in modern China that the government's influence should be pervasive because the government set the moral framework for the entire society is also a product of the imperial era."[17]

Meanwhile, even among the Chinese leadership, there is an unspoken realization that Communism is a failed philosophy that has left the country morally bankrupt.[18] The leaders will not acknowledge it publicly, or allow it to be acknowledged, since they have no other source of ideological legitimacy. When Deng decided to abandon socialism because it didn't work, to save face he called its replacement a "socialist free market," seemingly undisturbed by the contradiction in terms. Chinese intellectuals are earnestly searching for something to fill the moral vacuum. With the awareness of moral decline and the burgeoning economic prominence of China, nationalism is on the rise and history is once again being culled for an authentically Chinese source of cultural values. Since many are looking to Confucianism to supply that need, we will look at this element of Chinese history as another source of resistance to Christianity.

Extreme nationalism has long characterized China. The Chinese name for what we call "China" is Zhong Guo, which means "middle kingdom," suggesting that China is the center of civilization. This condescending attitude toward other nations, even with the notion that other cultures might taint them, has resulted in long periods of isolation. Nationalism is a historical constant. The recent resurgence has arisen from China's new-found status as a world-class player on the economic scene. A recent book which has gotten a huge reception within China is *China Can Say No*, followed by many sequels, like: *Why China Can Say No*, *China Can Still Say No*. What they are saying "no" to is the West. The work of these writers, many in their early twenties, is not orchestrated by the government, but the government finds it useful because nationalism is a powerful motivator and source of cohesion, whereas the party's goal of stability and control is not.[19]

China's intensely nationalistic history accounts for much of the appeal in Confucianism, though some contemporary scholars argue that China was originally, in its first three dynasties, monotheistic. The emperors practiced sacrifice somewhat similar to Old Testament Israel. But for millennia, an essentially secular Confucian culture developed in China. Buddhism and Taoism, like Confucianism, were not originally religions. Buddha made no claim to deity. Prayer, worship, and idols came later. Even as presently practiced, the goal is to manipulate the gods to serve human ends. There is no transcendence, no claim on the worshipper's life. If one god doesn't suit you, switch to another. As Chinese scholar Daniel Su observes, China has no "self-evident" truths, like those named in the U.S. Declaration of Independence.[20] There are no individual rights based on a starting point of good and evil or the idea of sin.

The practical result of the Confucian system was a feudal system in which most of society suffered severe oppression: the wife was the servant of the husband, the daughters-in-law were the servants of the patriarch's wife. In this pragmatic and conservative environment, the highest ideal for the Confucian scholar is to know the rules governing relationships, to pass them on, and to build the nation with its hierarchical relationships in place from the emperor to the various members of the family. The resultant lack of transcendent values is one of the barriers Christianity has to overcome, not only on the cultural level but the political. Christianity has both transcendent values and international ties, two reasons why the Chinese government fears it. It requires a higher allegiance than the government.

Here is a practical example of the difference Christianity would make in life at a grass roots level in China. On the Confucian model, obligations are only to people with whom you have direct relationships. There is no sense of widespread obligation on the basis of shared humanity, as there is in Christianity, believing that all bear the image of God. When an accident happens in China, a large crowd will gather, but only to gawk and perhaps even to laugh. Only the police will get involved. The sense of the onlookers is that "this person is nothing to me. I have no obligation by family connection or friendship," which would include favors exchanged over a period of time. A guide for Chinese visitors to the West produced in the early 1980s advised not standing around an accident and laughing.[21] A beggar passed often in the street who one day dies might be the source of jokes, instead of remorse.[22] Lieberthal's assessment is that "the fundamental nature of social obligation has been one of China's major obstacles to developing a sense of citizenship."[23]

Through the parable of the Good Samaritan, to cite one example, Jesus taught that the person in the accident and the beggar are our neighbors. For another, when Jesus boiled down all the law and prophets into a single sentence, he said we are to love God and our neighbors as ourselves. Does Christianity have an uphill battle to fight with Chinese culture? Absolutely. But, paradoxically, at this stage the stark cultural difference between China and the U.S. creates some of the greatest and most natural openings for presenting Christ as the basis for personal and cultural transformation. Let me give one illustration, the like of which could be multiplied many times over.

A short time ago, my wife and I said good-bye to a visiting Chinese scholar who stayed with us for a few months to get acclimated before commencing study at an Ivy League school. She was my wife's student, informally, for a semester during our second trip to China two years ago. We only recently learned from this scholar how she came to regularly attend my wife's English class. Early in our time at the Chinese school, we were walking out of a classroom building as this Chinese teacher was coming in with some friends. We held the door for them to go in first. She said to herself, "these foreigners are kind." And on the basis of that, she tracked down our schedules and went to my wife's class.

Here she is two years later, now having read most of the Four Gospels, living with a Navigator family, studying Luke every morning, and twice a week attending an English as a Second Language class based on the Bible. On her second day with us, in the context of a discussion about bribery, she remarked, "China is cruel." From business ethics to acts of courtesy, our culture has yet a potent residue from the Christian values that went into its making. Of course, our culture has many raw edges and it makes a great deal of difference where on the battlefield of our culture wars a foreigner lands. The point of this is not to look down our noses at China and thereby to sin. It is 1) to awaken our gratitude for the Christian heritage that has shaped our culture in ways we take for granted, and 2) to suggest that we have something to give which we too seldom think about. The love of Christ is transforming, and love plays well in every culture.

III. Why Should We Care?

Why should Westerners care about the relationship of Christ and culture in China? Let me give three reasons. Reason #1. The most obvious and important reason is that Jesus cares. From the great commission of Mt. 28:19-20, "make disciples of all nations," to Rev. 7:9, John's vision of heaven with people from "every nation, tribe, people, and tongue" standing before the throne of Jesus, it is quite simply the Christian's mandate. Concern for the poor and the oppressed is a constant in both the Old Testament prophets and the teaching of Jesus and the apostles. Even our political concerns are to be spiritually driven. Paul teaches us to pray for political stability so that the Gospel might advance. The most important reason for caring about culture is as a means of bringing the light of Gospel to those who are in spiritual darkness.

It is no small reassurance to observe that God has been at work in China, even through its culture, hostile though it has been to the Gospel. I don't know which of Niebuhr's categories this next observation fits, so I think I'll make up a new one: "Christ through and in spite of Culture." Don Richardson, one of today's premier missionary statesmen, has made the following observation about Mao Zedong and the spread of Christianity. Remember that this is the man responsible for more deaths than any other who has ever lived. I have seen estimates of up to 90 million if you include the effect of his monomaniacal policies. Like Satan in Milton's *Paradise Lost*, God frustrates the Devil by using even his most dastardly attempts to stop the kingdom of God to advance the kingdom. The death of Jesus on the cross would be the prime example. So, what did Mao do?

First, he unified the nation under one language. Most cities still have their own dialects, but the language for education and commerce, at his dictate, is Mandarin. Of course, Mao's intent was to insure a means for universal political training—indoctrination and control. Second, in an attempt to eradicate religion altogether, he eliminated false religions, then purified the true church through suffering. Third, after killing and imprisoning many Christians, he decided to destroy the remainder by dispersing them throughout China. Break up the groups, the churches, and Christianity will die out, he reasoned. So he sent the remaining 100,000 tested and proven Christians who were prepared to die for their faith around China to do menial tasks, like delivering mail and collecting garbage—both of which took them to people's doors.

Richardson's conclusion: Mao and the Chinese Communist Party became the largest missions-sending agency in the history of the world. Missionaries were expelled in 1949. When the doors began to open in the 1970s, it gradually became clear that Christianity had not died out; that it had, in fact, flourished, so that there were at least a million Christians. God's sovereign work in history should give us hope in thinking about the impact of Christ on culture.[24]

Reason #2. Though the following reason could be seen as strictly nationalistic and self-serving, it needn't be. We must care for reasons of our own survival, but we may also care for the nobler reason of thinking strategically about the kingdom of God. Respected futurist John Naisbitt in his recent *Megatrends Asia* predicts that by year 2000 Asia "will dominate the world politically, economically, and culturally. We are on the threshold of the Asian Renaissance."[25] Similarly, Kenneth Lieberthal observes that "according to the International Monetary Fund, China has the third largest economy in the world in terms of real purchasing power."[26] As Lieberthal aptly says, "When a country with 22 percent of the globe's population achieves real rates of economic expansion of more than 12 percent per year, everybody takes notice and accommodates to the changes underway."[27] The nations have also noticed that China has the largest military force in the world. This is no small reason to care.

Reason #3. China's culture needs Christians to, in Gertrude Himmelfarb's term, "moralize" it. The list of social ills in any country is arresting, but in China's case, it is staggering. Persecution has already been discussed. On the business scene, many find that planning for any project requires an additional 40 percent of a project's cost to allow for corruption.[28] On the social scene, the policy with the most far-reaching consequences for individuals, families, and society is the one child policy. The results of this brand of social engineering are mind-boggling. A country like ours can scarcely cast stones regarding abortion. The uniqueness of the Chinese practice is the pressure brought to bear on women who do not want to have an abortion and the social and family pressures to abort a female fetus. This accounts in large part for the popularity of ultra sound, which has been common for a decade, with 100,000 scanners already in use by 1990.[29] With the one child policy and with China's patriarchal family structure, couples want sons. The result is an 18 percent total shortfall in females; 12 percent when adjusted for the naturally occurring majority of male births.[30] Many female babies are allowed to die; others glut orphanages along with the deformed. As recent documentaries on Chinese orphanages have shown, with the resultant closure to Westerners, these institutions all have dying rooms where the ill-cared for, ill-treated, and abandoned are left to die as though they were human waste, a net loss to society.

Another result of the one child policy is a generation of spoiled brats. The Chinese call these pampered only children "little emperors." Something else new on the scene is obese Chinese. In 1995, we saw public service ads on TV with six people (parents and two sets of grandparents) stuffing one child with food as the child ballooned before our eyes. The point was to caution parents against raising obese children by showering them with candy treats and rich food. The prospect of a self-centered, sexually frustrated, predominantly male population in the next decade is a scary thought. Already women have become the object of mercenary free trade of the worst sort: a slave trade in women and children, kidnapped from villages and sold hundred of miles away, often after being raped by the handlers. Sheryl Wudunn reports that "in 1989 and 1990, a total of 65,236 people were arrested for trafficking in women and children" in China.[31]

As a related issue to the one child policy, who will take care of the aging? There is no welfare, since the extended family traditionally took care of that. Now, instead of transgenerational families living together with ten or more children and their spouses and a growing number of grandchildren, one child has to support the parents and two sets of grandparents. How will China deal with this? Euthanasia? Suicide? A further stress on the family is a growing divorce rate, which has tripled since 1990.[32] If ever there was a case tailor-made for arguing Model #5, "Christ Transforming Culture," here it is.

It would be foolish to try to delink Christianity and culture in the public debate for two reasons. The first is the simple reason that it's impossible. The Chinese leadership has researched the fall of communism in Eastern Europe, concluding that Christians played a key role in the largely peaceful fall of communism. They realize that having an ultimate loyalty to God and to biblical principles may severely limit their own authority, this despite the reality that most Chinese Christians are apolitical and want mainly to be left alone to worship God, study the Bible, and propagate the faith. But when the heart is changed, everything is changed. It is not for nothing that dictators throughout history have often persecuted the devout. Of course, it depends in the end upon what the government is after. If it wants a healthy work and business ethic and the many benefits of a moral society, then Christianity is an unacknowledged ally. But if the aim is a megalomaniacal control of minds and hearts like that which Mao aimed at, then, yes, Christianity is a formidable foe.

The second reason is the need for a common commitment to solve elemental social problems, like care for the poor. The kind of commitment required for such efforts can only come from the religiously committed. It will not work to suggest to people that religion is pragmatic. Distinguished historian Russell Kirk says: "No man sincerely goes down on his knees to the divine because he has been told that such rituals lead to the beneficial consequences of tolerably honest behavior in commerce. People will conform their actions to the precepts of religion only when they earnestly believe the doctrines of that religion to be true."[33] All human civilizations arise, says Kirk, from persons "joining together for worship."[34] It is simply a "myth" that some kind of civil religion based on public virtue is pragmatically possible. Culture takes on the cast of true belief, whatever it is. The only thing deep enough to insure peaceful cooperation among people is religious belief; the only way to renew culture is to renew the worshipping community.[35]

The book *Soul Searching* (1997) features ten essays by mainland Chinese intellectuals who have come to North America and converted to Christianity.[36] In one essay, Daniel Baida Su expresses the belief that, while many Chinese have been searching "for free and democratic institutions," the focus should be on "inner renewal" of the individual, which is a prerequisite to the "restructuring of culture." Rejecting the "historical determinist's" view that China is destined to totalitarian governments in the Imperialist tradition, Su affirms that Christianity is the way to genuine cultural renewal.[37] In another of the essays, Xian Rikui focuses on the transforming power of God's love as the only thing that will truly liberate China's basic social institutions.

"Forgiveness, humility, and a sound marriage become possible, as God's life and human life become intertwined."[38]

James Hitchcock's words in speaking of the need for religious and thence cultural renewal in our own country apply with equal force to China, suggesting an essential linkage among religion, culture, and society: "Salvation will not come through politics, and in a sense the renewal of the society must come from the renewal of culture, a task in which few Christians seem to be consciously engaged and for which perhaps few are suited. However, before Christians can even think about transforming culture, they must first act to protect culture from the voracious appetite of the Modernist state, must tenaciously affirm the autonomy of culture, which at the deepest level means affirming and securing the autonomy of religion. . . . Bold and radical actions alone will serve, inspired by that mysterious power that always holds out the promise of throwing off the old man, of making all things new."[39]

IV. On the Bright Side

If the hope for cultural renewal is revitalization of religious belief at the core, then there is hope for Chinese culture. Though statistics from the Chinese government on the number of Christians are at about 10 million, it counts only those in the officially recognized and registered church. There are many more in unregistered house churches. A conservative estimate is a total of 35 million believing Christians (with many using a figure twice that number), which means that, paradoxically, China is "home to the world's fastest growing Christian movement," yet "remains the world's largest mission field, with more than one-quarter of the world's unevangelized people living within its borders."[40] According to a China researcher, one house church group in central China has 8,500 full time itinerant evangelists with perhaps 40,000 converts each month. Six organizations collaborated to deliver 100,000 Bibles to them during 1995 and early 1996, a significant number, but far below the actual need.[41]

According to official United Front figures, in Tianjin, one of China's huge national cities located near Beijing, there are 610,000 Communist Party members and 620,000 Christians. Since 1991, the Christian population has increased by 50,000 per year, while the Party has increased by 30,000 per year. And these figures do not include the unregistered church, which is several times larger than the registered church. This phenomenon, called "Christianity Fever" by the government, holds countrywide (though with varying intensity) and is the cause for the government's anxiety.[42]

The transformation of culture is important, but not ultimate. It is important in the same way that every human endeavor is important. As C. S. Lewis reminds us: "Our leisure, even our play, is a matter of serious concern. There is no neutral ground in the universe: every square inch, every split second, is claimed by God and counterclaimed by Satan."[43] Culture is both the arena in which we make our witness and part of the witness itself. "Culture is a storehouse of the best (sub-Christian) values. These values are in themselves of the soul, not the spirit. But God created the soul. Its values may be expected, therefore, to contain some reflection or antepast of the spiritual values. They will save no man. They resemble the regenerate life only as affection resembles charity, or honour resembles virtue, or the moon the sun."[44] The purpose of the witness in and through culture is to bring the lost to Christ.

V. What Can We Do about It?

How can we not only influence the culture to "moralize" it, but reach the people to "Christianize" them? There are as many ways as people willing to go for periods of time ranging from the three-day conference to a career. There are people making a difference in China through fields as diverse as music, the military, business, law, medicine, and education. From English to computers to elementary schools, there are teaching opportunities by the thousands. In the universities, we have a chance to reach the elite 1 percent at the top of China's culture. What makes China such a unique arena for the engagement of culture at its spiritual root is the unprecedented hunger for God in this country. I will illustrate it with a closing story, which took place at an English corner gathering: a random gathering of Chinese interested in practicing English. The following conversation is reported by my wife Nita, who was the principal in the exchange.

Question: "Where are you from?"

Nita:	"Chicago."
Question:	"Isn't it dangerous?"
Nita:	"Well, it's not what you think, but, actually, I live in a suburb 25 miles west, and it's a largely Christian community and very safe."
Question:	"Are you a Christian?"
Nita:	"Yes."
Question:	"I have heard that Jesus can help Christians; how has Jesus helped you?"
Nita:	Silence, while the wheels turn. (What would you say?)

Helpful voice from the crowd: "Tell us a small way, and tell us a big way."

For the small way, she told how Jesus helped her not to be so shy at English Corner. For the large way, she began to tell how Jesus helped her when her mother died of cancer when Nita was a junior in high school. As she told the story, the tears ran, and she choked up with emotion, unable to continue. Three young men stood in the front rank of the circle.

First man: "Many of us do not believe in Jesus. I think this must make you very sad."

Second man: "Many of us do not believe in Jesus because we have never heard."

Third man: "Many of us do not believe in Jesus, but some of us think it would be a good thing if we did."

Several weeks later, we left China on forty-five minutes notice following the Tiananmen Massacre of June 4, 1989. We spent the preceding night with the third young man and his wife, not knowing it would be our last in that city. The following school year, a nineteen-year-old student from a midwestern university came to China to teach English for the year. The third man, along with five others, came to faith in Christ through a Bible study she conducted. Two years later his wife also came to faith. From that core of fewer than ten, a church took root and soon grew to forty. This scenario has been repeated throughout China for over twenty years now, since its opening in the

1970s. It represents the real hope for China. Out of the worshipping church, civilization flows.

Wayne Martindale is Associate Professor of English at Wheaton College, and a long-time visitor, teacher, and student of China.

Bibliography

Anon. "The Latest Signal of Ruthlessness." In *China Harvest*, vol. 8, July 1997, 1-2.

Aikman, David. "The Laogai Archipelago." In *The Weekly Standard*, September 29, 1997, 17-20.

Barrett, David. *World Christian Encyclopedia.*

Belz, Mindy. "Saving a Drowning Man: Can Religious Freedom Be Brought Aboard the Lifeboat of U.S. Foreign Policy?" In *World*, April 11, 1998, 19-20.

Chao, Jonathan. "The Church in China Today: Officially Registered Churches and House Churches." In *China Prayer Letter and Ministry Report*, No. 143, September-October 1997, 5-7.

_____. "Han Wenzhao Slanders House Church Leader." In *China Prayer Letter and Ministry Report*, No. 143, September-October 1997, 1-2.

FECCA Prayer Letter, April 1996.

Focus on the Family. James Dobson, host. "Sounding the Call for Persecuted People Today" (side 1, panel), "An Unforgettable Look at China's Persecution" (side 2). Audiocassette, BR276/20825, 1998.

_____. "International Persecution of Christians." "Information" sheet, 1998.

Hitchcock, James. "Christ & Culture: a Dilemma Reconsidered." *Touchstone* 10.1 (Winter 1997), 13-17, 13.

Jacobson, Jim. International Bible Society mailing, September 1996.

Kirk, Russell. "Civilization Without Religion?" In *Touchstone* 6.1 (Winter 1993), 5-9.

Knippers, Diane. "How to Pressure China." In *Christianity Today* (July 14, 1997), 13.

Lieberthal, Kenneth. *Governing China: From Revolution Through Reform.* New York: Norton, 1995.

Lewis, C. S. "Learning in War-Time," In *The Weight of Glory and Other Addresses*. Ed. Walter Hooper. New York: Simon & Schuster, 1996.

_____. "Christianity and Culture." In *Christian Reflections*. Ed. Walter Hooper. Grand Rapids, MI: Eerdmans, 1967, 12-36.

Ling, Samuel. Letter from Institute for Chinese Studies, Wheaton College, IL, July 19, 1996.

_____. "Introduction to Soul Searching." In *Horizon Letter*. April-June 1997, 18-21.

Naisbitt, John. *Megatrends Asia*. New York: Simon & Schuster, 1996.

Palmer, Brian. "Caesar vs. Christ in China," *U. S. News & World Report*, August 4, 1997, 41-42.

Richardson, Don. College Church in Wheaton (Illinois) Missions Conference, 1991.

Spence, Jonathan. *God's Chinese Son: The Taiping Heavenly Kingdom of Hong Xiuquan*. New York: W. W. Norton, 1996.

Su, Daniel. "Trends for Chinese Intellectual Thought: The Rise of Nationalism," a paper given for China Briefing '97 at the Institute for Chinese Studies, Wheaton College, April 25-26, 1997.

Wendling, Ken. English Language Institute video "Light at the Ends of the Earth."

Yancey, Philip. *Christianity Today*, October 7, 1996.

Zhiming, Yuan. *Soul Searching: Chinese Intellectuals on Faith and Society*. Wheaton, IL: China Horizon, 1997.

Notes

[1] Hitchcock, 13. The three distinctions were also pointed out to me in this article.

[2] Lewis, "Learning in War-Time," 44-46.

[3] Yancey, 136.

[4] David Barrett, *World Christian Encyclopedia*. While the 160,000 figure is the subject of some debate, the number is nonetheless staggering.

[5] International Bible Society mailing, Sept. 1996.

[6] Focus on the Family "Information" sheet, 1. Nina Shea's *In the Lion's Den* listed as source.

[7] Belz, 19. In light of the Clinton administration's call for such a resolution just a year ago, the White House's flat refusal to support this resolution seems perverse.

[8] Knippers, 13.

[9] Chao, 2.

[10] Belz, 20.

[11] Wendling, video.

[12] OMF *China Insight*, Sept/Oct 1996.

[13] Palmer, 42.

[14] Ibid.

[15] Ibid.

[16] Hitchcock, 13.

[17] Lieberthal, 4.

[18] Many Chinese, including non-Christians, have sensed that the roots of America's success had to be found in its historic beliefs. Throughout the opening of China, invitations to address this issue have come from many quarters. A current example would be the eagerness with which former Deputy Police Chief of Los Angeles, Vernon Grounds, has been received by leaders in the police and military establishment in China. His message to them is explicitly moral and explicitly Christian. As Angus Menuge pointed out to me, there is an analogous situation in U.S. prisons. Many governors, including non-Christians, have invited Chuck Colson and Prison Fellowship to minister in their facilities because faith in Christ demonstrably results in reduced recidivism. In the Czech Republic, Christian missionaries have been invited to teach Christianity in the state schools—for the good of the country. The moral vacuum, then, is another potential foothold for Christianity and competing ideologies alike.

[19] Su paper. The consequence of nationalism untethered to morality may be seen in Bosnia, Serbia, the splinter countries of the former Soviet Bloc, and factional tribes in Rwanda, where atrocities in the name of the state stagger the mind. In China today, persecution in the name of "stability" continues apace.

[20] Ibid. I am also indebted to Su for his discussion of Confucianism, Taoism, and Buddhism.

[21] Lieberthal, 15.

[22] Ibid.

[23] Lieberthal, 16.

[24] Richardson, speech.

[25] Naisbitt, 10.

[26] Lieberthal, 332.

[27] Ibid., 333.

[28] This number is anecdotal, coming from a friend in business. Kristoff, 187, reports that a 1992 survey of 3,300 people revealed an annual expenditure of "118 yuan, or several weeks income on graft, an amount that equates to a national annual total of $20 billion.

29 Kristoff, 229. Using ultra sound for sex selection of babies has been technically illegal from the mid-1990s, though Chinese law also requires prenatal screening.

30 Ibid.

31 Ibid., 218.

32 Naisbitt, 66.

33 Kirk, 7-8.

34 Ibid., 6.

35 Ibid., 7-8.

36 Ling, 18-21. The review by Samuel Ling is the source of my information on the contents of this book.

37 Ibid., 19.

38 Ibid., 20.

39 Hitchcock, 18.

40 Ling. Naisbitt notes estimates ranging from 20 million to 100 million with an official (registered) number of Protestants at 6 million (page 80). Chinese house church authority Jonathan Chao says that Christian leaders in China's house churches estimate their number at 70-80 million, not including the TSPM or registered churches ("Church" 5). Focus on the Family, referencing Nina Shea's *In the Lion's Den*, puts the house church range at 60 to 100 million.

41 Unpublished report from confidential source.

42 Anon. "Latest," 2.

43 Lewis, "Culture," 33.

44 Ibid., 23.

7

Eastern Metaphors for the Gospel

A. R. Victor Raj

This essay does not presuppose that certain metaphors of the Gospel are Eastern and, accordingly, others are Western. Nor does it propose that people who live on the eastern side of the globe have one kind of Gospel and residents of the West have another. For there is only one Gospel for all people everywhere, just as there is one Lord, one faith, one baptism, one God and Father of all, who is over all and through all and in all (Eph. 4:5, 6). Rather, this writer assumes that specific expressions of the Gospel in the Scriptures which might be dubbed "Eastern" speak directly to the people of the East. And they are many.

To be sure, with few exceptions, the major world religions today are of eastern origin. Though the Christian religion started out in the (Middle) East, its westward momentum increased significantly beginning with the apostle Paul's positive response to the "Macedonian call" (Acts 16:9). Eventually, over nineteen hundred years, the Christian religion spread rapidly among the people of the west to the extent that, at the turn of this century, all but five percent of Christendom lived in Europe and the Americas. Over the centuries much Christian theology was also developed in the West and its crowning glories found expression in predominantly western categories. Doubtless, from the layman's point of view, Christianity has the makeup of a western religion.

No less has been the impact of the Christian religion on western culture. Biblical names like John and Mary have become household nomenclatures in western culture to the extent that individuals who hold such names do not necessarily embrace the faith by which the biblical John and Mary lived. Biblical phraseology like "scapegoat" and "writing on the wall" has become very much a part of the average western person's everyday discourse. The Bible became an authority and source book for most westerners. "It's in the Bible" came to mean that the veracity of a certain statement remained uncontested; even though maxims like "God helps those who help themselves," pious as they sound, could not be traced to the Bible Christians know.

The above observations, and numerous others like them, have helped patronize the impression that all westerners are Christians, often against the desire and fancy of many westerners themselves. Arguably, the notion has also prevailed that western culture is Christian culture, and, by reason of association, that those who embrace the Christian faith would take in western patterns of behavior and lifestyle. Students of the Christian religion are required to become conversant not only in biblical languages, but in western languages in which interpretations of biblical texts have been made. The spiritual fathers of the majority of Christians in today's East have been westerners. Not a few of the Christian theologians and ministers of the Gospel in the East have gained mastery over the biblical languages through one or more of the European languages. This situation has emerged partly because those communities of Christians in the East which have the largest membership today resulted from the modern missionary movement from the West. Christianity today, however, is advancing its eastward drive at a faster pace. If numbers support an argument, sixty percent of the Christians of our day live in non-western countries, practicing the Christian faith in their indigenous culture and expressing the same faith in their own vernacular.

Language is by far the most effective means of communication humans have ever been known to cherish. Language enables peoples to express thoughts, ideas, emotions, and patterns of behavior. Language shapes a community. It unites a people, provides them with a sense of identity, and steers the course of interaction among them. Languages beget words, and cultures impregnate them with specific meanings and nuances.

"Language is culturally specific. . . . The way in which any person speaks is always rooted in a specific time and place, in a special historical culture, and in the words and idioms that are used follows the linguistic code of a particular community,"[1] writes Paul Raabe. Accordingly, when a message first shaped in one language in a specific historical culture is communicated to another language and culture, care must be taken to make sure that the original, intended meaning of the message is conveyed as accurately in the new language and to the new culture.

The meaning of words and phrases changes according to culture and context. We borrow words and phrases from other languages and cultures and make them our own by usage. In that process many such words lose their original, historical, and cultural intent and assume new definitions and nuances. While the idea of a spiritual leader is innate in the Sanskrit word *guru*, the colloquialism "computer guru" represents an expert in the art and science of computer technology. Similarly, while the title Czar (Tsar) originally referred to the emperors of pre-revolution Russia, the English rendition "drug czar" often stands for one who controls the operation of manufacturing and distributing illegal drugs.

Languages have words and phrases which convey meanings beyond the definitions given in standard dictionaries. The meaning of words is often determined by the context in which they are presented. Speakers and writers make up expressions that capture the attention of their listeners and readers, and leave lasting imprints on their minds by means of those expressions. Taken out of the specific context in which they are used, such expressions would generate notions which may be far removed from the original intention of their authors. A person who exclaims "holy cow!" during a conversation with a friend, for instance, gives expression to his sense of wonderment, and is not thinking of the sacredness which a certain religious tradition has attached to a domestic animal. When a newspaper reports that "the student body swelled up" in a regional chiropractic college, it means simply that there was a remarkable increase in the number of students who enrolled in that college that year.

Not all who speak the same language understand every expression in that language the same way. I would not have known that what many people in Pennsylvania call a "gum band" is exactly what others call a "rubber band," had I not been told that many Pennsylvanians are [descendants of] German immigrants, and until recently German continued to be the household language for them. My own children, who started learning English in India, have, not a few times, surprised their American friends and classmates by asking for a "rubber" when they needed an "eraser," and a "scale" when they wanted a "ruler"!

Again, context has a way of determining the meaning of words and phrases.

Communication is an important responsibility of any educator. Such a noble task has special significance for those who are engaged in the mission of proclaiming the Christian Gospel. The God in whom Christians believe communicates. By His very nature God speaks. "He spoke, and it came to be," wrote the psalmist, describing the awesome creative energy of God's Word (Ps. 33:9). He speaks by means of His Word. That Word, according to the New Testament witness, was made incarnate in Jesus Christ. In Jesus Christ God has spoken the final word to the world. That He would announce to the created order the depth of the love He lavished on the human race is the purpose of the incarnation. Jesus Christ then is God's unique message for all people everywhere at all times. While God has left no one without a witness of Himself, He desires all people to be saved and to come to the knowledge of truth in Jesus Christ.

God's design for the world moves forward to completion as much as the Gospel is proclaimed to all people. The ways and means by which the same Gospel is communicated to various peoples and cultures differ according to the nature of the language and culture into which the Gospel newly enters. When the Gospel enters and takes root in a new culture it is bound to find expression in the language of that culture. Wherever this has occurred, its effect has caused much excitement and no little unrest both to the missionary and to those among whom the Gospel has been proclaimed.

Communicating the Christian Gospel to new cultures often predicates various challenges. Christians are bearers of a unique message that does not and cannot change. With that message they enter a language and culture which is new to them. Their audience, the native speakers of the language, however new to the message, has a greater and deeper understanding of the way in which their mother tongue works. As a result both the communicators, confessors and interpreters of the Gospel, and the listeners for and among whom the Gospel is being proclaimed for the first time are called upon to engage in an intensive task. Together they are involved in identifying words and expressions in the language of the community into which the Gospel has newly entered.

Doubtless, this is no easy chore. The missionary has an uncompromising message to convey. He has a call to relate that message in all its truth and purity to an audience which is not accustomed to his way of thinking or speaking. His engagement in this noble task has present as well as future implications. The decisions he makes under the guidance of the native, new believers in Christ in selecting words and developing expressions for the Christian faith in the new context will become the incense from which the aroma of the Gospel will permeate that community.

When is the missionary task considered complete, especially as common knowledge assumes that missionaries are those who travel to faraway foreign lands to preach the Gospel to non-Christians? In modern times various Christian missionary movements were formed in the West which unleashed an intensive effort to evangelize all people all over the world. Christian missionaries took leadership in identifying the myriad of languages in which not a portion of the Christian Scripture was available and no theological literature had been developed. In many instances Christians ranked first in identifying a particular language and the science of its operation, and writing its first grammar book and lexicon.

As the missionary era was drawing to a close, as it were, the new believers were challenged to develop their Christian selfhood in their native lands. The infamous colonial era had ended. One by one nations which had been subjected to foreign government became independent. Expatriate missionaries started their homeward journey, most of them never to return to the mission field. New churches, under the laws of their lands, could no longer entertain the company of missionaries as proclaimers of the faith. The new churches had to be autonomous, which meant that they would generate sufficient resources to support themselves, exercise the gift of administration for the church's unity and integrity, and continue diligently in the mission of communicating the Gospel to those who are still alien to it.

Nevertheless, in recent years Christian churches which have taken root in the mission fields, as well as missionaries and missiologists, are taking a serious look into another dimension of the church's existence in a given community. That is, how is the faith, once delivered to them by "saints," nourished, nurtured, and yielding of fruit in the new situation? This aspect of the church's activity is termed "self-theologizing." At a glance this expression raises concerns in the minds of various people, for obvious reasons. Theology is primarily the study and formulation of doctrine. That being the case, one wonders if a community of believers which is struggling to flesh out its new identity should be allowed the privilege and the responsibility of engaging in theological discourse and decision making. The question also arises if, in doing so, the truth and integrity of the Gospel will not be undermined.

Theologizing entails teaching and practicing. It is interpreting and applying the non-negotiable biblical truth to human lives which change constantly and are contingent on the culture in which those lives are shaped and sustained. As God chose to share the same Gospel with all people, all people are given the opportunity to hear God's call and respond in faith. As Mattson observes, "To be self-theologizing means that the Church must be capable of answering the questions raised by its own cultural context in ways that make sense within that context. Of course, there is only one biblical message, but there are many ways in which that message is expressed."[2]

Self-theologizing is the church's privilege to witness the faith. While the church continues to remain rooted in and faithful to the truth that brought her into being, she also forges ahead into her surrounding community with the invitation for others to come to the knowledge of the same truth. By self-theologizing the church "takes hold of the eternal life" to which she was called and makes her "good confession in the presence of many witnesses" (1 Tim. 6:12)

Confessing the faith serves a dual purpose. While confession is the outward expression of the Christian's trust in God for salvation in Jesus Christ, it is also a witness to others of that same salvation. As Christians all over the world make their good confession in the presence of many witnesses, they do so from their heart in the language and cultural framework of the communities of which they are a part. For this they are obligated.

Languages have their own styles and figures of speech. Languages develop new words and phrases through speech and writing, through discourse and dialogue. Certain expressions disappear from a language while others emerge new and become unusually popular. A person who learns a new language in the setting of a classroom will recognize that in live situations the same language works in a somewhat different manner.

So also with culture. Our academic understanding and interpretation of a given culture may not be exactly the same as the way in which that culture is lived by the people of that culture. Ordinarily people do not live by the exact wording of the strict and stringent rules in the book, although they subscribe to them. In community, living rules become flexible. We make our home look unusually clean and tidy when we invite a special guest to come over for dinner, and pile up unwarranted excuses should a friend stop by our house without prior notice and see the mess in real life. In daily speech and conversation, written down rules of grammar and style become variable and flexible. In communication, the message, much more than the means, continues to be the focus. In Gospel witness, nevertheless, that message can not be messed up regardless of the untidiness of any language.

The Gospels, the primary witness of Jesus Christ and His work of salvation for the whole world, employ various figures of speech in order to communicate one Gospel truth. The Christian religion hinges on the authority of Scripture, the very Word of God. The Bible uses various figures of speech and countless literary devices as it describes God and mankind and the way in which they interact. Metaphor is one such figure of speech.

The *American Heritage College Dictionary* defines metaphor as "a figure of speech in which a word or phrase that designates one thing is applied to another in an implicit comparison." Metaphors play a key role in Christian theologizing. Theology is a human endeavor to describe divine truth in concrete human language. Theological metaphors represent the divine truth. By definition biblical metaphors transfer the divine truth to human moments of truth. As G. E. Veith observes, "Metaphors are ways of speaking about truth. In fact, all language . . . is metaphorical."[3]

"Since God chose to reveal Himself to us by means of human language, He employs metaphors as the best way of communicating truth."[4] "How else could we creatures of flesh and blood comprehend spiritual realities unless they are explained in terms of flesh and blood?"[5] The very incarnation of God in Jesus Christ is the supreme example of His will to speak to the human race in human terms. The

Bible makes use of a variety of metaphors to speak the good and gracious will of God, the Gospel. The makeup of metaphors depends on the life situation of the people among whom they are put to use. In other words, metaphors are culture sensitive. No metaphor relates equally well to all peoples and cultures. Fortunately, the Gospel has been described in a variety of ways so that the people of all cultures are able to understand it, in one way or another.

Sadhu Sundar Singh (1889-1929) was one of the most famous Christian evangelists of his time in India. As a child he was raised in the Sikh religious tradition, and his mother had hoped that Sundar Singh would grow up to become a teacher of the Sikh religion. Against her wish, and to his own surprise, Sundar Singh had a vision of Jesus (he compared it to the Apostle Paul's experience) which led to his conversion. "The water of life in an Indian cup" is a metaphor Sundar Singh popularized among Indians. In Sundar Singh's way of speaking, proclaiming the Gospel for the people of India is "the giving of the water of life in an Indian cup." It is obvious that this metaphor is derived from Jesus' discourse with the woman from Samaria in the Gospel of John chapter four.

"Living water as a metaphor for divine activity in quickening men to life occurs in the Old Testament."[6] Furthermore, in Judaism "living water" along with "the gift of God" signified the Torah. If, as Raymond Brown has proposed, the Samaritans shared this understanding of the living water, "the woman [from Samaria] could have understood that Jesus was presenting himself and his doctrine as the replacement of the Torah in which the Samaritans believed."[7]

To be sure, Jesus used the phrase "living water" in John 4:10 with reference to the gift of eternal life. Interestingly enough, in John 7:38 Jesus invites all those who are thirsty to come to Him and receive from Him the drink, which is an allusion to the Holy Spirit.[8] The cleansing and quickening power of water speaks directly to India's religious quest. "Living water" makes it especially biblical and Christian.

Other metaphors from the Gospel of John also have a greater appeal for easterners. Of unique significance here are the "I AM" sayings of our Lord. The predicates of such sayings are very familiar to most easterners. They have known them in real life, and experience them as concepts and objects which enter their minds and benefit their daily living. As a metaphor heightens and intensifies the truth it conveys,[9] it invites the listener to look beyond the verbal image and get to the truth it represents.

In the specific instance of the "I AM" sayings in John's Gospel, the intensity of the truth rests singularly on the person and authority of the speaker Himself. One of these sayings reads "I am the Way, the Truth and the Life" (John 14:6). The veracity and trustworthiness of that statement is reinforced as the speaker continues, "no one comes to the Father except through Me. If you really knew Me you would know My Father as well." By that statement Jesus is making the absolute claim that He is the absolute truth in person; and, apart from Him there is no way to eternal life. That announcement is an invitation for all truth seekers to come to Jesus to find what they are looking for. Elsewhere Jesus said that He came to bear witness to the truth, and those who are on the side of truth pay close heed to Him (John 18:37). Some may claim that they have the truth. Others may try to relativize truth by asking, "After all, what is truth?" Jesus places all truth seekers in an either/or situation. There is no truth but truth, and that truth is Jesus Christ.

The same principle applies to the other "I AM" sayings also. As a case in point, Jesus said, "I am the Good Shepherd" (John 10:11). The community Jesus addressed had known shepherds, good as well as bad. Many leaders had tried to put on an appearance of a shepherd in rather convincing ways. But Jesus stood among them as the Good Shepherd. His statement that the Good Shepherd lays down His life for the sheep was no figure of speech. Many of those who heard Him say that He was the Good Shepherd later saw with their own eyes how, on the cross, Jesus laid down His life for the sheep. He did that on His own for the sake of His people.

The woman of Samaria came to the well to draw water for her daily sustenance; but Jesus offered her water which would quench her spiritual thirst. Jesus assured that those who drink of the water He offered will never thirst. And that water will become in them a spring of water welling up to eternal life (John 4:14). Making use of the ordinary, familiar, and true-to-life, though temporary, elements and experiences Jesus was leading His listeners to the heavenly, real, and lasting truth of His life and message.

During His earthly life and ministry Jesus preferred for Himself the appellation "Son of Man"(Matt. 8:20). While in many places in the

Old Testament this figure of speech referred to just a man, or to a prophet, the spokesman of God, other specific references pointed to the coming messiah.[10] No doubt Jesus applied that title for Himself in the messianic sense, of God's designate who would usher in God's kingly reign by His suffering, death, and resurrection. As the climax of this way of speaking, toward the end of His public ministry, at His trial, Jesus declared that the Son of Man will be seen sitting at the right hand of God and coming in the clouds of heaven (Mk. 14:62). Thus he made it clear that His coming to the earth had its basis in history, and it has present as well as future consequences for all people.

The Gospels testify that those who encountered Jesus had a preference in applying specific titles to Him. While some called Him "Son of God" (Mk. 15:39), others addressed Him "Son of David" (Mt. 21:9), "Son of the Most High God" (Lk. 8:28), "the Holy One of God" (Mk. 1:24), "Lord" (John 20:13), "Lord and God" (John 20:28), "Teacher" (John 3:2; cf. 13:14), and "the Lamb of God" (John 1:29). If the writer of the Letter to the Hebrews called Jesus "the High Priest" (Heb. 2:17), the apostle Paul called Him "the Sacrifice" (Rom. 3:25), "the Firstborn over all Creation" (Col. 1:15), "the Firstfruits from the Dead" (1 Cor. 15:20), "the Chief Cornerstone" (Eph. 2:20), "the Head of the Church" (Col. 1:18), and "the Hope of Glory" (Col. 1:27). In the apostle Peter's words, Jesus is "the Shepherd and Overseer of Souls" (1 Pet. 2:25), and "the Chief Shepherd" (1 Pet. 5:4). In the Gospel of John, Jesus calls himself "the Temple" (2:19), and in the book of Revelation John sees Him as "the Alpha and the Omega", "the One Who Is, Was, and Is to Come" (1:8), and "the Bright Morning Star" (Rev. 22:16).

Just as a variety of metaphors are applied to Jesus Christ, so also the Gospel is given expression in different ways. The Gospel is the good news that God has provided salvation through the life, death, and resurrection of Jesus Christ. Paul called the same Gospel the power of God for the salvation of everyone who believes (Rom. 1:17). Spreading the Gospel is spreading the aroma of Christ, the fragrance of life (2 Cor. 2:16f.). The Gospel gives life, love, hope, peace, and purpose to those who embrace it in faith. It is good news to the poor, freedom for the prisoners, sight for the blind, and release for the oppressed. The Gospel is ultimately the celebration of God's way of redeeming the human race from eternal damnation. The Gospel is eternal and will be preached to the ends of the earth till the end of time.

Proclaiming the Gospel calls for a response from those among whom the Gospel is proclaimed. The most powerful, and perhaps the purest form of response is expressed in the form of poetry. Poetry brings out the best in the human mind with intensity, in very powerful, imaginative, and beautiful words. Poetic words speak the poet's conscience. Christian hymnody is a poetic rendition of Christian prayer, praise, and thanksgiving. Hymnody is poetry with an attitude. Hymns express best the believers' confession of their relationship with God. Christian poetry (and music) give expression to the inner workings of the heart touched and transformed by the Gospel.

It has been said that language is the poet's homeland. Hymn writers exercise poetic freedom as they craft words and phrases which bring out the biblical truths and relate them to human experience. Poets let their conscience speak in their own individualized styles of expression, sets of vocabulary, concepts, and images which reflect the human appropriation of the divine message. Accordingly, various hymn writers[11] have described Jesus as the Refuge of the Weary, and the Fountain in Life's Desert; Life of all the Living, and Death of Death; Priceless Treasure, Source of Purest Pleasure, and Trusted Friend; the Armor of His Soldiers, and Our Health While We are Living; Fruit of the Mystic Rose, and the Potentate of Time; Sacred Flame, and Joy of Heaven; and Pure, Unbounded Love.

Religious language has an experiential dimension to it. Such experience is founded in the knowledge of the Gospel, and expressed in feelings and emotions which stem from that knowledge. In speaking the Gospel, God speaks His heart out to His people. He speaks with desire and intention for the salvation of all people. Heart is the center of the human spirit, from which spring emotions, thoughts, motivations, courage, and action. When people respond to God's speaking they do so with an understanding of God's salvific act for them, by giving expression to their own feelings and emotions touched by God's love. If knowledge is associated with the head, and feelings and emotions with the heart, then religious language is both "head language" and "heart language."

Heart language is evident in the confessions of faith made by those who became Christians in South India, especially during the great mission century of the modern era. These were, for the most part, first generation converts to Christianity from Hinduism. Their spiritual sojourn had been nourished by the rich *bhakti* tradition of the religion in which they were born. Monism has been the dominant philosophical system of Hinduism. Monistic interpretation of life is built on the premise that the ultimate reality is one. Hence according to monistic thinking, ultimately God and the created order are held together in one mysterious unit. *Bhakti* tradition is a reaction to monism.

Bhakti means devotion. *Bhakti* is a relational word. In the bhakti tradition, therefore, personal piety is emphasized. Unlike monism, which in the philosophical sense identifies God with the universe, *bhakti* tradition distinguishes God and mankind, and allows room for a personal relationship between them. *Christian Bhakti* therefore developed among the new converts as a worshipful expression of their devotion to Christ the Savior. Devotees of Christ in India have given the Christian faith an attractive Indian form by offering the "water of life in an Indian cup."

Indian Christians have described Christ as River of Life from Heaven, the Mountain of Salvation, the Ocean of Bliss, the Cloud that Showers the Rain of Grace, Life-giving Medicine, and Gem of Gems. Christ's shed blood, shed for all, is the Heavenly Ganges that washes away human sin. *Bhakti* tradition duly emphasizes the sinfulness of man and does not compromise the uniqueness of Christ's substitutionary death as the appropriate payment for sin. It gives expression to the Gospel truth in a language that speaks meaningfully to a people who understand devotion as an expression of praise and thanksgiving to God.[12]

It is to be observed that while witnessing the Christian faith to a community which is new to the Gospel, not only people but their language and culture also are led through a "conversion" experience. Christian theology is speaking the life-giving word of God in true-to-life situations.[13] It is the human endeavor to interpret the divine truth in meaningful and understandable human language. Indian Christian theology is a witness of the Gospel primarily to the people of India put forth in the language(s) to which Indians are able to relate. Like others, Indian languages are contextual, developed and molded in the cultural and religious milieu of India. When the truth of the Gospel is communicated in such languages the messengers "baptize" the words and impress on them a unique Christian identity.

To resort to just one example from Scripture, one New Testament witness of the incarnation of God in Christ is put forth in the words "The Word became flesh and made His dwelling among us." The Greek word for "Word" referred to thought as well as speech. In the Hellenistic culture of the day, in the context in which the above verse was first stated in the Gospel according to John, however, "word" had a pantheistic connotation, signifying the rational principle that governed the universe and framed human lives. In the Christian theological sense, however, Word represents God's self-revelation and the communication of that revelation to people.[14]

When the Christian Scripture and the Christian Church use that word "Word," it acquires a specific meaning, and hence communicates a specific message. In the same way a church that is newly planted in a culture is bound to develop a Christian religious and theological language for it by adopting words and phrases from the native tongue and defining them with Christian meaning and theological content.

Proclamation of the Gospel is a mandate Jesus Christ gave His Church. That Gospel is authenticated by Jesus' own death and resurrection. Gospel proclamation, in its bare essentials, involves the call for all to repent and the offer of the free gift of forgiveness of sins in Christ's name (Lk. 24:47). In fact this is a continuation of Christ's own mission as the risen Christ has assured the Church of His ongoing presence with her as she engages in proclamation to the ends of the earth. The Christian Gospel is for all people. No doubt, God wants all people to be saved and come to the knowledge of the truth (1 Tim 2:4). When the Gospel is proclaimed to a people of another culture, the power of the Gospel transforms not only the people who receive the message, but their culture as well. Culture, too, repents, as it were, and goes through an experience of conversion and transformation. Renewal and reshaping is effected by the new faith.

In this connection, self-theologizing is the befitting upshot of the above transformation. By self-theologizing the community of believers makes confession of their faith in Jesus Christ rooted in Scripture, from their own conscience in their mother tongue and expressed in ways meaningful and relevant for them as a people of God and as a witness to those around them. Theologizing is simply expressing the faith in meaningful and relevant language that communicates.

Confessing the faith is applying the message of salvation to human lives in relevant and meaningful ways. In applying the Gospel to specific contexts many in the East have preferred the language of mysticism and transcendence. They are better able to relate to God's redemptive act of reconciliation than to justification. They understand well the heart of the Shepherd who seeks after the lost sheep, the Father who runs with open arms to embrace the returning prodigal son, and the woman who sweeps the house clean in search of the lost coin.

The strength of the Christian Gospel is its simplicity. That is also its apparent weakness in the eyes of the modern sophisticated mind. No mention needs to be made of the myriad ways in which Jesus Christ and the Gospel have been interpreted in modern times. Christ has been made literally all things to all men. Yet whatever manner Christ and His Gospel are presented to any community or people, Christian proclamation could not be considered complete unless Jesus Christ is presented to the world as the Savior from sin. That is what the name Jesus means (Mt. 1:21).

Victor Raj is Missions Professor of Exegetical Theology and Aisstant Director of the Institute for Mission Studies at Concordia Seminary, St. Louis

Bibliography

Barrett, C. K. *The Gospel According to St. John.* 2nd. Edition. Philadelphia, PA: The Westminster Press, 1978.

Boyd, Robin H. S. *An Introduction to Indian Christian Theology.* [Indian Society for Promoting Christian Knowledge & Indian Theological Library, 1976 (1975)].

_____. *Khristadvaita: A Theology for India.* Madras: The Christian Literature Society, 1977.

Brown, Raymond E. *The Gospel According to John* (2 vols). Garden City: Doubleday, 1966, 1970.

Lindars, Barnabas. *Jesus Son of Man.* London: SPCK, 1983.

Lutheran Worship. St. Louis: Concordia Publishing House, 1982.

Marcus, Joel. "Rivers of Living Water from Jesus' Belly (John 7:38)," *Journal of Biblical Literature* 117/2 (1998) 328-330.

Mattson, Daniel L. "Church Planting through Leadership Formation," *Missio Apostolica* III: 2.

Raabe, Paul R. "Cross-Culture Communication and Biblical Language," *Missio Apostolica* IV: 2.

Ramachandra, Vinoth. *The Recovery of Mission: Beyond the Pluralist Paradigm.* Grand Rapids, MI: Eerdmans, 1996.

Veith, Gene Edward Jr. *Reading Between the Lines: A Christian Guide to Literature.* Wheaton, IL: Crossway Books, 1990.

Notes

[1] Paul R. Raabe, "Cross-culture Communication and Biblical Language," *Missio Apostolica* IV: 2, p. 97.

[2] Daniel L. Mattson, "Church Planting through Leadership Formation," *Missio Apostolica* III: 2. p.81.

[3] Gene Edward Veith, Jr., *Reading Between the Lines: A Christian Guide to Literature* (Wheaton, IL: Crossway Books, 1990), p. 84.

[4] Ibid., p. 85.

[5] Ibid., p. 84.

[6] C. K Barrett, *The Gospel According to St. John.* 2nd edition (Philadelphia, PA: The Westminster Press, 1978), p. 232.

[7] Raymond E. Brown, *The Gospel According to John* (2 vols.; Garden City: Doubleday, 1966, 1970) 1. 176.

[8] For various interpretations of this verse, linking its roots to the prophecy in Isaiah 12:3, "With joy you will draw water from the wells of salvation," see Joel Marcus, "Rivers of Living Water from Jesus' Belly (John 7:38)," *Journal of Biblical Literature* 117/2 (1998), 328-330.

[9] Veith, p. 85.

[10] For a scholarly discussion of this title as it applies to Jesus see Barnabas Lindars, *Jesus Son of Man* (London: SPCK, 1983).

[11] These references are from *Lutheran Worship* (St. Louis: Concordia Publishing House, 1982). These titles are used for Jesus in the following hymns in the order of their occurrence: 90, 94, 270, 271, 278, 280, 286. Hymns 270-286 focus on the Redeemer. Readers will find it interesting to research how different hymn writers describe God, Christ, and the Gospel by

means of poetic imagery, although by no means compromising the Gospel truth.

[12] For a summary description of the *bhakti* movement and its historical development among Christians of South India see Robin H. S. Boyd, *An Introduction to Indian Christian Theology,* [Indian Society for Promoting Christian Knowledge & Indian Theological Library, 1976 (1975)], pp. 112-143. For an illustrative account of the formation of various strands of Indian Christian theological discourse see also R. H. S. Boyd, *Khristadvaita: A Theology for India* (Madras: The Christian Literature Society, 1977).

[13] Contextualization is a word employed in this connection. While this is a popular world-wide phenomenon in the Christian theological enterprise, classical writings in the nature of the works cited in the footnote above are literally absent today. For a critique of various approaches to Christian theologizing in India see Vinoth Ramachandra, *The Recovery of Mission: Beyond the Pluralist Paradigm* (Grand Rapids, MI: Eerdmans, 1996).

[14] C. K. Barrett, *The Gospel According to St. John,* p. 152.

8

Am I My Brother's Keeper?
Individualism and Community in
Colonial American Churches

William R. Cario

The tension between the one and the many is a common one in history. The stress can arise in a large system; for example, national legal systems work to balance an individual's right to freedom with the right of society to safety, security, and stability. On a much smaller scale, a significant tension within families is that between an adolescent asserting her individuality and the parents attempting to protect her. Individuals in virtually every culture deal with such tensions, and all cultures, in the end, establish basic ground rules between the one and the many.

One of the most common sources for such tension between the one and the many arises in the context of the individual and his community. The concept of community has always been a rather slippery term to define, although we tend to know it when we see it. For the purposes of this essay, we will use the definition of Robert Bellah and his colleagues in their pathbreaking book, *Habits of the Heart*. Bellah recognizes that community develops over time; he defines community as a "group of people who are socially interdependent, who participate in discussion and decision-making, and who share certain practices that both define the community and are nurtured by it." He also articulates that community is not necessarily homogeneous. Unlike lifestyle, which encourages uniformity and private life, people in community are necessarily heterogeneous and must interact in the public sphere.[1] Thomas Bender reminds us that the concept is flexible and dynamic rather than rigid and static; in a sense, community is as community does, and its evolving nature forces us to constantly reexamine its qualities.[2]

The purpose of this essay is to use paradoxical vision to look at the role of community in the Christian church. As we examine the relationships between Christ and culture, it becomes obvious that in this instance the goals of the two kingdoms are not identical. While the goal of culture is to build community, Christ in His High Priestly Prayer set a different standard, that of unity. In one sense, as a result of the life, death, and resurrection of Jesus, Christians already have unity as members of the invisible church. At the same time, however, He promises full unity with Him and other believers in eternal life. Therefore, Christians can begin to look at community from the basis of the unity that all believers share.[3]

Christians have also had to explore the relationship between the one and the many in practical terms as they struggled to build congregations, church bodies, and denominations. Throughout its history the Christian church has experienced the struggle balancing the demands of community with the needs of individuals. The church has also struggled with the relationship between the local community of saints and the church militant. A more specific examination of the tensions between community and individuals in eighteenth-century North American religious communities highlights the healthy paradox implicit in our understanding of what the Christian church is about. People in colonial North America used both old and new means to develop community in the New World. At the same time, out of those religious communities came a new impetus for the value of the individual. Thus, Christian churches nurtured and promoted both community values and individual values in a uniquely American perspective.

The Christian church has traditionally used Scripture to define the relationship between the individual and the community. While there are several analogies for the church mentioned in the Bible, the most common model is the comparison of Christ and the church to the human body. Paul most fully articulates the relationship between the individual and the community in 1 Corinthians 12:12-30. He identifies the paradoxical nature of the relationship in verse 27 when he states, "Now you are the body of Christ and individually members of it." The apostle states that the church is composed of individuals who in and of themselves have worth. He emphasizes that "the parts of the body which seem to be weaker are indispensable." At the same time, Paul argues, the parts of the body are not independent. The individual parts must work together towards a common goal. Individual members cannot attempt to do what they are not made for. Thus, at the same time Paul emphasizes the roles of both community and individuals in the church.[4]

How that tension between body and members played out makes up much of the history of the Christian church. The New Testament Book of Acts describes the early Christian church in Jerusalem striving to share all material possessions in a communal fashion; that sense of community lingers for a time, perhaps because of the persecutions. At the same time, however, church doctrine did not ignore individuals. The early Christian response to abortion shows a nuanced understanding of the rights of individuals. While many Mediterranean societies had condemned abortion long before the development of Christian doctrine, they tended to condemn the practice based on property rights or the right of the father to control his family. Christian theologians were among the first to argue the immorality of the practice because it destroyed an individual human being. Christian theology, while stressing the church as community, did not always lose sight of the individual.[5]

A quick examination of the Christian church during the Middle Ages shows that the balance between the two was weighted toward community. In the early Middle Ages, especially in Western Europe, the church provided much of the community that people experienced. Not only had the Roman Empire fallen, but it had also taken many local institutions and mores with it. Legal systems, educational systems, and commercial systems were swept aside by various foreign invasions and the internal weaknesses of the imperial system, destroying virtually anything more than the most local sense of community. Feudal ties became one response to the breakdown of community. But the church provided more community ties than any other institution. It encouraged and sponsored local worshipping communities. It provided opportunities for even closer communities in the form of monastic orders and educational institutions. Latin provided a means of communication among different groups. Church hierarchy provided some of the strongest ties throughout Europe for the whole period.[6]

That does not mean that individualism was totally ignored during the Middle Ages. One of the hallmarks of western society has been, as a historian has recently stated, its willingness to put "so high a value on the soul and conscience of the individual person." The church's emphasis on saints demonstrates a willingness to identify the significance of individual action. And while the monastic orders were built on a communal ideal, their very separation from the outside world encouraged individual initiative and action. For example, Abélard and Heloise were able to develop their ideas in the context of monastic living. It is out of a monastic tradition that Martin Luther came to challenge the hegemony of the church. And while Luther did not set out to destroy the church as community, one lasting mark of Protestantism has been his emphasis on the priesthood of all believers, which some took to mean a sense of spiritual equality. Luther did not encourage individualism either within the church organization or in the political realm, but his ideas encouraged other, more radical Protestants toward a strong individualistic impulse. Perhaps most famously, Max Weber has pointed out that the Protestant, and specifically Calvinist, emphasis on the doctrine of vocation or calling encourages individual initiative rather than group action.[7]

The paradoxical pull of community and individual is especially evident in the study of Christianity in the United States. One of the longer lasting debates in early American historiography is the dispute between those who find individualism an important factor in the incipient American colonies and those who see individualism as a later and more dangerous phenomenon. Did immigrants leave medieval, feudal, and "catholic" institutions, mores, and goals in the Old World when they landed in the New World? What communitarian beliefs and values made their way across the Atlantic Ocean? Did the circumstances in North America foster community values or did they encourage individualism? This question becomes more pointed as scholars have examined the eighteenth-century North American colonies and especially the era of the American Revolution, when colonists found the opportunity to fundamentally shape their own political, social, economic, and even religious systems.[8]

Thus religion becomes a useful way to look at the eighteenth-century relationship between individual and community. For Christian congregations provided the loci for many communities in colonial British America. This is most recognizable in New England, where church and community were virtually synonymous in the seventeenth century, although by 1700 a diversity of factors was breaking up any semblance of homogeneity of the "New England way." The New England experience was not based on such traditional forms of organization as a hereditary monarch, titled nobility, hierarchical church organization, or even a landlord class. The Puritans established what Stephen Foster has called a "radical voluntarism" based on a social contract. Thus, covenant theology helped to shape these new community relationships. In some New England towns where 60-70 percent of the white adult males were freemen, there was a broad involvement in voting and participating in congregational affairs. Despite that involvement, freemen generally deferred to their magistrates and to their pastors. And Massachusetts law mandated community financial support of Congregational churches until the early nineteenth century.[9]

In British colonies south of New England, congregations also provided community, and those communities were also often based on voluntary, exclusive associations. Throughout the Middle Colonies and the South, ethnic groups used their churches to bring people together and provide mutual support and community. Henry Muhlenberg, a Lutheran minister who immigrated to North America in 1742, arrived to find German Lutherans scattered throughout communities in New York, Pennsylvania, and Virginia. He spent the rest of his life encouraging those fellow country people to form distinctly Lutheran congregations.[10] The growing ethnic diversity of the eighteenth-century colonies was a partial result of the migration of Christian sects looking for opportunities to establish worshipping communities. French Huguenots in South Carolina, Welsh Baptists and Quakers in Pennsylvania and Delaware, and Scots-Irish Presbyterians on the Pennsylvania and Virginia frontier are only a few of the ethnic groups whose settlement patterns were influenced by religious motives. Charles Woodmason, an Anglican minister who spent some of his ministry itinerating in the Carolina backcountry, grudgingly acknowledged the existence of dissenting communities in western

South Carolina. In a backhanded compliment he recognized the power of those congregations to oppose—or at least circumvent—his work for the Church of England. Even the larger settlements in eighteenth-century America were made manageable by the divisions among ethnic and denominational congregations. The divisions in eighteenth-century New Castle, Delaware, for example, a town of approximately 1000 people, followed the fault lines of the Anglican, Baptist, Lutheran, Presbyterian, and Quaker congregations in and near town.[11]

Barry Shain has recently argued that the influence of a Calvinist/Protestant communitarian ethos was both more pervasive and more powerful in shaping American life, especially the Revolutionary era, than was either individualism or republicanism. According to Shain, most eighteenth-century Americans lived in communities of "overlapping circles of family—and community—assisted by self-regulation and even self-denial, rather than by individual autonomy and self-defining political activity."[12] For most Americans who lived in the late eighteenth century, the question was not whether the needs of the individual were met; instead, people questioned whether the individual was better off free from "familial, communal, and religiously imposed traditional limits." Shain posits that congregational connections were—for most people—some of the most defining relationships they were to develop.[13]

Nevertheless, the connection of congregation to community was not nearly as straightforward as it might first seem. Early in seventeenth-century North America, the religious landscape took on a shape that still marks our twentieth-century religious culture. Both Roger Williams and Anne Hutchinson attacked both the theology and the community of Massachusetts Bay Colony. Although their efforts did not make lasting changes to the Puritan order, they were not the last ones to challenge the religious community. The colonial landscape encouraged such individualism. Because of the wide variety of Protestant churches in the colonies, people were empowered to choose their congregations. Finding one's own faith was sometimes more important than preserving the unity or even the community of the saints. When people did not find congregations of their own liking, they were not averse to start their own congregations. In the late seventeenth century, New Castle, Delaware, experienced a period where inhabitants moved from the defunct Reformed congregation in town to the newly organized Anglican and Presbyterian churches in town and the older Lutheran church outside of town. Throughout the eighteenth century, those congregations competed with each other for members, local recognition, and status. In addition, small groups within each congregation attempted periodically to establish their own congregations apart from the mother churches. Sometimes the reason was to provide religious services closer to home; at other times, as during the Great Awakening, the impetus was doctrinal. Such factionalism later led to the denominationalism of the American republic, and eventually—in the last part of our own century—to an approach to faith nicknamed "Sheilaism," after an interviewee in *Habits of the Heart* who saw little need for organized religious life and a public expression of belief.[14]

Even in eighteenth-century New England, where ties between church and state were still quite strong, an individualistic impetus can be found. The case of the abortion and death of Sarah Grosvenor in 1742 Pomfret, Connecticut, discovered and written about by Cornelia Hughes Dayton, demonstrates the changing sense of community, the development of a gendered understanding of individualism, and the complexity of communitarian values.[15] When Sarah discovered that she was pregnant by her boyfriend Amasa Sessions, he pressed her to attempt to terminate the pregnancy by taking an *abortifacient*, and then by submitting to a surgical abortion by a visiting doctor. While neither the out-of-wedlock pregnancy nor the abortion attempts were terribly unusual in colonial Connecticut, several aspects of the community reaction are enlightening. Dayton advises us that Grosvenor, Sessions, and their friends were able to successfully keep the pregnancy a secret and hide their activities from Pomfret's older generation, including parents and church leaders. Reading through the records, it is amazing to see how little Pomfret's church or its leaders were involved in this crisis, even though Sessions's father was a leader in the church. Unlike the seventeenth century where New England towns would have pressured an unwed father to marry the mother, Pomfret residents refused to pressure Sessions into marrying Grosvenor; indeed they seemed to forgive him, as he later became a town leader. Finally, Dayton posits the development of individualism in this eighteenth-century Puritan community. Not only did several of the males make decisions out of self-interest—which occurs in virtually every point in American history—but the community appeared not to hold it against them, and they were elevated in later life in the community. Amasa Sessions seemed to have gotten away with looking out for his own self-interest without having community opprobrium fall upon him too harshly.

This incident indicates the growth of a sense of individualism in colonial North American religious communities. That observer of eighteenth-century American life, J. Hector St-John de Crevecoeur, wrote about the effect of individualism on colonial life as a whole. In the selection entitled "What Is an American?" Crevecoeur's major indicator of an American as someone who is governed in part by self-interest is followed by his discussion of the uniqueness of religion in North America. While religious sects had arisen in Europe, he argued, in America sectaries were under less pressure to adhere to their beliefs. Over time, because of the emphasis on self-interest, religious people in the colonies had become more indifferent in their beliefs. According to the Frenchman, distance and space encouraged people of various faiths to intermingle; "the fury of making proselytes is unknown here . . . and it may happen that the daughter of the Catholic will marry the son of the Seceder, and settle at a distance from their parents." Thus, he predicted, environment and pluralism would conspire to tear down the religious communities that he saw so destructive in the Old World, and along with them such qualities as "[p]ersecution, religious pride, and the love of contradiction."[16]

Of course, the religious sphere was not the only locus for either community or for individualism. There were many sources for the growth of an individualistic impulse in eighteenth-century America, and those sources tended to affect religious development as well. The development of capitalism and its ensuing recognition by those who examined their world showed the importance of individuals in their economic world. While strands of capitalism had been in western society for centuries, it is clear that the eighteenth century saw all of the pieces come together; a dependable money supply, institutions that would be able to facilitate capitalistic enterprises, and a conscious recognition of this new economic system. Already in the seventeenth century, English, Scottish, and French writers identified "individuals seeking satisfaction of their personal goals" to be a more powerful economic force than traditional institutions' efforts to shape the world. These writers justified self-interest because it encouraged general welfare and prosperity. In 1776, Adam Smith articulated a theory of self-interest and economic competition in his landmark, *Wealth of Nations*. Smith and others recognized that individual self-interest in economic matters had encouraged European exploration and expansion and thus was in great part responsible for the economic boom that followed. One modern historian has identified a change in economic motivation among colonial New Englanders. While Weber's Protestant work ethic thesis works for seventeenth-century Puritans, James Henretta identifies a more secular, individualistic ethos driving New England business in eighteenth-century New England. It is also clear that traditional attempts to control economic power—especially in urban areas—were challenged throughout the British North American colonies.[17]

Another impulse toward individualism in the eighteenth century came from the Enlightenment experiment. As a purpose of this essay is to identify the wide variety of sources of individualism in the history of American churches, it would be remiss if this paper omitted the influence of the Enlightenment. A strong emphasis in the Enlightenment was the distrust of tradition. Isaac Newton encouraged people to empirically test things rather than trust ancient explanations. Both Thomas Hobbes and John Locke discounted religious mandate for government, seeking the basis for political structure instead ultimately in the free will of individual citizens. Benjamin Franklin was one of the earliest Americans to articulate the "American Dream" of individual upward mobility through hard work, perseverance, intelligence, and a little bit of luck. His autobiography demonstrates the influence of both capitalism and the Enlightenment in eighteenth-century British America.[18]

Thus, it is clear that various secular influences such as capitalism and the Enlightenment encouraged the growth of individualism in British North America. But it is important to recognize the theological and spiritual influences on the American churches toward individualism. For example, the Great Awakening did much to impart among church-going Americans the ideals and the usefulness of the individual Christian. This religious revival, which affected the British Atlantic world between 1720 and 1750, shook traditional religious structures in several ways. First, while its leaders included such clergy as George Whitefield, William and Gilbert Tennent, John Wesley, and

Jonathan Edwards, the Great Awakening tended to challenge the power of the clergy by making the individual the arbiter of his own salvation. The message of the Awakening preachers was that the individual was responsible for his own religious faith.[19]

This message is shown clearly in the sermons of the Awakeners. Jonathan Edwards's most famous sermon, "Sinners in the Hands of an Angry God," demonstrates his emphasis on individual regeneration. Edwards stresses—first—that individuals deserve punishment because of their own sinfulness; "they are liable to fall of themselves without being thrown down by the hand of another." According to the Congregational minister, "[a]lmost every natural man that hears of hell, flatters himself that he shall escape it; he depends on himself for his own security." Edwards then moves on to place the saving work of God in individual terms. "And now you have an extraordinary opportunity, a day wherein Christ has flung the door of mercy wide open, and stands in the door calling and crying with a loud voice to poor sinners; a day wherein many are flocking to him. . . . How awful it is to be left behind at such a day!"[20] Edwards puts the onus for salvation on neither the church nor the congregation nor the family but squarely on the individual.

In a sermon preached a few years earlier, Edwards explains the need for "A Divine and Supernatural Light" that changes people's lives, focusing again on the work of God upon individuals. Edwards distinguishes the different ways that God acts on the unregenerate and on the regenerate. Edwards recognizes that people can be affected by "the story of Jesus Christ" in many ways. He emphasizes that by reason people may develop a "sensibleness of the excellency of divine objects." But it is by God's Word that He brings His Light to people. As in the more famous sermon, Edwards encourages the listener to see this as an activity God gives to individuals rather than to congregations or families. There is little in either of these sermons of the seventeenth-century emphasis on people gathered together into covenants. Instead, Edwards emphasizes the covenant that God makes with individuals.[21]

By such means, the Great Awakening encouraged individualistic values in eighteenth-century American religious communities. It is possible to over-emphasize the influence of this series of events. Not all sects were equally affected by the revival movements; Anglican and Lutheran congregations, for example, did not experience the upheavals experienced among other sects. Nevertheless, as Patricia Bonomi has argued, the cumulative effect of the Awakeners was to "emphasiz[e] individual values over hierarchical ones." The revival message was anti-institutional, encouraged greater lay participation, and "insisted there were choices, and that the individual himself was free to make them." The Great Awakening further exacerbated the trend in Protestant America of factionalism and individualism. It encouraged colonists to take religion into their own hands and to make it a private issue. While the Awakening did not destroy Christian communities in America, it gave lay individuals more power to shape and mold those religious communities.[22]

As we look forward from the late twentieth century, we can surely see continuing effects of individualism on Christian churches. Despite the efforts of people involved in ecumenical movements, Protestantism has continued to fracture into more denominations. The continued use of revivalism in a number of churches speaks to the perceived need to reach individuals as the Awakeners did. Luther's "priesthood of all believers" has been used to challenge traditional relationships within the church structure. Since the Great Awakening, women have been more active and have taken greater leadership roles in many Protestant churches in the United States; many denominations encourage women as ordained ministers. Some scholars have described the result as the feminization of American Christianity. Singles in the late twentieth-century United States are much more likely to go without a church home than are couples or families with children. Individuals increasingly transfer among congregations and even denominations looking for the community that would best fit their perceived religious needs. Indeed, culture has affected the church.[23]

But what can the church do in such a world of individualism run rampant? First, it must continue to declare God's goal of true unity in Christ Jesus. As the world cries out for greater meaning and for greater compassion, Christian congregations must heed the call to provide hope for individuals who find themselves without community and without meaning. The church must proclaim the cause of disunity—human sin—and the solution to that problem—God's grace through the atoning work of Jesus Christ.

The church also needs to remember that it models Christian community here on earth. While complete unity is impossible in this world, the church can provide an example of community in a world searching for such ideals. While such institutions as governments have been able to provide order in society, they have been much less successful at promoting community. The two institutions most useful in balancing individualism and community are God-ordained: religious communities and the family. And those institutions appear to be inextricably tied together. As members of the body of Christ, we can promote and participate in both fixtures in our society. Our congregations can provide a sense of community while encouraging us to look forward to the hope of unity with Christ and all believers in heaven. As with all paradoxes, we are discovering again that the church cannot have community without individuals but that individuals cannot exist well without community. The body of Christ is not complete without its members; the members cannot exist outside the body.

William Cario is Associate Professor of History at Concordia University Wisconsin

Bibliography

Appleby, Joyce. *Capitalism and a New Social Order: The Republican Vision of the 1790s*. New York: New York University Press, 1984.
_____. "The Social Origins of American Revolutionary Ideology." *Journal of American History*, 64 (1978): 935-58.

Bellah, Robert N., Richard Madsen, William M. Sullivan, Ann Swidler, and Steven M. Tipton. *Habits of the Heart: Individualism and Commitment in American Life*. Berkeley: University of California Press, 1985.

Bender, Thomas. *Community and Social Change*. New Brunswick, NJ: Rutgers University Press, 1978.

Berthoff, Rowland and John Murrin, "Feudalism, Communalism, and the Yeoman Freeholder: The American Revolution Considered as a Social Accident." *Essays on the American Revolution*, eds. Stephen G. Kurtz and James Hutson. Chapel Hill: University of North Carolina Press, 1973. 256-88.

Bloch, Marc. Feudal Society, vol. 1, *The Growth of Ties of Dependency*, tr. L. A. Manyon. Chicago: University of Chicago Press, 1961.

Bonomi, Patricia U. *Under the Cope of Heaven: Religion, Society, and Politics in Colonial America*. New York: Oxford University Press, 1986.

Breen, T. H., and Stephen Foster, "The Puritans' Greatest Achievement: A Study of Social Cohesion in Seventeenth-Century Massachusetts." *Journal of American History*, 60 (1973): 5-22.

Bushman, Richard. *From Puritan to Yankee: Character and Social Order in Connecticut, 1690-1765*. Cambridge: Harvard University Press, 1967.

Butler, Jon. "Enthusiasm Described and Decried: The Great Awakening as Interpretive Fiction." *Journal of American History*, 69 (1982), 305-25.

Cario, William R. "Anglicization in a 'Frenchified, Dutchified, Damnified Place': New Castle, Delaware, 1690-1750." Ph.D. dissertation, New York University, 1994.

Cohen, Charles. "The Post-Puritan Paradigm of Early American Religious History." *The William and Mary Quarterly*, 3rd Series, LIV (October 1997): 694-722.

Crevecoeur, J. Hector St. John de. *Letters from an American Farmer*, ed. Susan Manning. New York: Oxford University Press, 1997.

Dayton, Cornelia Hughes. "Taking the Trade: Abortion and Gender Relations in an Eighteenth-Century New England Village." Hartz, Louis. *The Liberal Tradition in America*. New York: Harcourt, *Colonial America: Essays in Politics and Social Development*, eds. Stanley Katz, John Murrin, and Douglas Greenberg, 4th ed. New York: McGraw-Hill, 1993. 398-431.

Foster, Stephen. *Their Solitary Way: The Puritan Social Ethic in the First Century of Settlement in New England*. New Haven: Yale University Press, 1971.

Franklin, Benjamin. *The Autobiography and Other Writings*, ed. L. Jesse Lemisch. New York: New American Library, 1961.

Gay, Peter. *The Enlightenment: An Interpretation*, vol. 1, *The Rise of Modern Paganism*. London: Wildwood House, 1973.

Gorman, Michael. *Abortion and the Early Church: Christian, Jewish, and Pagan Attitudes in the Greco-Roman World*. Downers Grove, IL: Intervarsity Press, 1982.

Greene, Jack P. *Pursuits of Happiness: The Social Development of Early Modern British Colonies and the Formation of American Culture*. Chapel Hill: University of North Carolina Press, 1988.
Brace, and World, 1955.

Hatch, Nathan. *The Democratization of American Christianity*. New Haven: Yale University Press, 1989.

Heimert, Alan, and Perry Miller, eds. *The Great Awakening*: *Documents Illustrating the Crisis and Its Consequences*. New York: Oxford University Press, 1967.

Henretta, James. "The Protestant Ethic and the Reality of Capitalism in Colonial America," in *Weber's Protestant Ethic: Origins, Evidence, Contexts*, eds. Hartmut Lehmann and Guenther Roth.New York: Cambridge University Press, 1995: 327-46.

Lewis, C. S. *The Weight of Glory and Other Addresses*, rev. ed. New York: Macmillan, 1980.

Lockridge, Kenneth. *A New England Town. The First Hundred Years— Dedham, Massachusetts, 1636-1736*, enlarged edition. New York: Norton, 1985.

McClay, Wilfred M. "Mr. Emerson's Tombstone," *First Things*, No. 83 (May, 1998).

Muhlenberg, Henry. *The Journals of Henry Melchior Muhlenberg in Three Volumes*, tr. Theodore Tappert and John Dobberstein. Philadelphia: The Muhlenberg Press, 1942.

Shain, Barry A. *The Myth of American Individualism: The Protestant Origins of American Political Thought*. Princeton, NJ: Princeton University Press, 1994.

Silk, Mark. "Something New, Something Old: Reflections on a Conference Held at The Harvard Divinity School September 5-8, 1996." *Program in American Religious History*, Cambridge, MA: Harvard University, 1998.

Smith, John E, Harry S. Stout, and Kenneth Mikkenen, eds. *A Jonathan Edwards Reader*. New Haven, CT: Yale University Press, 1995.

Weber, Max. *The Protestant Ethic and the Spirit of Capitalism*, tr. Talcott Parsons. New York: Charles Scribners' Sons, 1958.

Woodmason, Charles. *The Carolina Backcountry on the Eve of the Revolution*, ed. Richard J. Hooker. Chapel Hill: University of North Carolina Press, 1953.

Notes

[1] Robert N. Bellah, Richard Marsden, William M. Sullivan, Ann Swidler, and Steven M. Tipton, *Habits of the Heart: Individualism and Commitment in American Life* (Berkeley: University of California Press, 1985): 333, 72.

[2] Thomas Bender, *Community and Social Change* (New Brunswick, NJ: Rutgers University Press, 1978).

[3] John 17:20-26.

[4] C. S. Lewis deals with the paradoxical relationship of individual and community in his essay "Membership," in *The Weight of Glory and Other Addresses*, rev. ed. (New York: Macmillan, 1980): 106-20.

[5] Acts 4:32-37; the subsequent story of Ananias and Sapphira (Acts 5:1-11) indicates the importance placed on living within the norms of that community. For practices and understandings regarding abortion in the centuries around the birth of Christ, see Michael Gorman, *Abortion and the Early Church: Christian, Jewish, and Pagan Attitudes in the Greco-Roman World* (Downers Grove, IL: Intervarsity Press, 1982), especially chapter 4.

[6] Marc Bloch, *Feudal Society*, vol. 1, *The Growth of Ties of Dependency*, tr. L. A. Manyon (Chicago: University of Chicago Press, 1961), gives the now classic explanation of the breakdown of imperial ties and the development of newer ties during the Middle Ages.

[7] For the quotation, see Wilfred M. McClay, "Mr. Emerson's Tombstone," *First Things*, No. 83 (May, 1998): 21. McClay has included a very insightful look at the balance between the individual and community in this article. Max Weber, *The Protestant Ethic and the Spirit of Capitalism*, tr. Talcott Parsons (New York: Charles Scribners' Sons, 1958), 79-92, 98-128. For a recent and wide-ranging series of critiques of Weber's thesis, see Hartmut Lehmann and Guenther Roth, eds., *Weber's Protestant Ethic: Origins, Evidence, Contexts* (New York: Cambridge University Press, 1993).

[8] Louis Hartz, *The Liberal Tradition in America* (New York: Harcourt, Brace, and World, 1955) argues for an America born individualistic; on the other hand, Richard Bushman, *From Puritan to Yankee: Character and Social Order in Connecticut, 1690-1765* (Cambridge: Harvard University Press, 1967) shows a colonial America quite tied to European mores. For an essay which lays out many of the issues raised in the study of colonial American religion, see Charles L. Cohen, "The Post-Puritan Paradigm of Early American History," *The William and Mary Quarterly*, 3d Series, LIV (October

1997): 695-722. For a description of the historiographic debate over community and individualism, see Barry Alan Shain, *The Myth of American Individualism: The Protestant Origins of American Political Thought* (Princeton, NJ: Princeton University Press, 1994), 9-26. For an example of an attempt to find feudal institutions in colonial North America, see Rowland Berthoff and John Murrin, "Feudalism, Communalism, and the Yeoman Freeholder: The American Revolution Considered as a Social Accident," in *Essays on the American Revolution*, eds. Stephen G. Kurtz and James Hutson (Chapel Hill: University of North Carolina Press, 1973): 256-288.

[9] Stephen Foster, *Their Solitary Way: The Puritan Social Ethic in the First Century of Settlement in New England* (New Haven: Yale University Press, 1971); T. H. Breen and Stephen Foster, "The Puritans' Greatest Achievement: A Study of Social Cohesion in Seventeenth-Century Massachusetts," *Journal of American History*, 60 (1973): 5-22; and Jack P. Greene, *Pursuits of Happiness: The Social Development of Early Modern British Colonies and the Formation of American Culture* (Chapel Hill: University of North Carolina Press, 1988): 24-5. For a description of the closed, consensual nature of rural New England colonial communities, see Kenneth Lockridge, *A New England Town. The First Hundred Years— Dedham, Massachusetts, 1636-1736*, enlarged edition (New York: Norton, 1985).

[10] *The Journals of Henry Melchior Muhlenberg in Three Volumes*, tr. Theodore Tappert and John Doberstein (Philadelphia: The Muhlenberg Press, 1942) I: 57, 169-72, 188-200.

[11] Patricia U. Bonomi, *Under the Cope of Heaven: Religion, Society, and Politics in Colonial America* (New York: Oxford University Press, 1986), especially chapters 2 and 4, gives a description of the variety of religious practices in colonial America. Charles Woodmason, *The Carolina Backcountry on the Eve of the Revolution*, ed. Richard J. Hooker (Chapel Hill: University of North Carolina Press, 1953), 56-59 and passim. For the New Castle example, see William R. Cario, "Anglicization in a 'Frenchified, Dutchified, Damnified Place': New Castle, Delaware, 1690-1750" (Ph.D. dissertation, New York University, 1994).

[12] Shain, xvi.

[13] Ibid., 14.

[14] For the challenge of Williams and Hutchinson to Massachusetts Bay Colony's corporate community, see Edmund Morgan, *The Puritan Dilemma: The Story of John Winthrop* (Glenview, IL: Scott, Foresman, 1958), chapters 9 and 10. For New Castle, see Cario, chapters 3 and 4. For "Sheilaism," see Bellah, 221.

[15] Cornelia Hughes Dayton, "Taking the Trade: Abortion and Gender Relations in an Eighteenth-Century New England Village," in *Colonial America: Essays in Politics and Social Development*, eds. Stanley Katz, John Murrin, and Douglas Greenberg, 4th ed. (New York: McGraw-Hill, 1993): 398-431.

[16] J. Hector St. John de Crevecoeur, *Letters from an American Farmer*, ed. Susan Manning (New York: Oxford University Press, 1997): 45-6, 48-51.

[17] For an overview of the development of capitalistic institutions, see Fernand Braudel, *Civilization and Capitalism, 15th-18th Century*, vol. II, *The Wheels of Commerce*, tr. Sian Reynolds (New York: Harper and Row, 1979). Joyce Appleby, "The Social Origins of American Revolutionary Ideology," *Journal of American History*, 64 (1978): 944-5. See also Appleby, *Capitalism and the New Social Order*, for a description of the eighteenth-century attempts to explain and describe the strengthening capitalistic impulse. Henretta, "The Protestant Ethic and the Reality of Capitalism in Colonial America," in *Weber's Protestant Ethic: Origins, Evidence, Contexts*, eds. Hartmut Lehmann and Guenther Roth (New York: Cambridge University Press, 1995), 327-46.

[18] Franklin, "The Way to Wealth," *The Autobiography and Other Writings*, ed. L. Jesse Lemisch (New York: New American Library, 1961) 188-97. See also Peter Gay, *The Enlightenment: An Interpretation*, vol. 1, *The Rise of Modern Paganism* (London: Wildwood House, 1973), for an interpretation of the Enlightenment and Christianity which traces their roots to ancient Rome. For a darker view of the Enlightenment, see Patrick Riley, "Discriminating Multiculturalism," in this volume.

[19] For a survey of the Great Awakening, see Bonomi, chapter 5, and Alan Heimert and Perry Miller, eds., *The Great Awakening: Documents Illustrating the Crisis and Its Consequences* (New York: Oxford University Press, 1967). For a contrary view of the revival, see Jon Butler, "Enthusiasm Described and Decried: The Great Awakening as Interpretive Fiction," *Journal of American History*, 69 (1982), 305-25. For an interpretation that the Great Awakening encouraged community rather than individualism, see Henretta, 340-1.

[20] Jonathan Edwards, "Sinners in the Hands of an Angry God (1741)," in *A Jonathan Edwards Reader*, eds. John E. Smith, Harry S. Stout, and Kenneth Mikkenen (New Haven, CT: Yale University Press, 1995): 89-105. Quotations from pp. 89, 94, and 103.

[21] "A Divine and Supernatural Light, Immediately Imparted to the Soul by the Spirit of God, Shown to be Both a Scriptural, and Rational Doctrine (1734)" in *A Jonathan Edwards Reader*, pp. 105-124; quotations on pp. 112 and 113.

[22] Bonomi, p. 147. Bonomi further extrapolates this growing sense of religious individualism, social leveling, and challenging of authority into a foretaste of the patriot justification for separation from Britain during the Revolutionary War era; see chapter 7. Nathan Hatch extends the connection as he shows the effect of the American Revolution on Christian churches and denominations in *The Democratization of American Christianity* (New Haven: Yale University Press, 1989).

[23] For some of the trends that scholars have begun to identify in American religious history, see Mark Silk, "Something New, Something Old: Reflections on a Conference Held at The Harvard Divinity School September 5-8, 1996" (Cambridge, MA: The President and Fellows of Harvard College, 1998). McClay, pp. 20-21.

9

The Greatest Story Ever Told: Christianity and Film

Michael Ward

The Greatest Story Ever Told is the story of Christ, not the ponderous 1965 film of that title.[1] To the earliest exponents of what has come to be called 'narrative theology,' this story has importance in two main ways. To Karl Barth it primarily reveals things about God; to H. Richard Niebuhr it reveals things about mankind, as the Christ-story intersects with the lives of individuals and communities. For the purposes of this present chapter, a third area of importance will be addressed: what the story of Christ reveals about stories.

First of all I will try to define what is meant by "the story of Christ." Then I will explore the relationship between this greatest story and stories which are (necessarily) less great, looking first at Old Testament stories, then at the stories of first-century paganism, and finally at modern contemporary stories. For the sake of brevity only films will be addressed in this last section, though the approach, if plausible, should apply equally well to other forms of story-telling, such as novels and plays.

The Greatest Story Defined

"Beginning with Moses and all the prophets, He interpreted to them in all the Scriptures the things concerning Himself." Thus Luke records Jesus as speaking to Cleopas and another disciple on the road to Emmaus (Luke 24:13-35). Hermeneutically, it is probably the most important statement in the Bible, for it authorizes, as no other single verse does so explicitly, the Christian interpretation of the Old Testament. To be sure, when Jesus applied to Himself the imagery of

Jacob's ladder,[2] Moses' serpent,[3] and Jonah in the whale,[4] He deliberately provoked His hearers into reinterpreting the received view of the Hebrew Scriptures. He did so too, but more implicitly, in such statements as "I am the Vine" (alluding to the prophet Isaiah)[5] and "I am the Good Shepherd" (alluding to Jeremiah).[6] But it is only in Luke that Christ is reported as giving to His followers the example of interpreting from all the Scriptures the things concerning Himself.

The Emmaus-bound disciples presumably knew the Scriptures well already, but they did not properly understand them. Nor would they have understood the term "Old Testament typological prefigurations," but that was what, in effect, they were about to learn from the resurrected Christ. They were going to discover whose story lay behind all those ripping yarns they had known since childhood such as of a father building a boat under lowering skies; a boy, trussed up, listening to the sound of metal on stone; a midnight wrestler; a dreamer wearing a special coat; a baby watching the rushes sway above him in a stream; lamb's blood dripping from door frames; a young buck choosing five pebbles for his sling; a fool standing up in a mess of fish vomit. The stories of Noah and Isaac and Jacob and Joseph and Moses and the Passover and David and Jonah (not to mention many others) were suddenly to acquire a new and unexpected meaning.

It must have been a bewildering experience for the disciples. The "recontextualisation" of all they held most sacred must have sounded fantastic, if not blasphemous, until they realized it was true. For Christians today, after the passage of twenty centuries, the practice of interpreting the Old Testament through the eyes of the New has become obvious and natural, but it cannot have been so at first. If we wish to put ourselves in the shoes of the Emmaus travelers we must imagine some favorite national legend of our own suddenly reapplied in an unexpected fashion. It is as though Americans had to believe that the story of George Washington and the hatchet was really about John F. Kennedy, or as though the British had to believe that the story of King Alfred burning the cakes was about Winston Churchill. If one wants to experience this sort of sudden shift in meaning, one could not do better than read John Irving's novel, A *Prayer for Owen Meany*.[7] It is a brilliant example of typological story-telling. The final fifty pages cast a fresh light over all that has gone before and it is a disturbing, but exhilarating, experience. One trembles at the realization of unseen potentialities.

The disciples' hearts "burned" within them as they heard how the Old Testament stories exemplified the great story of Christ. But what was that story and does it make sense to describe as "a story" something which apparently ramifies into everything else in the Scriptures? In one way it is impossible and this may be what John meant when he said the world was not big enough to hold the books that could have been written about what Jesus did (John 21:25). Nevertheless, a summary was (and is) necessary and the early Christian hymn we find recorded in Paul's Letter to the Philippians (2:6-11) provides a good example:

> Christ Jesus, though He was in the form of God, did not count equality with God a thing to be grasped, but emptied Himself, taking the form of a servant, being born in the likeness of men. And being found in human form He humbled Himself and became obedient unto death, even death on a cross. Therefore God has highly exalted Him and bestowed on Him the name which is above every name, that at the name of Jesus every knee should bow, in heaven and on earth and under the earth, and every tongue confess that Jesus Christ is Lord, to the glory of God the Father.

This hymn sets out very clearly the three major movements of the "Christ-event": descent, absolute zero, re-ascent; equality, humility, glory; love, death, exaltation. If we wish to visualize the shape of this story in our minds, we should think of the letter "v". The downstroke represents Christ humbling Himself; the point represents His death; and the upstroke represents His resurrection. Of course, we could complicate matters at the beginning if we wanted by talking about the eternal pre-existence of the Son; and we could complicate matters at the end by bringing in the *parousia* and things eschatological. But however much we elaborate things either side of the main event, the center holds its v-shape: that is the hinge about which the whole of human history turns. The Great Story is like a Victorian three-volume novel with V for victory at its heart. So, working with this triptych model, we will now briefly examine three Old Testament stories which clearly exhibit it:

1. The story of Noah. God's love streams out towards the world in the form of rain—rain to purify the world from wickedness. Death

results: the deluge drowns every living creature, except the man God had prepared beforehand and the remnant he had been told to rescue. In the midst of utter destruction Noah achieves fame as the father of all succeeding generations.

2. The story of Joseph. God's love is modeled by Jacob who sends his favorite son, Joseph, out into the fields to see how his brothers are faring with their flock. Death strikes (symbolically) when Joseph is bundled into a pit, then sold as a slave. Exaltation comes when he is appointed the right-hand man of Pharaoh, and his famine-struck family bows down before him, begging for grain.

3. The story of the Exodus. This is full of triadic patterns. In love God provides Moses, 'a goodly child'; his familys lose him when he is taken away by foreigners; but he rises to prominence in Egypt. In love God decides to purify Egypt; plagues come upon the whole land; but the Israelites escape because every family has killed a lamb. In love God drives the Israelites out of Egypt; their way is fatally blocked by the sea; but Moses parts the waters and the people cross on dry land. In love God leads the people through the desert; sickness comes upon them; but they recover if they look at a bronze snake.

All these stories (and many more besides) are presumably what Jesus was referring to when he spoke on the Emmaus road. They all structurally prefigure Jesus' own story because in every case the forward flow of the narrative is slashed across by a crisis, a disastrous and ever-worsening crisis, which irreversibly and irremediably destroys the protagonists' expectations until, in the moment of complete calamity, a calmer, broader, greater story unfolds, raising the tale to unforeseen heights. The resemblance between these stories and Christ's own incarnation, crucifixion, and resurrection is obvious and need not be labored. A more pertinent question is "Which way round does the resemblance work?" In other words, are the Old Testament stories "just stories" (however historical) which may conveniently be allegorized in order to furnish us with a greater understanding of Christ's story? Or are they, first and foremost, Christologically significant, and only secondarily about Noah and Joseph and Moses and the rest?

The Relationship between the Great Story and Other Stories

The Great Story and the Old Testament

I would say that the Bible as a whole favors the latter view unquestionably. We have already seen how Jesus told the disciples everything in the Scriptures "concerning Himself." Admittedly, "concerning Himself" (*peri eautou*) is not a particularly precise expression, and by itself it might do no more than suggest an allegorical approach to the Old Testament. But set alongside, for instance, John 8:58 ("Before Abraham was, I am") and Matthew 22:45 ("If David thus calls Him Lord, how is He his son?"), it demonstrates that, although Christ's story is chronologically secondary to the Old Testament stories, it is logically primary, because we are dealing not just with chronology, but eternity. "He is before all things, and in Him all things hold together" (Col. 1:17). "Without Him was not anything made that was made" (John 1:3). We have to escape the fashionable concept of time as a linear progression from A to B to C, and remember that time is a thing created by God who places Himself, like a huge tent-pole, at the center and then stretches the canvas out on either side. Christ dropped into the formless waters of history like a rock into a pool, sending ripples both before and after. Therefore the Old Testament stories do more than allow or invite a Christian reading: they demand it, if they are to be understood aright.

So it is probably wise not to rely exclusively on words like "prefigurations" and "foreshadowings" when discussing the Old Testament stories. The prefixes "pre-" and "fore-" mislead us into thinking too much in terms of chronology and not enough in terms of eternity. That way, Noah and Moses and the others tend to be seen as mere ancillary figures, acting their part until they are eclipsed by Christ. At first glance, that might seem a good consequence because it magnifies Christ. Indeed, it would seem to be the very raison d'être of a prophet that he must work towards his own abdication ("he must increase, but I must decrease"[8]). But, in the long run, this approach, if unqualified, is profoundly un-Christian. Men do not exist so that they may love God, however self-denyingly. They exist so that God may love them, and what He has called clean they must not call unclean. He is not interested in perpetuating inferiority complexes. When Christ was transfigured between Moses and Elijah, they were not buttressing Him, He was legitimizing them, confirming their reputations in Law and Prophecy. For God is no man's debtor. He does not reap where He has not sown, and we should not think of the Old Testament as "feeding into" the story of Christ like tributaries flowing into a river where they are instantly swallowed up and overwhelmed. The reward promised for the faithful is eternal life, not annihilation.

So when Christ retold the Scriptures He was not defending Himself with "corroborative detail designed to give artistic verisimilitude to an otherwise bald and unconvincing narrative."[9] He was not saying, "I am genuine because the Scriptures speak of Me." He was saying, "The fact that I am genuine means the Scriptures are bound to speak of Me." Of course! How could it be otherwise? As the fountainhead of all life, it is obvious that it is He who feeds into the Old Testament stories, not the other way round. He is the great original, they the copies. One realizes that they speak of Him because He speaks through them. Christ in His grace allowed His story to be introduced by His children, all of whom fluffed their lines in one way or another: Noah was a drunkard, Abraham a liar, Moses a murderer, David an adulterer. It magnifies Christ far more to see Him giving life to copies of Himself, especially to copies that are in various ways blind or lame or dumb, than to see Him as an upas tree in whose shadow nothing can grow. "If even a beast touches the mountain, it shall be stoned" is yesterday's law.[10] To be sure, Peter's awareness of his own inadequacy ("Depart from me O Lord, for I am a sinful man"[11]) was a good sign, but Christ did not act on his advice. Though Peter was right to think that no one could see the face of God and live, the miracle was that God had come to save men from that God.

From the vantage point of the twentieth century, it is easy to think that this miracle was predictable. Indeed, Jesus rebukes the Emmaus road disciples for being "foolish and slow of heart to believe all that the prophets have spoken." But they were not alone. John the Baptist seems to have had his doubts,[12] Peter's declaration of faith at Caesarea Philippi was undercut only moments later,[13] and Jesus' own neighbors turned against Him.[14] The sad fact was (and is) that religious people, the prophet's countrymen, can be perversely imperceptive, blinded by their privileged knowledge, rich and therefore unable to enter the kingdom of God. The greatest faith Jesus found in Israel belonged to a

Roman centurion, a Gentile without the Law. And we now turn to look at how the Bible views the relationship between the Great Story and paganism.

The Great Story and First-Century Paganism

In Acts 17 we see Paul interacting with pagan "stories"—the myths and beliefs surrounding the idol-worship of the Greeks. Imitating Christ's own practice on the road to Emmaus, he listens before he speaks. Just as Christ twice asked the disciples what they were speaking of, so Paul spends time observing the objects and practitioners of Athenian worship. His patience means that, when at last his provoked spirit moves into action, he has a foothold for the Gospel in the Athenians' worldview. Similarly, after hearing out the disciples on the Emmaus road, Christ was moved to rebuke them, knowing (and being seen to know) where their ignorance lay.

"What you worship as unknown, this I proclaim to you." Thus Paul speaks to the men of Athens in the Areopagus. He had found an altar dedicated "To An Unknown God" and uses it in his speech as a springboard to talk about the God he knew "who made the world and everything in it." Later he quotes the Cretan poet of the sixth century B.C., Epimenides, and the third century Stoic Aratus. Paul has two audiences here: one who says God is unknown, the other who says God is the father of us all, in whom we live and move and have our being. Both groups need to come to the resurrected Christ, the judge of all. Both need to have their stories retold to them so that they can realize unseen potentialities. Paul is anxious to reinterpret their positions so that they can see their beliefs not as end-points, but as starting-points on the road to the God who is knowable in Christ.

Paul's task here is both easier and harder than the task facing Christ on the road to Emmaus. It is harder because, where Christ was faced with two people who knew almost everything there was to know about him, including evidence of His resurrection, Paul is faced either with people who proclaim their ignorance of God or whose knowledge of God is very basic and limited. But Paul's job is easier because, as everyone knows, it is easier to teach a child who knows nothing or very little than an adult who thinks he knows everything.

As regards the altar inscription, Paul had an excellent piece of straw with which to build the first brick of edification. The Athenians knew something about God: they knew He was not known to them. This is a great step gained. As a modern writer has said, "If we cannot 'practice the presence of God,' it is something to practice the absence of God, to become increasingly aware of our unawareness till we feel like men who should stand beside a great cataract and hear no noise, or like a man in a story who looks in a mirror and finds no face there, or a man in a dream who stretches out his hand to visible objects and gets no sensation of touch. To know that one is dreaming is to be no longer perfectly asleep."[15] The Athenians who worshipped an unknown God are good examples of people practicing the absence of God. True, it is somewhat perverse to celebrate one's ignorance, but all truth is God's truth, and the truthfulness which drives a pagan to admit his ignorance is a good sign. "The pressure of truth or meaning upon our minds is nothing other than the impact of God upon us, even though we may not have learnt to call him by his proper name. It is one of the activities of God in his self-manifestation which is included under the heading of general revelation."[16]

If we should be in any doubt that Christ is present in this general revelation, we need only check the question against His special revelation. As John Stott says in his commentary on this passage, "Special revelation must control and correct whatever general revelation seems to disclose."[17] Isaiah 45 reveals a God who acts though He is unknown, a God who deliberately hides Himself. And Jesus' own cry from the cross, quoting Psalm 22, provides the strongest evidence necessary to show how God can be present in ignorance. Where the fool says in his heart, "There is no God" and where the Nietzschean says, "God is dead," Jesus says to God, "Why have You forsaken Me?" At that moment of the crucifixion, Jesus apparently felt that God had withdrawn from Him or abandoned Him in some way. For Jesus, for a while, there was no God, He was as good as dead. God had become completely absent from Him, and He knew it.

This serves as a reminder that the Great Story is the origin and strength of all stories, not just the stories of the Old Testament, but also the stories God gives to every man. There is no way out of the Great Story. "If I make my bed in Sheol, Thou art there!"[18]

Admittedly, the likeness Moses bears to Christ is far greater than that which an idol-worshipping Athenian bears, but the Athenian shares something with Christ and it is Paul's recognition of that sharing that underpins his response to them. Paul knows that Jesus Christ is "the Life," and any life, however embittered or ignorant or faltering, insofar as it is life, reflects something of Christ. It can be fanned into flame. God does not quench the smoldering flax. Paul knows he can work with their ignorance because he recognizes it as having a counterpart in the Great Story.

If this approach works for those who say God is unknown, then *a fortiori* it must work for those who claim to know *something* about God. They are the next to be addressed in Paul's sermon. Their positive, but incomplete, knowledge of God is also shared by Christ. At first sight it would seem unorthodox to suggest that Christ's knowledge of God is incomplete, since He taught that He and the Father "are one."[19] However, He also acknowledges that He does not know at least one thing known by the Father—the date of the Last Day. So when the Greeks reveal a positive, but limited, knowledge of God, again, the Great Story—in the unfathomable mystery of the Trinity— has got there first.

Wherever we look, in fact, we find the universe ringing with the story of Christ, not only loudly in the Old Testament and quietly in paganism, but silently in the very life of nature. The sun dies to the world each night and is reborn each morning. Autumn dies into winter and is reborn as spring. Seeds die into the ground to be reborn as crops (Paul's own figure for the resurrection in 1 Cor. 15:36-37). The heart dies at each systole to be reborn at each diastole. Lovers die at the moment of sexual extremity to be reborn in the life of their child. The pattern of Christ is the grand theme of the cosmos. Karl Barth puts it in terms of the general (the world and humanity) existing for the sake of this particular; that in this particular the general acquires its meaning and significance. And C. S. Lewis observes that, "The whole Miracle [of the Incarnation], far from denying what we already know of reality, writes the comment which makes that crabbed text plain: or rather, proves itself to be the text on which Nature was only the commentary."[20] It is Jesus Christ, not Joseph Campbell's factitious and non-existent construction, who is the hero with a thousand faces.[21] We should therefore not be hesitant in looking for the pattern of the Christ-event in contemporary stories—in particular, for our purpose, in films.

The Great Story and Films

The first movement of the Great Story is that of descent, love descending freely from God to man in Christ to tackle the problem of sin. Here are some examples of episodes in film that seem to parallel that movement. They are drawn from a wide variety of sources, some serious, some not so serious. Schindler offering to help the Jews in his factory in *Schindler's List*. Keanu Reeves trying to save the busload of passengers in *Speed*. Captain Kirk tackling his enemies in any *Star Trek* film you care to mention. A certain nun called Maria leaving her convent to serve the family Von Trapp in *The Sound of Music*. Tim Robbins taking on the corrupt prison authorities in *The Shawshank Redemption*. The bridge-building love of Emma Thompson in *Howards End*. Kevin Costner obeying the mysterious voice in *Field of Dreams*. Various versions of the Pygmalion story such as *My Fair Lady* where Henry Higgins improves Eliza Doolittle, where Richard Gere improves Julia Roberts in *Pretty Woman*, where Julie Walters improves Michael Caine in *Educating Rita*. The list could go on and on. Now, it may be claimed that lumping together such diverse films as *Speed*, *Schindler's List*, and *My Fair Lady* is so loose a categorization as to be worthless. But it cannot be denied that all the characters mentioned above do, in some form or other, put themselves out, freely, on behalf of others, out of a sense of service or love or self-sacrifice. Any such positive, outgoing concern conveys something, however refracted or diluted, of the love shown in the Incarnation. It is the Incarnation that is the Christian's controlling narrative. Only by imitating God's love in Christ are human loves at all.

Then there is the low point of the Great Story, the crucifixion, the loading of Christ with sin, the apparent abandonment by God. Some cinematic examples spring to mind: the jilting of Marianne by Willoughby in *Sense and Sensibility,* the torture of Mel Gibson in *Braveheart,* the loss of contact with earth in *Apollo 13*, the wrongful accusation of Hero in *Much Ado About Nothing,* the collapse at the piano of David Helfgott in *Shine*, the shouting of Anthony Hopkins in *Shadowlands*, the parting of the lovers in *Brief Encounter*, the death of

Leonard Bast in *Howards End*, the return to the convent of Maria Von Trapp, the two months spent in solitary by Tim Robbins in *The Shawshank Redemption*. Again, these examples are extremely varied, but they all show characters or events running into the ground, metaphorically speaking, hitting the buffers, drawing a blank. Our power to sympathize with such personalities and such occurrences springs, I would suggest, from the recognition, conscious or sub-conscious though it may be, that God too has suffered, has felt deserted, has known death.

And then thirdly, the turn, the movement upward or forward again, the change in quality, the resurrection movement in the Great Story. Here are some parallels from the movies: the boys standing on their desks in *Dead Poets Society*, Kevin Costner playing catch with his dad in *Field of Dreams*, the start of the day after *Groundhog Day*, Juliette Binoche journeying down a sunlit avenue at the end of *The English Patient*, the flooding of the screen with color in *Schindler's List*, the escape of Tim Robbins from *Shawshank Prison*, the helicopter flight at the end of *Jurassic Park*, the journey into the mountains at the end of *The Sound of Music*, Kate Winslet rejoining Leonardo Di Caprio at the end of *Titanic*, Linus Roache returning alone to Venice at the end of *The Wings of the Dove*. Some of these examples no doubt are more successful than others, but all are intended to be uplifting or at least are indicative of a change of direction for the better. If they move audiences it is because, I suggest, they remind them of that new life they have found, or wish they could find, in Christ, who has Himself been changed and raised to the right hand of God.

Very few films manage to reproduce uniformly well each of the three movements in the Great Story. Some movies, often they are what we call political films or social message films, the films of Oliver Stone for instance, tend to get stuck in the first movement. They are full of energy and engagement with issues, confronting enemies and taking on conspiracies. But as Yeats said, when we argue with our enemies we produce only rhetoric, when we argue with ourselves we produce poetry. These films tend not to have poetic depth because the finger of accusation is too often pointing away from the protagonists. The story line rarely gets near a crucifixion moment and never as far as a resurrection moment. One leaves the cinema full of unfulfilled emotion, brewing with indignation at the waste of war or the criminality of government or the evil of capital punishment, but the feeling is febrile and unstable. One has been whipped up, but not made wise. High-octane thrillers and shoot 'em up adventure yarns (Bond films, for instance), not to mention pornographic films, similarly allow one to "get off," but they do not follow through. They are, narratively speaking, contracepted. They cannot leave one imaginatively pregnant because they have not died. At the worst (*Natural Born Killers*, for instance) they leave one feeling raped.

Interestingly, Martin Scorsese's film, *The Last Temptation of Christ*, deals with just this issue of avoiding death. The film asks what would have happened if Christ had not been "obedient unto death, even death on a cross"? As Scorsese has said, "The last temptation of Christ is not to have sex with Mary Magdalene, it is to get off the cross and live his life as a normal human being."[22] In a dream-sequence, Christ is seen coming down off the cross and growing to be an old man with a wife and children. But He overcomes the temptation and returns to the cross, supplying the film with the most unusual ending: rather than the crucifixion being the low point of the story it is actually the temptation which takes that dubious honor and the return to the cross has that quality of relief and new life which we would normally associate with the resurrection. But Scorsese is not the first to have asked this question. Dorothy L. Sayers does so too in *The Mind of the Maker* where she writes: "We may ask ourselves how much power would be left in the story of the crucifixion, as a story, if Christ had come down from the cross."[23] And she concludes that it would have lost all its power, because such an outcome would have been irrelevant, separating the consequences of the plot from its causes. As Bonhoeffer wrote: "The life of the spirit is not that which shuns death and keeps clear of destruction: rather it endureth death and in death it is sustained. It only achieves its truth in the midst of utter destruction."[24]

The problem with many violent and disturbing films is that they are not violent and disturbing enough. They lack the courage of their convictions. If they could be prepared to plumb the depths, they would find the route up the other side. Such films leave one feeling bleak because they do not go down to utter destruction. *Seven*, with Brad Pitt and Morgan Freeman, is like that. The story gets one as far as the crucifixion, but not as far as the "It is finished." David Jones's *The Trial* and Scorsese's *Taxi Driver* are other examples. One is reminded of the fate of vampires (in *Interview with the Vampire*, for instance) who are forever destined to feed off the dead but unable to die themselves. Perhaps the clearest example of this problem is to be found in David Cronenberg's controversial film *Crash*. This is a story of people who derive sexual pleasure from car crashes and the resulting mutilation. The final scene depicts a crashed car and a couple copulating on the ground next to it. At the end of the scene, the man whispers to the woman, "Maybe next time." But the viewer knows that "next time" will be no better because this couple is not interested in death, only in narrow escapes. They are a pair of rutting animals, desperate to achieve some form of self-escape, but condemned always to come down from the cross of their story. As Erich Fromm says: "Despair can be overcome only if it has been fully experienced."[25] Or, to put it in Jürgen Moltmann's terms: Christianity supplies the hope which is not the hope of the optimist, but the hope of the hopeless.[26]

In some films which get bogged down in the second movement the problem is not just with content but also with style. The director Peter Greenaway (*The Cook, The Thief, His Wife and Her Lover, Prospero's Books,* etc.) is an example of a film-maker whose very style is trapped in the darkness of the crucifixion:

> My cinema, deliberately, is very artificial. I draw your attention to the frame, to the artificiality of the editing . . . witness the association with music—and lately I have tried very hard to draw attention to the whole device and pretense of acting. . . . Hollywood so often offers a world which, if it's not romanticized, is somehow deodorized, somehow sentimentalized. I know a lot of people find the hard edge of sex and death in my films far away from that picture of the world. I am very eclectic—I homage and borrow, quote and reprise. I am suspicious of so-called truths—the multiple meanings, the hidden meanings.
>
> I object to the simplistic moral positions of so much Hollywood cinema—its notion that we should have happy endings, the very notion that cinema can provide some sort of solution to a narrative. I'm not very interested in narrative. I think cinema is a poor narrative medium—certainly if you compare it with literature. The film director, after all, can only relay one interpretation of an event by his choice of camera position and art direction and so on. His position is very subjective, and it permits the viewer no alternatives. . . . The ability of the written word to conjure up a thousand million different possibilities is so much richer than anything the cinema can do. So, I feel suspicious about narrative in

cinema and try either to subvert it or minimalize it or to be extravagant about it in ways that draw attention to it.[27]

If post-modernism is correctly defined as "antipathy to the meta-narrative," then these remarks of Greenaway's are a classic statement of it. The eclecticism, the self-consciousness, and the non-judgmentalism of his position are, in themselves, not bad things. But they become bad if they are pushed too far. The Christian can and must sympathize with those going through the valley of the shadow of death. In that valley meaning evaporates and honest filmmakers will want to draw attention to this, perhaps in the stylistic ways described by Greenaway. Where they part company with Christian thought is when they claim to be the whole picture. Because, of course, being antipathetic to the meta-narrative is just a new meta-narrative, but an inverted one. Greenaway is suspicious of narrative solutions: this means his narrative solution is to leave things wriggling on "the hard edge of sex and death." Admittedly, this will at first prove exciting and varied to those who have tired of the clichéd and the romanticized, but to stop there is self-indulgence, indulgence in gall rather than in saccharine. Greenaway's description of his films as "pinned butterflies" neatly encapsulates his fixation with crucifixion. But the Christ story teaches that one needs to get off that "hard edge" and plummet into the depths of death, to "sleep indeed, then wake indeed,"[28] as the protagonists in *Crash* are so desperate to do. Then, and only then, can one open up "a thousand million different possibilities." Unlike previous generations of artists who would deal with madness and artificiality, but within a larger context of sanity and sincerity, Greenaway and his school have embraced the hollow middle of the Great Story while rejecting its beginning and its end. They have thrown out the baby and are trying to nurse the bathwater.

But Greenaway's distaste for the "deodorized" Hollywood with its "simplistic" happy endings is something which Christians must surely respect. Though joy, not sorrow, is a fruit of the Holy Spirit, it was for the joy set before Him that Christ endured the cross. For Him, the joy of resurrection was attainable only through the bitter waters of death, and just because death was overcome does not mean it was sweet to experience. There was a real death which made a real difference. Films like *Indecent Proposal*, which end with a reconciliation that seems to take too little account of the foregoing conflict, are no better, perhaps worse, than those bleak films which see no possibility of redemption. Like a dog to its vomit, they return to the very problem the conflict was designed to free them from.

Most filmmakers do, in fact, attempt to cover the three movements of the Christ-story, even if unwittingly. They may, for instance, be working to Aristotle's system of *hamartia, catharsis,* and *peripeteia,* or to the modern script editor's demand for setup, conflict, and resolution—formulae which replicate the patterns of the Great Story, though grounded at a less fundamental level. The better the filmmaker is at storytelling the more closely will he follow these formulae and the more nearly, therefore, will he imitate the structure of the Christ-event. There is an amusing anecdote that, during the production of *E.T.*, Melissa Mathison, its writer, discovered many similarities between her screenplay and the story of Christ. Mathison, educated in a Catholic convent in Hollywood, went to the director, Steven Spielberg, and told him what she had found. "I'm Jewish and I don't want to hear anything about this," was Spielberg's reaction.[29] But the shape of the story remained.

Another example of a film closely imitating the Great Story is *The Shawshank Redemption.* Given the word "redemption" in the title, one might expect to find the presence of a Christian hand behind it, but, as far as I know, neither the director/screenwriter, Frank Darabont, nor Stephen King who wrote the novella from which the film comes, is a Christian. It apparently provides a perfect example of a non-Christian story speaking better than it knows and imitating with uncanny exactitude the movements of another, greater story. Of course, as Erich Auerbach and Northrop Frye have shown, Western literature (and therefore films) have been enormously influenced by the Bible and the makers of *Shawshank* will not have escaped that influence. The interesting thing is how strongly the influence can work without making itself explicit. If Darabont and King did indeed arrive at this story without conscious imitation, then they would do well to listen to George Herbert: "There is in love a sweetnesse readie penn'd: / Copie out onely that, and save expense."[30]

Which is not to say that all human art should merely and explicitly regurgitate the Great Story. There may be good reasons for diverging from the pattern in a given film or for emphasizing one movement over another. But I suggest that the best films are usually those that mirror most closely the three major strands of the Great Story, because, after all, it is not just a great story, but the Greatest Story, the Greatest Story Ever Told. As J. R. R. Tolkien remarked, "There is no tale ever told that men would rather find was true. . . . To reject it leads either to sadness or to wrath."[31] In other words, to reject it means one either gets stuck in the first movement, full of unfulfilled emotional activity, which must ultimately turn in frustration to wrath, or else one gets stuck in the second movement, full of unregenerate emotional passivity, which must ultimately turn to sadness. Either way, Christ is in the cultural expression, but He is cut off from completing His mission. For those artists who go through to the third movement, their persistence allows them imaginatively to traverse that path which is the path of Christ and the path of Christian commitment. Here Christ transforms the cultural response, whether the reader/writer realizes it or not, for imagination is, as it were, the shadow of faith. Whether faith can ever embrace and raise imagination to a level of spiritual response is not a question for this present chapter. My purpose here is only to argue for the formal resemblance between the Great Story and these other stories. But even at the formal level, where the response is imaginative and far from salvific, these stories may be of some spiritual efficacy, for one can only be a Christian if one is a human being first, and any good exercise at the merely natural level of a human faculty such as imagination presses upon one's mind the limitations of nature and one's need of supernature. Thus the good enjoyment of a good film may be, among other things, a useful preparation for salvation.

And for the Christian who is having his need of supernature met in the faith that transcends imagination, imagination may yet remain a useful tool to encourage salvation in others or as a helpful reminder or explicator of aspects of the salvation that is already being experienced. Here Christ is above the cultural expression, directing it and controlling it, but not disregarding it. As the Second Council of Nicaea proclaimed, only God deserves worship (*latreia*), but images of Him (among which we may include imitative stories) may be venerated (*proskynesis*) as aids in devotion and in teaching the confessions of the Church.

The Christian who wishes to engage with or contribute to his culture recognizes, along with the writer of Psalm 87, that all the springs of artistic expression are in Zion, for the Christian and the non-Christian alike. His special knowledge of the source of those springs must not blind him to its presence in pagan art, for God works there too, incognito. Just as Christ came into the world, not to condemn the world, but to save it, so the Christian must try to save the stories told in our culture. The Christian must take captive every story presented to him and allow it to be embraced by Christ's greater story. He must listen before he responds. If the story is deficient, he must say so, and sublimate it after the manner of Paul. Preachers must take such stories and make up the deficit in their sermons; reviewers must diagnose the narrative weaknesses; movie-goers must deter or warn in word-of-mouth recommendations. But if the story is sufficient, the Christian must admire it, give thanks for it, and worship the God whose story echoes within it, taking care not to deserve the rebuke that came to the Emmaus road disciples: "O foolish men, and slow of heart to believe all that the prophets have spoken!"

Michael Ward is head warden of C. S. Lewis's former home,
"The Kilns," in Headington, England.

Bibliography

Bonhoeffer, Dietrich. *The Cost of Discipleship*. New York: Macmillan, 1961.

Campbell, Joseph. *The Hero with a Thousand Faces*. London: Fontana, 1993.

Dougan, Andy. *Martin Scorsese Close Up*. London: Orion Media, 1997.

Herbert, George. *The English Poems of George Herbert*. Ed. C.A. Patrides. London: Dent, 1974.

Irving, John. *A Prayer for Owen Meany*. London: Black Swan, 1989.

Kreitzer, Larry J. *The New Testament in Fiction and Film*. Sheffield: JSOT, 1993.

Lewis, C. S. *The Four Loves*. Glasgow: Fount, 1991.

Lewis, C. S. *Miracles*. Glasgow: Fount, 1980.

MacDonald, Alan. *Films in Close-Up*. Leicester: Inter-Varsity Press, 1991.

MacDonald, George. *George MacDonald: An Anthology*. Ed. C. S. Lewis. London: Fount, 1983.

Marsh, Clive & Gaye Ortiz. *Explorations in Theology & Film*. Oxford: Blackwell, 1997.

Martin, Joel W. & Conrad E. Ostwalt, Jr. (eds.). *Screening the Sacred*. Oxford: Westview Press, 1995.

May, John & Michael Bird. *Religion in Film*. University of Tennessee Press, 1982.

Moltmann, Jürgen. *Theology of Hope*. Trans. J. W. Leitch. London: S.C.M. Press, 1967.

Richardson, Alan. *Christian Apologetics*. London: S.C.M. Press, 1950.

Sayers, Dorothy L. *The Mind of the Maker*. London: Mowbray, 1994.

Stott, John R. W. *The Message of Acts*. Leicester: Inter-Varsity Press, 1990.

Third Way, Harrow: Third Way Trust Ltd., December 1995.

Tolkien, J. R. R. *The Monsters and the Critics*. London: George Allen & Unwin, 1984.

Walker, John, ed. *Halliwell's Film Guide*. London: HarperCollins, 1995.

Notes

[1] *The Greatest Story Ever Told*, directed by George Stevens, was originally over four hours long. *The New Yorker*, in its review, said that, "If the subject matter weren't sacred, we would be responding to the picture in the most charitable way by laughing at it from start to finish."

[2] John 1:51. Cf. Gen. 28:12.

[3] John 3:14. Cf. Num. 21:9.

[4] Matt. 12:39.

[5] John 15:1. Cf. Isa. 5:1-7.

[6] John 10:11. Cf. Jer. 23:1.

[7] Irving, John. *A Prayer for Owen Meany*. London: Black Swan, 1989.

[8] John 3:30.

[9] Gilbert, W. S., *The Mikado*, 1885.

[10] Heb. 12: 20. Cf. Exod. 19:12.

[11] Luke 5:8.

[12] Matt. 11:3.

[13] Matt. 16:16,23.

[14] Luke 4:16-30.

[15] Lewis, *The Four Loves*, 128.

[16] Richardson, *Christian Apologetics*, 121.

[17] Stott, *The Message of Acts*, 285.

[18] Ps. 139:8.

[19] John 10:30.

[20] Lewis, *Miracles*, 134.

[21] Joseph Campbell's book, *The Hero with a Thousand Faces*, attempts to unite the myths and religions of the world into a "monomyth." His theories deeply impressed George Lucas, who made use of Campbell's work when writing *Star Wars*.

[22] Dougan, *Martin Scorsese Close Up*, 88.

[23] Sayers, *The Mind of the Maker*, 67.

[24] Bonhoeffer, *The Cost of Discipleship*, 33.

[25] Quoted in May and Bird, *Religion and Film*, 122.

[26] Moltmann, *Theology of Hope*, quoted in Marsh and Ortiz, *Explorations in Theology and Film*, 243.

[27] Interview with *Third Way*, December 1995, 12.

[28] MacDonald, *George MacDonald: An Anthology*, 149.

[29] MacDonald, *Films in Close-Up*, 19.

[30] Herbert, 'Jordan (II)', *The English Poems of George Herbert*, 117.

[31] Tolkien, *The Monsters and the Critics*, 156.

10

The Impact of Origin Paradigms on Culture

Gary H. Locklair

Why is there a conflict between the demands of Christ and human culture? This book has demonstrated the tension and conflict between Christ and culture and offered insightful answers to the diverse questions which are generated. This present chapter aims to elucidate one possible root cause of the conflict between Christ and culture.

I propose that a foundational reason for the conflict between Christ and human culture stems from two opposing and radically opposite views of ultimate origins. These disparate origin paradigms are evolution and creation. These different origin paradigms result in opposing mindsets and worldviews. The tension between Christ and the "world" is partially explained by different worldviews and cultural values which flow from different origin paradigms.

One's view of his origins has an effect on his personal mindset and beliefs. One's beliefs naturally shape behavior. Collectively, a view of origins plays a dominant role in a culture. Behavioral differences between Christians and the postmodern culture at large can be traced to differences in beliefs about origins. This chapter outlines the two fundamental origin paradigms or models, evolution and creation, and demonstrates the effect these two belief systems have on culture.

A different perspective on this chapter would be to consider the following question. Are origin paradigms (ideas about evolution and creation) merely insignificant scientific issues, or are questions about ultimate origins foundational to a worldview and culture? I propose that models of origins form a foundation on which other "cultural" issues are built. That foundation, then, determines the direction a culture will pursue.

This chapter outlines issues of evolution and creation and the impact these ideas have on culture. Christ beside culture results in a sometimes paradoxical view for Christians. The paradoxical relationship is rendered slightly less perplexing once the cultural role played by origin paradigms is understood.

Importance of Origins

When my oldest son first joined his Boy Scout troop, I was surprised to see that the other scouts did not wear the scout neckerchief. The scoutmaster explained that the scouts had voted not to wear the neckerchief or scarf. My son was happy to forego the additional expense of buying a neckerchief. While we both enjoyed the troop, the scoutmaster did seem to have one quirk. At the end of each troop meeting he would announce a "belt check." All of the scouts would line up and any scout who was not wearing a belt would be fined! I wondered about this strange behavior. Why was the scoutmaster so concerned about his scouts wearing a belt? Was it some deep-seated psychological scar from his past? I finally asked the scoutmaster about the belt rule. He explained that the scout's neckerchief is not merely decoration but serves a purpose as a scout's tool. The neckerchief can be used as a makeshift sling or a temporary rope among other things. A scout must always "be prepared" and the neckerchief would serve as a useful tool. Since the scouts had decided not to wear the neckerchief, it was important to have a substitute tool. The belt became the tool that the scouts would always have in place of the neckerchief. Thus, if a scout was not wearing his belt, he was not in uniform as he was not prepared for an unforeseen emergency.

I could not understand the reason for mandating the wearing of a belt because I did not understand its origin. This simple story illustrates a larger truth: the meaning of anything is linked to its origin. It is difficult to understand something without knowing its origin. Arriving late to a movie or play usually results in confusion for the viewer because the beginning has been missed. Reading a book by starting in the middle usually results in less than perfect understanding of the characters and plot.

Since the meaning of anything is intimately linked to its origin, it follows that ultimate meaning is derived from ultimate origins. Are ideas of origins important? Consider the importance placed on historical origins in the academy. Most liberal arts universities require a "cross cultural" component in their core requirements. One primary way a student can satisfy the cross cultural component is by taking a course in history. Professors believe that students can learn about another culture by understanding the history of that culture. This is true because the meaning of anything, including a culture, is tied to its historical origins.

Competing Origins Paradigms

There are two competing views of ultimate origins with different descriptions of human history. These two paradigms of origins are the evolution and creation models. Because these two paradigms are radically different, subscribers to the different models possess radically different worldviews.

The evolution model states that ultimate origins are solely the result of natural processes. The scientific designation for natural processes is secondary causes. Examples of secondary causes include water erosion forming a canyon and chemical reactions spontaneously producing amino acids from organic compounds. Secondary causes act without plan or purpose. Hallmarks of the evolution model include the concepts of long, slow, gradual development over immense periods of time. Billions of years were necessary for the universe to form into its present state. The transformation of the initial state of the universe into its present state was accomplished solely by secondary causes such as gravitational and nuclear forces. In a similar fashion, the evolution model states that all life on planet earth is related via common descent over billions of years of organic evolution. Immense periods of time were required for natural selection to produce all of the variety of extant living things from initially less complex life forms.

The basic evolution model is quite old historically. While many assume that Charles Darwin was the first to propose an evolutionary origin for living things, evolutionary concepts predate Darwin by thousands of years. The Greek philosophers had speculated on evolutionary themes for centuries prior to Lucretius's synopsis of the evolutionary paradigm in his six-book work *On the Nature of the Universe* (circa 55 B.C.).[1] Lucretius's work has many modern-sounding evolutionary elements, including the foundational concepts of secondary causes for origins (i.e., gods did not make the world, but it and all living things arose naturally). It is worthwhile to note the origin of the evolution model itself. It originated "in the minds of men."[2]

The creation model states that ultimate origins are the result of an intelligent creator. The scientific designation for the act of an intelligent creator is a primary cause. Examples of primary causes include the production of a computer system and the writing of a book. Primary causes are actions with plan and purpose. Hallmarks of the creation model include the concepts of design and production of systems in a fully formed and functional condition. The creator produced a "ready to run" universe complete with a huge diversity of fully formed and functional kinds of life on planet earth. The act of an intelligent creator was necessary to infuse living things with the information content of their DNA. Once created, the genetic code allows living things to live, grow, and reproduce.

The basic creation model is quite old historically. Moses recorded God's Word of creation in Genesis circa 1400 B.C. While the concepts of the creation model are recorded throughout the Bible, Genesis 1 is chronologically the first record of the creation model. It is instructive to note that the first book of the Bible is the book of origins (genesis means origin). Genesis is the first book of the Bible as the result of a deliberate plan. In other words, there is a reason that Genesis is the first book of the Bible. The Book of Genesis is foundational to understanding the Bible and its message. God had a purpose when He "recorded" Genesis 1 as the first chapter. There is a reason that "In the beginning, God created the heavens and earth" is the first verse in the Bible. The meaning of anything is linked to its origin. For a Christian, ultimate meaning is derived from ultimate origins as they are presented in the book of Genesis. Ultimately the origin of the creation model itself is the "mind of God."

The debate that rages between proponents of the two models of origins can be confusing to the interested, outside observer. If evolution and creation concern science, why is there a debate at all? Why hasn't one side proven its case scientifically? After all, no one accepts the idea that the earth is flat as we have scientifically proven the earth is a sphere. One reason for the debate concerns the nature of origin paradigms. Both evolution and creation are models, not theories, as they deal with past, unobserved events. Empirical science deals with ideas which can be directly observed and tested such as the shape of the earth. Origin science, on the other hand, deals with past, historical events.[3] There can be no scientific "proofs" when dealing with origins. Origin science is analogous to the proceedings in a court of law. Instead of scientific proofs, evidence is introduced in the framework of a model. The evidences and models are critically analyzed as to their validity. Although the preponderance of evidence may favor one side versus the other, the fact remains that no one can be absolutely certain of past, unobserved events. The evolution and creation paradigms are scientific, yet neither can be proven to be true using empirical scientific techniques. Therefore the debate between adherents to the two competing models rages on.

Evidences for the Creation Paradigm

Although the creation model can not be proven (just as the evolution model can not be proven), there are a number of scientific evidences which support the claim "In the beginning, God created the heavens and the earth."

The first law of thermodynamics states that matter and energy can not be created or destroyed in a closed system.[4] As an analogy, consider a glass bottle with a cork stopper in its opening. If one day a ship appeared in the bottle, what would your conclusion be as to the origin of the ship? Would you conclude that the bottle had somehow birthed the ship? I doubt you would, but if so your conclusion would be invalid as it would violate the first law of thermodynamics. Obviously the closed system of the bottle didn't create the ship naturally; rather, some intelligent (and perhaps devious) person put the ship into the bottle. In a similar fashion, our closed universe could not have "birthed" itself as the evolution model states. Instead, our fantastically complex and diverse universe must have been created by an outside intelligence, a transcendent God.

Polonium-218 halos are cited as strong evidence of the instantaneous creation of planet earth by Dr. Robert Gentry.[5] Dr. Gentry has studied and published about this fascinating evidence for nearly three decades. Because the formation of Polonium-218 halos requires a rapid crystallization of the rocks containing them, Dr. Gentry and many others believe the earth was called into existence and formed rapidly as the creation model states. As an analogy, consider Alka-Seltzer™ dissolving and producing bubbles in water. Polonium-218, like Alka-Seltzer bubbles, is extremely short lived. How quickly would the water have to be solidified (e.g., frozen) in order to capture the bubbles? Of course, the water would have to be frozen very quickly in order to preserve the bubbles. In a similar fashion the earth must have solidified quickly in order to preserve Polonium-218 halos. This evidence conflicts with the evolution model which states that the earth formed slowly and gradually over a multimillion-year period.

Information theory states, among other things, that information can only arise from intelligence.[6] The living cell is an awesome storehouse of information. The information content of even the "simplest" bacteria's DNA is enormous. Living cells store information chemically in the form of a genetic code. The genetic code allows living cells to use energy for growth, repair, and reproduction. The presence of information encoded within living things is evidence that living things were created by an intelligent designer. As an analogy, consider the words in this book. Even if you have never met or seen any of the authors in this volume, the words convey information to you. English words are a standard code for conveying information from one person to another (at least to English-speaking persons!). The words in this chapter are the direct result of a primary cause (me) creating them using a word processor. The words did not arise naturally or spontaneously. In a similar fashion, the genetic information in living things must have ultimately originated from an intelligent God. This evidence conflicts with the evolution model which states that information arose naturally via secondary (non-intelligent) causes. As troublesome as the information question is for the evolution model, it is particularly difficult for the evolution model to explain how meaning arose from intrinsically meaningless events.

There are many other scientific evidences which support the creation model of origins.[7] But the debate over origins is not primarily a debate over scientific paradigms and evidences. If the debate were merely scientific, why would it be so emotional? The debate over origins is sometimes heated precisely because it is not merely a scientific debate. It is a philosophical, a theological, a worldview debate. The evolution and creation models are the scientific views of ultimate origins for two competing worldviews. Why is there a struggle between Christ and culture? The paradoxical tension of Christ beside culture can be understood by viewing this foundational struggle between competing views of origins.

The Impact of Origins Paradigms on Culture

Culture shapes human behavior. In a positive sense culture shapes behavior by affirming good behavior. In a negative sense culture shapes behavior by stigmatizing bad behavior. How do we ascertain good and bad behavior? What is right and wrong? What is truth? The meaning of anything is linked to its origin. A person's or a culture's determination of right and wrong is dependent upon a view of ultimate origins. Differences in behaviors, in definitions of right and wrong, and in cultural norms can be attributed directly to differences in worldviews. Worldviews are built upon the foundation of origin paradigms. Consider the following emotionally-charged cultural clashes that pit the Christian and Christ's Word against a postmodern culture.

Abortion. Could the debate over this issue have it roots in paradigms of ultimate origins? There is certainly a tension between Christ's Word and popular American culture over the issue of life.

Much pro-abortion rhetoric and justification of abortion is derived from an evolutionary paradigm of ultimate human origins. In a popular account entitled *Life Doesn't Begin, It Continues*, author Elie Schneour justifies abortion on the basis of an evolutionary idea.[8]

> Ontogeny recapitulates phylogeny. This is a fundamental tenet of modern biology that derives from evolutionary theory, and is thus anathema to creationism as well as to those opposed to freedom of choice. Ontogeny is the name for the process of development of a fertilized egg into a fully formed and mature living organism. Phylogeny, on the other hand, is the history of the evolution of a species, in this case the human being. During development, the fertilized egg progresses over 38 weeks through what is, in fact, a rapid passage through evolutionary history: From a single primordial cell, the conceptus progresses through being something of a protozoan, a fish, a reptile, a bird, a primate and ultimately a human being. There is a difference of opinion among scientists about the time

during a pregnancy when a human being can be said to emerge. But there is general agreement that this does not happen until after the end of the first trimester.[9]

Schneour claims that since all life evolves, there can not be an actual event identified as the beginning of human life. It flows logically from that premise that abortion is not the termination of human life— apparently, at least, not during the first trimester of a pregnancy.

In his work *Darwin's Dangerous Idea,* Daniel Dennett makes it clear that evolution allows human culture to make definitions and set standards for issues of life and death:

> At what "point" does a human life begin or end? The Darwinian perspective lets us see with unmistakable clarity why there is no hope at all of discovering a telltale mark, a saltation in life's processes, that "counts." We need to draw lines; we need definitions of life and death for many important moral purposes.[10]

In a similar fashion, others have attempted to secure a justification for abortion on the basis of the evolutionary paradigm. The evolution model dictates that a culture will focus on "quality of life issues." Life has meaning and value and worth if . . . if what? What is the basis for determining if someone (or some "thing" such as the "conceptus") possesses a significant quality of life? The real question is: who determines quality of life issues? Schneour, Dennett, and many other evolutionists agree that humans make the definitions. Under an evolutionary paradigm, life has meaning and value if humans say so. Abortion is an acceptable cultural practice due to our (supposed) evolutionary heritage.

Margaret Sanger, founder of Planned Parenthood, was influenced by evolutionary concepts. Sanger combined evolutionary views of eugenics, derived from Darwinian "survival-of-the-fittest," with her socialist ideas to build her platform of birth control. Eugenics, the science of improvement of the hereditary qualities of a race, was founded by Francis Galton, a cousin of Charles Darwin. Galton was not concerned about breeding animals, but about improving the "race of men." Sanger likewise argued for the purity and existence of the race by defending itself against the "less healthy, less intelligent, less discriminating mothers" and "the children of the feebleminded, the diseased, and the mentally dwarfed [who] drag down the standards of schools and society."[11] The scientific justification for eugenics is derived from evolutionary concepts where only the fittest survive.

Abortion is a perfectly logical and rational cultural practice if the evolution model is true. There is no meaning behind life in the evolution model. There is nothing but the material world and natural forces in the evolution model. There is no god with a purpose or plan for human beings and human life.

The creation model paints a radically different view of life. The creation model dictates that Christians will focus on "sanctity of life" rather than on "quality of life." Life has meaning and value and worth because God declared so. God is the author and creator of life. In Jeremiah 1:4, 5, the prophet records "The word of the Lord came to me saying, 'Before I formed you in the womb I knew you.'" Abortion is wrong from a Christian perspective because God created and sanctifies all human life. God created the first two human beings in His image. He commanded them to be fruitful and multiply. In Malachi 2:15, the prophet records Christ's view, "Has not the Lord made them one? In flesh and spirit they are His. And why one? Because He was seeking godly offspring." Christians do not promote or condone abortion because God's act of creation decries abortion as an illegitimate cultural practice.

From a macroscopic perspective, it is possible to claim that differences in behavior are due to differences in worldviews; yet, foundationally the cultural tension and conflict over abortion derives from competing views of origins. I am not saying that people always make the conscious connection between evolution and abortion. But at the same time, the evolutionary worldview does permeate our current culture and does have an impact on people's actions.

Homosexuality. Could the debate over this issue have it roots in paradigms of ultimate origins? There is certainly a tension between Christ's Word and popular American culture over the issue of life-styles and "sexual orientation."

In a homosexual publication, the author writes:

> Homosexuality is seldom discussed as a component of evolution, but it undoubtedly plays a role. Homosexual behavior has been observed in

most animal species studied, and the higher we climb on the taxonomic tree toward mammals, the more apparent homosexual behavior we see.[12] In other words, since animals engage in homosexual behavior, it is a natural part of the evolutionary process which produced humans. Homosexual behavior is a natural part of human culture within an evolutionary paradigm.

John Money has stated:

> Any theory of the genesis of either exclusive homosexuality or exclusive heterosexuality must address primarily the genesis of bisexuality.[13]

According to Money, understanding the origins of sexuality will give us insight into the nature of homosexuality and heterosexuality. Evolutionists speculate that organisms "invented" sexual reproduction at some stage in evolutionary development. Neither homosexuality nor heterosexuality can be considered wrong from an evolutionary perspective.

To emphasize the "naturalness" of homosexuality, Michael Ruse stated:

> Is homosexuality biologically unnatural? Modern evolutionary theory suggests that this claim is highly questionable.[14]

In a similar fashion, others have attempted to secure a justification for homosexuality on the basis of the evolutionary paradigm. Notice the use of the word "natural" implying that natural tendencies are good. Christians understand that sin is "natural" yet is not good. Under an evolutionary paradigm, "sexual orientation" is an accident. There is no plan or purpose for human sexuality. Accepting a moral basis for sexual activity would acknowledge an "outside force" which sets standards of human behavior. In the evolution model, there is no "outside force"; thus, homosexuality is an acceptable cultural practice due to our (supposed) evolutionary heritage.

Homosexuality is a perfectly logical and rational cultural practice if the evolution model is true. There is no meaning behind sexual expression in the evolution model. There is nothing but the material world and natural forces in the evolution model. There is no god with a purpose or plan for human beings and human sexuality.

The creation model provides a radically different view of human sexuality. To understand why homosexuality is wrong, a Christian merely needs to review the account of creation. In the beginning God created the first male Adam and the first female Eve. "So God created man in His own image, in the image of God He created him, male and female He created them" (Genesis 1:27). Jesus Christ emphasized that the meaning of anything is linked to its origin when He responded to the Pharisees question about divorce in Matthew 19,

> Some Pharisees came to Him to test him. They asked, "Is it lawful for a man to divorce his wife for any and every reason?" "Haven't you read," He replied, "that at the beginning the Creator 'made them male and female,' and said 'For this reason a man will leave his father and mother and will be united to his wife, and the two will become one flesh'? So they are no longer two, but one. Therefore what God has joined together, let man not separate."

Homosexuality is wrong because it does not coincide with the will of the Creator. As Ken Ham has stated,

> Understanding the biblical basis for marriage makes the question of homosexuality an easy one for Christians to solve. It is not a matter of personal opinion. . . . God made Adam and Eve. Not Adam and Steve! He made a man and a woman, not a man and another man.[15]

God created a woman for man and not another man because it was not good for man to be alone.

Foundationally the cultural tension and conflict over homosexuality originates in the two competing views of origins. I am not saying that people always make the conscious connection between evolution and homosexuality. But at the same time, the evolutionary worldview does permeate our current culture and does have an impact on people's actions.

Racism. It is unfortunate that some have used an evolutionary foundation to promote racism. Henry Fairfield Osborn, a leading American evolutionist in the early twentieth century, was outspoken in his beliefs about different human races and their progression along evolutionary lines.

> The Negroid stock is even more ancient than the Caucasian and Mongolian. . . . The standard of intelligence of the average adult Negro is similar to that of the eleven-year-old youth of the species *Homo sapiens*.[16]

Osborn would not even classify human beings with dark skin as Homo sapiens! The concept of different human races springs from the evolution model. Christ does not speak about different human races. Indeed the creation model teaches that all human beings are the direct descendants of Adam and Eve. Paul preached to the men of Athens, "The God who made the world and everything in it is the Lord of heaven and earth. . . . From one man he made every nation of men" (Acts 17:24, 26).

In like manner, contemporary social and cultural conflicts can be shown to have their roots in different models of ultimate origins. While not everyone makes the connection between origins and culture, many do. Consider the following letter to the editor published in the *Milwaukee Journal Sentinel* newspaper:

> On the bright side, potholes: a lesson in nature.
>
> Be happy the next time you bump through a pothole as you drive along the roadway. It's just the result of Mother Nature practicing her miraculous law of expansion and contraction without which none of us would exist. We all should know that most substances expand with heat and contract with cold temperatures. Fortunately, water does the opposite —it expands with the cold. Thus, ice floats instead of sinking. This prevented the earth from being a huge solid icebox, which incidentally would have canceled the evolution of mankind. Look at those pesky potholes as just a very insignificant side effect of a glorious natural phenomenon.[17]

This is a cultural "impact" of another sort, of course! Unfortunately, not all connections are so benign. For example, Wrangham and Peterson in their book *Demonic Males: Apes and the Origins of Human Violence* argue that violence is inherent in human males due to evolutionary descent. What is the logical conclusion to be drawn from this thesis? To a consistent evolutionist, it would be that violence is inbred and natural. Would that not mean that violence should not always be suppressed, that perhaps violent acts are actually beneficial to the evolutionary process? The implications to a culture should be self-evident.

There is a true difference in mindsets between adherents of the two competing origin paradigms. Christians need to understand that the postmodern culture is being brutally logical by condoning sin since there is no such thing as sin if evolution is true. Christians need to understand the real issue behind the competing origin paradigms.

The Real Issue

Authority. Who decides what is good and bad? What do we use as a yardstick for determining right and wrong? What are acceptable cultural norms, mores, and values? What is truth? The paradoxical tension between Christ and culture is the tension that results over a question of authority. There are two fundamental answers to the question of authority. Ultimate authority is derived from ultimate origins.

For a culture based upon an evolutionary paradigm, there is no "outside" authority. The famous Sophist dictum, "Man is the measure of all things," is apropos to the evolution model. In his debates with creationists, the evolutionist William Provine states that consistent Darwinism implies "No life after death; No ultimate foundation for ethics; No ultimate meaning for life; No free will."[18]

For a culture based upon a creation paradigm, God is the ultimate Authority. God created humans for a unique purpose. He has the authority to set the standards of cultural conduct. For many Christians this is obvious, yet they fail to understand the deep root of cultural conflicts. Not everyone shares the same foundation! How often do Christians assume that the answer to many cultural issues is a philosophically soft one? In other words, "If I just explain to them that God says abortion is murder, then they'll change their minds and clean up their act." This line of reasoning falsely assumes that everyone shares the same philosophical foundation, based upon a common view of origins. Christians sometimes have difficulty dealing with cultural clashes because the problems are philosophically hard ones. In other words, Christ and the world do not share the same foundation regarding ultimate origins. Communicating at the "issue" level will have little impact on the prevailing attitude of a culture since it does not address the foundational issues of origins and authority. Truly, as Christians, we find Christ and culture in paradox.

In our postmodern, humanistic culture, man is the measure of all things. And why not? It is perfectly logical to take such a position if evolution is true. An evolutionary foundation followed to its rational conclusion implies that human beings are the sole source of authority in culture. If people are the result of a blind, natural, purposeless process, then we subject our culture to no outside forces.

Jeremy Rifkin stated the evolutionary conclusion eloquently in *Algeny*:

> We no longer feel ourselves to be guests in someone else's home and therefore obliged to make our behavior conform with a set of preexisting cosmic rules. It is our creation now. We make the rules. We establish the parameters of reality. We create the world. And because we do, we no longer feel beholden to outside forces. We no longer have to justify our behavior, for we are the architects of the universe. We are responsible for nothing outside ourselves, for we are the kingdom, the power, and the glory forever.[19]

The Humanist Manifesto affirms the following among its fifteen tenets:

> First: Religious humanists regard the universe as self-existing and not created. Second: Humanism believes that man is a part of nature and that he has emerged as the result of a continuous process.[20]

The foundation of religious humanism, then, is evolution. The evolution model has a profound impact upon a humanistic culture by denying the existence of any outside authority (God) and allowing humans to make the rules. The terrifying question is, of course, which humans get to make the rules? The cultural impact of that question is clearly seen in postmodern human behavior.

The Ultimate Issue

Origin paradigms not only have an impact on culture, but they have an impact on the very nature of Christianity itself.

As this chapter has shown, Christians sometimes incorrectly assume that the answer to the "culture clash" is a philosophically soft one. That is, the problem of various evils found in modern culture can be solved by presenting God's Law. A Christian might argue against homosexuality by citing God's prohibition of it in Leviticus and demonstrating how homosexuality corrupts God's created order. Sometimes Christians are heard to say, "If only they knew what God says about homosexuality, they would change their evil ways." The person arguing from a philosophically soft position believes that education is the answer. Education from a sound biblical perspective is an answer, but only for someone who shares a biblical worldview, rooted in the creation paradigm.

This approach is inadequate outside of Christian circles as it does not address the fundamental worldview assumptions involved. A person who has rejected the creation paradigm has rejected the creator God. Someone with an evolutionary foundation has a completely different worldview than a Christian. People with evolutionary foundations operate with wholly different mindsets than Christians, since their thinking is radically opposite from ultimate first principles. Presenting God's Law to a person who does not believe in a god will have very little impact on that person's behavior. The answer to the "culture clash" is a philosophically hard one. No change can take place in people's behavior, unless they experience a radical paradigm shift!

What difference do evolution and creation make? Does it really matter what I believe about origins? Hopefully the reader is able to understand the foundational difference paradigms of origins make in a person's behavior.

The ultimate issue for a Christian, though, is the reality of Jesus Christ. Christ is fundamental to Christianity, but creation is foundational. Christians do not always realize the foundational importance of the creation paradigm to the message of Jesus Christ. However, subscribers to the evolution paradigm do understand the connection between creation and the Christ. That is precisely why they attack the creation model. It is understood that to destroy the structure of Christianity, there is a need to destroy the foundation of creation. The humanist G. Richard Bozarth expressed the sentiment well when he said:

Christianity has fought, still fights, and will continue to fight science to the desperate end over evolution, because evolution destroys utterly and finally the very reason Jesus' earthly life was supposedly made necessary. Destroy Adam and Eve and the original sin, and in the rubble you will find the sorry remains of the Son of God. If Jesus was not the redeemer who died for our sins, and this is what evolution means, then Christianity is nothing.[21]

Evolution indeed destroys the purpose of Christ's redemptive act. If creation is not true, then Jesus is a fraud and His work is meaningless.

But thanks be to God that Jesus Christ is the way, the truth, and the life. He is not only the Redeemer of the world but the Creator of the world also. The truth of the creation foundation assures us that Jesus is indeed the Savior and we can derive ultimate meaning from His redemptive and creative acts!

As Jesus' parable about the two builders in Luke 6 demonstrates, a building needs a strong foundation. Worldviews and cultures are built on the foundation of origin paradigms. The foundational issue of origins has a profound impact on culture as reflected in human behavior. The paradoxical tension of Christ beside culture will not be resolved in this present age. But once understood, Christians will find the postmodern culture slightly less perplexing. This knowledge will allow Christians to develop an effective strategy for interacting with and witnessing to those who do not share a creation foundation.

Gary Locklair is Chair of Computer Science at
Concordia University Wisconsin and a member of
the Board of Directors for the Creation Research Society.

Bibliography

Behe, Michael. *Darwin's Black Box: The Biochemical Challenge to Evolution*. New York: The Free Press, 1996.
  Behe demonstrates how the complexity of living things argues strongly against an evolutionary origin for life.

Geisler, Norman and J. Kerby Anderson. *Origin Science: A Proposal for the Creation-Evolution Controversy*. Grand Rapids, MI: Baker Book House, 1987.

Geisler and Anderson outline the concepts of origin science and explain
why origin paradigms are not empirical science and therefore can not be
proven.

Gentry, Robert. *Creation's Tiny Mystery*. Knoxville, TN: Earth
Science Associates, 1986.
Gentry describes his work with Polonium-218 and demonstrates how it is
an evidence for the creation model.

Gish, Duane. *Evolution: The Fossils Still Say NO!* El Cajon, CA:
Institute for Creation Research, 1995.
Gish shows that the historical fossil record is in accord with the creation
model of origins.

Johnson, Phillip. *Darwin on Trial*. Washington, DC: Regnery
Gateway, 1991.
Johnson examines the evidence of evolution from a lawyer's perspective
and finds it wanting.

Lubenow, Marvin. *Bones of Contention: A Creationist Assessment of
Human Fossils*. Grand Rapids, MI: Baker Book House, 1992.
Lubenow demonstrates that the scientific evidence points to a
creation origin for human beings.

Morland, J. P., editor. *The Creation Hypothesis: Scientific Evidences
for an Intelligent Designer*. Downers Grove, IL: InterVarsity Press,
1994.
A panel of scholars assert there is scientific evidence for the creation
paradigm.

Morris, Henry. *The Long War against God*. Grand Rapids, MI: Baker
Book House, 1989.
Morris demonstrates the deleterious effect of evolution on religion,
ethics, and morals.

Taylor, Ian. *In the Minds of Men: Darwin and the New World Order*.
Revised Edition. Toronto, Canada: TFE Publishing, 1987.
Taylor demonstrates the humanistic origin of evolution.

Wilder-Smith, A. E. *The Scientific Alternative to Neo-Darwinian
Evolutionary Theory: Information Sources and Structures*. Costa
Mesa, CA: TWFT Publishers, 1987.
Wilder-Smith shows how information theory points to a creation origin.

Williams, Emmett, editor. *Thermodynamics and the Development of
Order*. St. Joseph, MO: Creation Research Society Books, 1981.
A panel of scholars demonstrates the scientific validity of the
creation model.

Zacharias, Ravi. *Can Man Live Without God?* Dallas, TX: Word, 1994.

Zacharias demonstrates how the reality of God's existence matters in all arenas of life.

Notes

[1] A readable translation of the Roman's work is R. E. Latham's published by Penguin and revised by John Godwin in 1994.

[2] Ian Taylor's book, *In the Minds of Men*, demonstrates the humanistic origin and reasoning behind the evolution model of origins.

[3] See the excellent discussion on the different kinds of science in *Origin Science*.

[4] See the discussion of thermodynamics in *Thermodynamics and the Development of Order*.

[5] Gentry's work is described in *Creation's Tiny Mystery*.

[6] Information Theory is discussed in Wilder-Smith's and Behe's works.

[7]Reference the bibliography for many fine works on the creation model. A good starting point might be *The Creation Hypothesis*.

[8] It is worth noting that the claim that ontogeny recapitulates phylogeny, although considered a law (the biogenetic law) in the nineteenth century, is no longer asserted in such an unqualified way by evolutionary biologists. Nonetheless, such ideas, since they are entrenched in popularizations of evolution, continue to have considerable influence on culture.—Ed.

[9] Schneour, Elie. "Life Doesn't Begin, It Continues," *Los Angeles Times*. 29 January 1989.

[10] Dennett, Daniel. *Darwin's Dangerous Idea: Evolution and the Meanings of Life*. New York, NY: Touchstone, 1995. Dennett is one of the leading proponents of Neo-Darwinianism today.

[11] Sanger, Margaret. "No Healthy Race without Birth Control," *Physical Culture*. March 1921.

[12] Smit, Jacob. "In the Beginning: Homosexuality and Evolution," *International Northwest Guide Magazine*, Issue 19 (August 1987).

[13] Money, John. "Agenda and Crescenda of the Kinsey Scale," *Homosexuality/Heterosexuality: Concepts of Sexual Orientation*, New York: Oxford University Press, 1990.

[14] Ruse, Michael. "Evolutionary Theory and Christian Ethics: Are They in Harmony?" *Zygon*, Vol. 29. March 1994.

[15] Ham, Ken. *The Genesis Solution*. Grand Rapids, MI: Baker Book House, 1988.

[16] Osborn, H. F. "The Evolution of Human Races," *Natural History*, Jan/Feb 1926.

[17] Letters to the editor, *Milwaukee Journal Sentinel*, 31 January 1998.

[18] Provine has debated creationist Phillip Johnson on several occasions. He made these statements in a debate at Stanford University on 30 April 1994. See *Darwinism: Science or Naturalistic Philosophy*. Colorado Springs, CO: Access Research Network, 1996.

[19] Rifkin, Jeremy. *Algeny*. New York, NY: Viking, 1983.

[20] American Humanist Association, *Humanist Manifesto I*, 1933. Contained in *Humanist Manifestoes I and II*. Buffalo, NY: Prometheus Books, 1973.

[21] Bozarth, G. Richard. "The Meaning of Evolution" in *American Atheist*. February 1978.

Part III

The Church

and

Church-Based Education

in Culture

11

The Transcultural Nature of Liturgical Worship

Timothy Maschke

Introduction

"If the stupid Germans can learn the liturgy, anyone can." That comment by an Anglican medievalist awakened me from the parochial stupor of believing the inaccurate, though oft repeated, axiom that Lutheran liturgical worship is Germanic. As I began to muse over whether there was a cultural bias in our Lutheran liturgical worship, I asked myself several questions. Among them was the following: Is liturgical worship a culturally-bound relic of the past which needs to be thrown out for more contemporary expressions of the faith or is it something higher, grander, even elevating? In my pursuits and studies I discovered that "the claim that Lutheran music and liturgy is Germanic"[1] was indeed false. But, I discovered something even more eye-opening: liturgical worship, particularly as practiced in the context of confessionally Lutheran congregations, is powerfully transcultural. This present chapter is an attempt to highlight my discoveries on the peculiar relationship of worship to culture and culture to worship in the context of Lutheran liturgical worship, theology, and practice.

Initially, I will point out that although Lutheran worship is liturgical, it has deep roots in the broader catholic-evangelical history of Christian worship. In the context of our larger topic of the relationship of Christianity to culture, I discovered that liturgical worship creates its own (new?) Christian culture. Liturgical worship in general, and Lutheran liturgical worship in particular, brings together a variety of cultural traditions. A key reason for this is that liturgical worship offers opportunities for a variety of cultural expressions within our ever-renewing Gospel communities. However, rather than legislating or coercing or even manipulating culturaltransformation, I rediscovered that it is the centrality of this transcultural Gospel in Lutheran worship which transforms the cultures from which the various worshippers come. Therefore, Lutheran liturgical worship is and must remain conscientiously transcultural in the most profound senses.

1. Lutheran Worship Is Liturgical

In comparison to most other Protestant denominations, Lutherans are identified with "liturgical" denominations. For instance, in his detailed book on world religions, Theodore Ludwig states,

> Liturgical denominations include the Roman Catholic, Eastern Orthodox, Anglican and Lutheran churches; non-liturgical groups would be Baptists, Quakers, and the variety of free evangelical churches. Somewhere in between are such groups as the Methodists, the Calvinist (Presbyterian, Reformed) churches, who do not emphasize the traditional liturgies and sacraments, but do follow commonly accepted forms of worship.[2]

Because of its catholic roots and the greater significance placed upon the sacraments, Lutheranism is most comfortably associated with the historically liturgical churches of Christendom.

This Lutheran comfort with liturgy is rooted in its catholic and ecumenical tradition. This tradition is most evident in the words penned by Philip Melanchthon in the Apology to the Augsburg Confession, which clearly affirms the Lutheran stance toward the liturgy. Confessional Lutherans still subscribe to his statement:

> we do not abolish the Mass but religiously keep and defend it. In our churches Mass is celebrated every Sunday and on the festivals when the sacrament is offered to those who wish for it after they have been examined and absolved. We keep traditional liturgical forms, such as the order of the lessons, prayers, vestments, etc.[3]

Notice how the liturgical emphasis in Lutheranism is connected with the sacramental understanding of worship. Another Lutheran author more recently described the liturgy as a vehicle through which a dynamic dialogue occurs between God and His people.[4] God comes to

His people through the means of grace and they respond in worship. Thus, the strong emphasis on Word and Sacrament is underscored and encouraged by the use of liturgy in Lutheran congregations.

Another reason why Lutherans appropriated the traditional liturgical worship of Luther's day was that liturgical worship enables people to participate. Martin Luther strongly encouraged the use of hymns in worship as an expression and manifestation of the doctrine of the "priesthood of all believers." Liturgical worship was not for Luther, nor is it for Lutherans, a vehicle for entertaining people, nor a rote routine mindlessly (and heartlessly) followed by the worshippers, but instead provides an opportunity for people to hear God's Word of promise and express appreciations for the blessings received from a great and gracious giver—God. This pattern is not a Germanic need nor a culturally rooted expression, but a biblically evangelical opportunity and privilege which God gives to His people.

An interesting phenomenon which is being seen more and more in recent years is that those Protestant churches that traditionally have been non-liturgical, or even anti-liturgical, are becoming attracted to liturgical worship. Several leaders of Campus Crusade for Christ (not a known liturgical organization) joined the Apostolic Orthodox Church because of its liturgical structure and historically Christian roots. Recently an Assemblies of God pastor visited with me and spoke of his own movement away from (in his own words) the "shallowness" of Pentecostal free worship along with the commensurate "deception" of many evangelical mega-churches.

Many people in our society today are attracted to and focus on spiritual journeys in a multitude of directions—most often in the form of human attempts to reach up to God. On the other hand, Lutheran worship is liturgical because God's gracious encounter with us through Word and Sacraments is central to our Lutheran spirituality. Over and over, Luther repeated the need for good liturgical structure so that the people would grow through their contact with the Gospel. For example, he wrote in his German Mass:

> Such orders [of worship] are needed for those who are still becoming Christians or need to be strengthened. . . . They are essential especially for the immature and the young who must be trained and educated in the Scripture and God's Word daily so that they may become familiar with the Bible, grounded, well versed, and skilled in it, ready to defend their

faith and in due time to teach others and to increase the kingdom of Christ.[5]

Luther here recognized the significant educational dimension of worship, a tool for discipling and preparing evangelists and apologists of the Christian faith. Worship is to be in the service of extending God's kingdom. Worship is not the theological equivalent of "pooled ignorance" in education, but is a God-given means for communicating the biblical truths to the world. Therefore, Lutherans appreciate and celebrate God's incarnate love in Christ and His gracious condescension to us as they continue to utilize the historic liturgical forms of worship.

2. Liturgical Worship Has Deep Roots in Christian History

Throughout the centuries, Christian worship has been predominantly liturgical. As we look at this concept, we need to have a clear definition of what is meant by "liturgy." According to The Lutheran Church—Missouri Synod's Commission on Worship, liturgy is "the design or pattern through which the congregation gathers to hear and receive anew the Gospel promise in Word and Sacrament, and then to respond collectively to the abundant gifts and gracious presence of the Triune God."[6] As one evangelical author put it, "Liturgy is logical. . . . The Scriptural pattern of revelation and response is followed and emphasized."[7]

Christian worship has always had some kind of a structure. St. Paul exhorted the Corinthian congregation to do things "decently and in order" (1 Corinthians 14:40). The early records of Christian practices in the time of the apostolic fathers indicates a desire to follow set patterns of worship so that aberrations and heresies would not seep into the foundations of the nascent Christian communities.[8]

Throughout the centuries, the Christian church has retained a sense of structure in its worship that is the basic liturgy. The liturgical historian John Harper has noted that "in spite of the constant flux and variation, it is possible to perceive six principle phases in the history of worship in the Western Church."[9] He delineates the first five centuries as the formative period, followed by several adaptive centuries as Christianity spread and adapted to the outer limits of the Roman

Empire particularly under the dominant influence of monasticism. During the eighth and ninth centuries there was a movement toward a codified (medieval) Roman-Frankish rite under Charlemagne. A unitive period followed in which the "late medieval Roman" rite of the twelfth century curia was distributed throughout Christendom by mendicant friars, especially the Franciscans in the thirteenth century. With the Council of Trent's response to the Protestant Reformations, a normative period was established in Catholicism, although a kind of confessional individualism marked most Protestant services. During the last half of the twentieth century western Christianity experienced a period of renewal of the major western liturgical traditions with a greater diversification and multiplicity of expression.

Thus, the liturgy is not some stagnant pool, but a living stream, constantly forming and being formed by Christian believers who desire to express their faith and to worship their Savior. In his work "Concerning the Order of Public Worship," Luther wrote: "The service now in common use everywhere goes back to genuine Christian beginnings, as does the office of preaching."[10] Lutheran liturgical worship follows a great tradition that extends long before the Reformation and will continue long after we are here—if the Lord does not return to take us to heaven tomorrow. This tradition leads us all the way back to the Scriptures and the Words of our Lord who invited us to worship God "in Spirit and in truth" (John 4:24).

3. Liturgical Worship Brings Together a Variety of Cultural Traditions

America has increasingly been described as a pluralistic society. There is no one culture which can claim dominance.[11] Therefore, it is imperative that Christians understand the great blessing of liturgical worship to bring together these pluralistic peoples into a particular unity of faith. This is true because Christians have always recognized and experienced diversity, yet there is a higher unity that also can be realized in worship. This is the unique harmony in diversity which Christians can experience in corporate worship. In many ways it is a more valid expression of unity than the American claim of *E pluribus unum*.

In the past, the Lutheran church has utilized the term *concordia* to describe this concept of external unity and harmony of diversity. *Concordia* refers to the outward expression of an internal reality. Such *concordia* is based upon a unity (*unitas*) which Christians find through faith in Christ Jesus alone. We may not always see the *concordia*, and so it is something to set as a goal. *Concordia* expresses itself most obviously in the working together of polyphonic and polyethnic and polycultural melodies and rhythms (to use a musical analogy) into a miraculous symphony of worship and life.

A look at the hymn selections of several recent Lutheran hymnals, for example, will show hymns with Hebrew, Greek, Latin, African, African-American, African Angoni, American folk, Basque, Danish, Dutch, English, Finnish, French, Gaelic, German, Irish, Israeli, Jewish, Norwegian, Polish, Russian, Silesian folk, Spanish, Swedish, Swiss, Slovak, and Welsh cultural sources. Lutheran worship and hymnody reflects the eschatological depiction of unity without uniformity portrayed most profoundly in the prophetic Book of Revelation by St. John the Divine. In the pages of the Book of Revelation, significantly in chapter seven, we find an eschatological presentation of people from every nation, tribe, and tongue who have come together in praise of their great and gracious God who created, saved, and sanctified them.

Although somewhat misleading in many of its details, David Luecke's book, *The Other Story*, is correct in one significant and pertinent way. He underscores the great diversity of expression that is possible within Lutheranism as it seeks to bring together all the people of God into the communion of saints as the Church on earth joins the hosts of heaven.

A Lutheran author writing on "Liturgy and Evangelism," in *Lutheran Worship: History and Practice*, says the following:

> It is a great mistake to think that the traditional forms of the Lutheran liturgy represent 16th-century Saxon (or Swedish, or Norwegian, etc.) culture, and must now be Americanized, Africanized, or what have you. . . . It did not originate in Wittenberg, or in Uppsala, or for that matter in Rome. Whenever the orthodox church is planted in a new country or culture, its liturgy must not arise "from scratch," or by happenstance, but it is to be lovingly adapted to confess the new church's continuity with the "deep structures" of the pure Gospel throughout space/time.[12]

In that sense, we can say that Lutheran worship is not only transcultural but also trans-temporal—we worship not only with those around us, but with the hosts of heaven. The great liturgical hymn of the Church, the *Te Deum Laudamus* of Matins,[13] and the Proper Prefaces of the Communion Liturgy express this unity of worship "with angels and archangels and with all the company of heaven."

The content of our worship resources is drawn from many times and from many places. There is no one culture that can claim exclusivity to Lutheran worship practices. Lutheran worship invites continuing cultural inclusion in its liturgical structures.

4. Liturgical Worship Creates Its Own (New?) Christian Culture

In an earlier chapter of this book, Angus Menuge noted H. Richard Niebuhr's definition of culture as something "artificial"—"language, habits, ideas, customs, social organization, inherited artifacts, technical processes, and values."[14] Yet Niebuhr identified such a viewpoint as embodying "the world" from the perspective of the New Testament writers, who understood those social elements as being alien from a Christian's world view. The issue of which culture is dominant becomes an issue.

Culture is always something that is passed down from generation to generation. In a sense it is a form of tradition. As the Church continues to hand down the central Gospel message of salvation by grace through faith in Christ's redemptive work, its tradition will be good and beneficial. Yet, such a tradition will also be divergent from that of contemporary society. Marva Dawn has shown this very clearly when she distinguishes between the church's worship and our cultural setting of our society at the end of the twentieth century.[15] There is a culture *surrounding* our worship as well as the culture *of* worship. This distinction needs to be maintained, and she claims, even emphasized, for the sake of retaining the Gospel's faith-empowering message.

Liturgy's relationship with culture has always been in flux. Throughout the centuries the Church has struggled with avoiding two poles, cultural capitulation and cultural irrelevancy. Frank Senn has written much in the area of worship and recognizes the cultural dilemma faced by the church over the centuries—especially how various cultural accretions have been identified with Christianity—yet how the Church has also been able to transform culture through its liturgical worship.[16]

We have already mentioned how Luther approached worship as a teaching tool and a proclamational opportunity. Thus, he revised the established Roman Mass of his day with his *Formula Missae et Communionis* in 1523 as a purification of Christian worship. Three years later, he introduced a German-language service, *Deutsche Messe und Ordnung Gottesdienst*,[17] so that the "simple and the young [may] . . . be educated in the Scriptures and God's Word."[18] This service emphasized congregational participation in the liturgy through the use of the vernacular and congregational singing. Through such participation, a Christian culture was being taught, practiced, and lived.

Following Luther there has always been much variety in the specific forms of worship,[19] yet the basic "catholic" structure remained constant in Lutheranism. Particularly, the emphasis upon the Gospel-content of Word and Sacrament remained a central feature of Lutheran worship experiences.

In America, Henry Melchior Muhlenberg was a prominent leader in early Lutheranism. After serving many years in various colonial congregations and becoming a leader in American Lutheranism, he wrote a letter to his constituents. In it he said, "It would be a most delightful and advantageous thing if all the Evangelical Lutheran congregations in North America were united with one another, if they all used the same order of service."[20] Over the next several decades, Lutheran leaders worked toward a Common Service and in 1888 produced a text for use among English-speaking congregations in America, reflecting "the consensus of the pure Lutheran liturgies of the sixteenth century."[21] This desire to bring conformity in worship practices to American Lutherans was not some legalistic attempt to control the multitude of new immigrants, but aimed to serve as a unifying resource for a common confession of faith.

It must be admitted that there will always be those who feel "inside" and those who feel "outside" of the church, or more specifically, the local congregation. Some of that is proper, since some people are not yet people of faith. But for others we need to utilize the spiritual gift of hospitality through our use of ritual. Patrick Kiefert has done much research and teaching in this area and I commend his little booklet, *Worship and Evangelism: A Pastoral Handbook*, where he underscores the importance of ritual for forming a sense of community.[22] His experience as a visitor in Germany began his recognition of the benefits of ritual and hospitality.

> . . . Public worship is the single most important factor in active church participation for the first-time visitor as well as the vast majority of members of any congregation. . . . Many who recognize the importance of public worship in a vibrant congregation and of effective evangelism decide to make radical changes in their public worship. . . . This approach, although it meets with some success, is not entirely sound. . . . When this approach succeeds, it does so primarily because it rediscovers ancient wisdom about public worship. . . . The beginnings of Christian liturgy around the Lord's table emphasized hospitality to the stranger. . . . The gospel's vision affirms impersonal, public interaction, since the gospel is primarily a public event. It is a public announcement of God's word. It opens the private to the public and builds a bridge between them. . . . In short, ritual, which according to the intimate society is the enemy of healthy human interaction, is instead a key ingredient to good public worship.[23]

By recognizing and properly utilizing ritual in the setting of a worshipping congregation, the church expands its expression of the inclusivity of the Gospel. In a sense, we could argue that with no liturgy there is no sense of "home," so that although outsiders initially may be more easily assimilated into a non-liturgical setting, they continue to feel "homeless."[24] The liturgy, however, provides a comfortable home, once the newcomer is integrated into the congregation's life.

Language provides a connection with and a distinguishing factor of a culture. We often speak of cultures by the languages with which the culture is connected—American, Chinese, French, German, Spanish, etc. In our computer age there is also a continued awareness of the use of jargon in various subcultures, which gives identity to that subculture as well as facilitates communication within that culture. Liturgical language is a peculiar kind of language. The liturgy provides us with a biblical vocabulary that will influence our lives. Philip H. Pfatteicher says the following about the vocabulary of worship:

> The language of the liturgy is not poetry. . . . The liturgy is prose, or perhaps more precisely, not quite prose either but a third kind of

language—ritual—in which words and gestures are joined in a flowing, moving, suggestive action which celebrates and proclaims the central affirmations of the Christian faith. The wholeness of words and music and movement meets and involves the wholeness of human life—mind, body, and spirit.[25]

This is the grammar of faith, the vocabulary and the communication structures by which we confess our wholistic biblical faith and express through enactment our incarnational Christian life.

Similarly, the Church year parallels yet counters the contemporary culture.[26] Our religious holidays are set in stark contrast to our secular (and often pagan) environment, yet they parallel them closely. Easter celebrates the resurrection of our Lord, while the images of the pagan festivities of springtime fertility are also evident in Easter eggs and rabbits. The Advent season is a time of solemn preparation for Christmas, which radically contradicts the frenetic shopping season of our corporate entrepreneurial society. The church year was designed to draw the believer from the culture of the day into the culture of the Church, to a renewed sense of time and to an elevated and eternal sense of life.

We know that cultures are passed down from generation to generation. The liturgy is also a kind of teaching tool for future generations of believers. Luther recognized this and stressed the benefits of repetition for teaching[27]—as do contemporary Wall Street advertisers in television commercials.[28] He emphasized that we are to be teaching our theology through our worship. One author on worship suggested that liturgical services should be viewed as apprenticeships for members to learn and understand and experience important relationships with Jesus Christ. [29]

The question we need to ask is this: "Whose culture or theology are we teaching?" Peter Brunner wisely suggests the following:

The Reformation has demonstrated impressively that far-reaching dogmatic decisions are involved in the manner in which we appraise the form of worship and especially in the concrete form in which we conduct worship. Consequently, there must be a doctrine of the form of worship. The task of such a doctrine is not to fix the order of worship in detail; it is, rather, to establish the critical boundaries within which every concrete form must be contained, lest the purity of the Gospel be impaired.[30]

Worship is affected by the teaching of the church and the teaching of the church should affect the doctrine. I use the following two in my worship classes to illustrate the contrasting, yet complementary, quality of our worship and our teachings: "How we worship indicates what we believe!" and "As people believe, so they worship!" What this means is that there is an intimate connection between the two.[31] Our worship practices must reflect the theology we proclaim. And just as significantly, what we do in our worship will affect what we believe.

This close connection between worship and doctrine is perhaps most evident in the Roman Catholic Church. In 1950, the teaching that Mary had gone bodily into heaven was declared to be an official doctrine of the Roman Catholic Church. Many Lutherans wondered how that could ever have happened. The fact is that for generations, Catholics were praying to Mary as one who was in heaven. The doctrine was merely expressing what many Catholics had held to be true in their personal devotional lives. Their worship or devotional life thus affected (created) this doctrine.

Luther, similarly, made some changes in the worship practices of his congregation in order to communicate more clearly the centrality of the Gospel word. He knew that the Gospel created a new Christian culture. If there are to be "new creations" in Christ, then there will be a new culture created by those gathered around Word and Sacrament to receive and respond.

5. Lutheran Liturgical Worship Offers Opportunities for a Variety of Cultural Expressions within the New Christian Culture

Medical doctors and nurses tell us that our skeletons are fairly similar, yet the outside—our flesh color, fat content, hair quality, etc.—is very different. Individually we appear in a multitude of shapes, sizes, colors, and styles—not to mention the fact that our clothing selections add even greater diversity. That image may help us understand our liturgy better. The liturgical structure of worship provides us with a marvelous framework or skeleton on which to hang the substance of our theology and the variety of our cultural expressions.

We have already noted that Lutheran liturgical worship has a long tradition of drawing from a multitude of cultural expressions and sources. Listen to this description of an early Christian service:

> After the entrance song (Introit) ended with the "Glory Be to the Father," the litany ("Lord, have mercy") was followed by the worship leader singing the hymn, "Glory to God in the Highest." He then greeted the people with "Peace be with you," and the words, "Let us pray," as he led the Collect. After an appointed reading, a singer stood up with his music book to sing the Gradual. Then another reader would read the Gospel and the Service of the Word was abruptly brought to an end. (There was no sermon.) The second part of the service opened with a Prayer of the Community and the gathering of the offerings. The worship leader, after saying, "The Lord be with you," called out to the assembly, "Lift up your hearts," and received in reply the acclamation, "We lift them to the Lord." He continued with a prayer which included the Words of Institution and concluded with the Lord's Prayer. The communion then began. After the clergy were communed, the bread was placed into the hands of the faithful and they put it in their mouths. A prayer was finally said at the end of the distribution and an assisting minister called out, "*Ite missa est*," to which the congregation replied, "Thanks be to God."[32]

Reread this paragraph and ask yourself how similar this service sounds to the service you attended this past Sunday. What is striking is that this description comes from the eighth century. The general form of the liturgy is a structure that has remained relatively the same over a thousand years.

The structure of the liturgy offers opportunities for diversity. The basic form of the liturgy has two parts—the Service of the Word and the Service of the Sacrament. Over the centuries these have been called the Service of the Catechumens and the Service of the Faithful or the ante-Communion and the Communion Services. Whatever they are called, the structure has remained remarkably consistent. Part of the reason for this is that the first part of the service, the Word, prepares the worshipper for the second, the Sacrament. With only the Sacrament, worshippers would miss the Gospel message in all its beauty. Without the first part of the service, that is the Word of Law and Gospel, the believers would participate in the Sacrament without understanding the full blessings of God's gracious presence and gift of forgiveness, life, and salvation. Both parts of the service are important in the structure of worship. The basic pattern of the liturgy is not some kind of a rigid relic from the past, but a solid framework on which to dress the diversity of our Christian community.

When looking at this structure in more detail, there are several key places where cultural dimensions and diversity can be manifested. Consider, for example, the Entrance rite in the Lutheran liturgical tradition. Whether one uses a Psalm, Entrance hymn, or Introit depends upon the cultural context of the congregation. Whether there is a procession or not is also culturally determined (although sometimes the liturgical calendar may provide some encouragement for a procession, such as the celebration of Palm Sunday). The Hymn of Praise for which two selections are available in *Lutheran Worship* may be adapted to a variety of praise hymns and songs—including many songs from the ubiquitous contemporary songbooks. In the Service of the Word, the readings and sermon are set, yet offer clear opportunities for some cultural expressions and diversity. Significantly, the Offertory is one place where many congregations could utilize more cultural sensitivity. Some African Lutheran congregations have the whole congregation process to the front of the church as they clap their hands to their native drums during the time of offering. Other possibilities include encouraging children of various ages to present their musical offerings to the Lord during this time of the service.

Similarly, in the Service of the Sacrament, two places could be utilized to express cultural particularity. The activities during the Distribution of the Lord's Body and Blood could span complete silence to chorale motets to individual solos to instrumental presentations. Finally, our response to the Eucharist need not be limited to a post-communion canticle (actually, the practice of singing Simeon's Song, the *Nunc Dimittis*, is a uniquely Lutheran element in the Service of Holy Communion). Many other responses could be used to express the thankfulness of our hearts and lives to God's gracious gift of Himself in the sacrament of Christ's Body and Blood.

In another sense, the liturgy provides us with the "bar lines" in a musical score. We don't need musical notations if we all sing exactly the same, or if we sing simple songs with little depth, but if we want to sing together in harmony we need some guidelines. The Gospel is always the central melody of faith. But the potential of cultural harmonies are many and diverse, albeit some can be discordant and in some situations, clearly inappropriate and disruptive.

The liturgy forms the structure for new cultural expressions. Consider the following. A small Lutheran congregation in Kentucky offers a summer outdoor service utilizing local Bluegrass instrumentalists. A Jamaican drummer provides rhythmic beats on his bamboo drum for a funeral dirge in a New York congregation. A Catholic congregation in Wisconsin celebrates with a Polka Mass. A university chapel service uses songs specifically composed by students from the school of music with a variety of student-played instruments. This is all possible within the context of the basic structure of the liturgy.

Sometimes American Christians express a Eurocentric idea by separating the sacred and the secular. The black historian, Albert J. Raboteau, points this out when he writes the following:

> Categorizing sacred and secular elements is of limited usefulness in discussing the spirituals because the slaves, following African and biblical tradition, believed that the supernatural continually impinged on the natural, that divine action constantly took place within the lives of men, in the past, present and future.[33]

A recent "buzz" word in cultural awareness is "inculturation." The Roman Catholic Church has officially designated the process of bringing culture into their worship with the Italian term, *aggiornamento*. This is the idea that cultures grow and change as they come into contact with other cultures. To separate culture from life is to make the Christian faith something irrelevant and inconsequential. Just the opposite is true.

The Christian faith is an important element for all cultures. Integrating other cultural expressions of the Christian faith into local congregation's liturgy can only come when we strive for integrity, that is, having the whole body "fit together." St. Paul uses this image in Ephesians 4 as he encourages the church to utilize the variety of gifts God has given, "so that the body of Christ may be built up until we all reach unity in the faith and in the knowledge of the Son of God and become mature, attaining to the whole measure of the fullness of Christ" (Ephesians 4:12-13). The integrity of the body depends upon the skeleton and a body cannot be "built up" without a strong skeleton upon which the various parts are "fitted together" and finely dressed for service.

The reason that Lutheran liturgical worship appears to be Germanic at times is that Lutherans have recognized the freedom within the liturgical tradition to express cultural particularities—such as German chorales, but also African-American spirituals, and Irish folk songs—within a larger unity of faith.

6. The Transcultural Gospel Is Central in Lutheran Worship

The integration with integrity mentioned in the previous section of this chapter comes only through the centrality of the Gospel. Luther's Smalcald Article on "The Gospel" (iii, IV) suggests that there are various forms of the Gospel which provide for greater integration into the life of the believer—the spoken word, baptism, communion, keys, and "finally, through the mutual conversation and consolation of believers."[34]

Lutheran worship is clearly oriented around Word and Sacrament; in both of these the Gospel emphasis is certainly preeminent. The Word is always centered in the message of Christ's life, death, and resurrection that provides our justification and reconciliation with the Father. The Sacrament is a visible means of that same grace, which assures us of the same forgiveness accomplished by Christ on the cross. In all of our worship, our focus is on God, not on ourselves.

As a result, central to Lutheran liturgy is the sermon and essential for Lutheran preaching is the double-edged preaching of Law and Gospel. Several years ago a book on worship by two evangelical Christians was entitled, *Worship, the Missing Jewel.* While the content of the book was good, the title was certainly not Lutheran, but it does provide an illustration for this chapter. For Lutherans, the jewel is not worship, but the Gospel. The Gospel is a precious jewel which is always in need of an appropriate setting—not something distracting and overly gaudy, yet not something cheap or tawdry. The jewel of the Gospel must always be placed into a liturgical setting which communicates the beauty, truth, and power of the Gospel-centered word.

The liturgy also provides a vital vehicle for moving the church out into the world with the Gospel. Because the liturgy is scripturally-based and Gospel-centered, those who hear the Word will be moved to follow Christ's commission to make disciples of all nations. The double emphasis on Word and Sacrament provides food for the soul as well as Gospel-motivation for Christian action. Through the liturgy, believers recognize their sinfulness, hear God's gracious word of Absolution, respond with praises, hear again selections of God's message to His people through the Scripture readings and an exposition in the sermon, respond with a bold profession of faith, offer their firstfruits of money, petition God for the future, and receive the benefits of Christ's work in the Sacrament, and thus are readied for the next week of service in His kingdom. Through it all, it is the very purpose of the liturgy's Gospel emphasis to transform us, to change us, to show us what God has in mind for us so that we can carry the mind of Christ out into the world.

We could even say that the liturgy can be used to train us with the proper words to use as we evangelize throughout the week. Perhaps it is time, once again, to practice "creedal evangelism," the utilization of the Apostles' Creed as an outline for witnessing and personal evangelism. One of the significant functions of the creeds is to provide a succinct outline of the faith for easy profession. This is using the liturgy's Gospel center for the extension of Christ's kingdom.

7. Lutheran Liturgical Worship Is Transcultural

Lutheran Worship: History and Practice said it succinctly: "The liturgy is already transcultural, or cross-cultural."[35] Because the liturgy has its roots in the history of the church, because it brings together a wide variety of cultural traditions, because liturgy creates its own new and Christian culture, because the structure of the liturgy provides opportunities for a variety of cultures to express themselves, and because the transcultural Gospel is central in Lutheran Worship, we can conclude that Lutheran worship is transcultural.

Frank Senn several years ago reflected this transcultural nature of Lutheran liturgical worship:

Christian liturgy retains traces of the various cultures through which it has passed and to which it has been adapted. We chant a Hebrew "Amen," sing Greek canticles, pray the rhythms of Latin rhetoric, assemble in Gothic buildings, listen to German chorale preludes, and extend an American handshake at the greeting of peace.[36]

That short paragraph encapsulates the transcultural or multicultural dimension of Lutheran liturgical worship.

Recall my opening statement in this chapter: "If the stupid Germans can learn the liturgy, anyone can." The Germans were pagans who were Christianized and learned the liturgy. I am extremely uncomfortable when I increasingly hear racist statements about African Americans being unable to understand the liturgy. Or paternalistic arguments which suggest that Asian persons shouldn't seek membership in a Lutheran church because it's so European. This is sad, if not anti-Christian. Liturgical churches need to show the cross-cultural and multicultural and transcultural nature of worship.

The transcultural nature of Lutheran worship is underscored by the following comment by a Lutheran pastor as he wrote to some of his pastoral colleagues:

In one way, such attitudes are quite chauvinistic. Does anyone really think that the Lutheran liturgical tradition represents a unique Lutheran way of conducting public worship? The same basic tradition is shared by three quarters of a billion Roman Catholics, the many Eastern Orthodox Churches, the pre-Chalcedonian Churches, the Anglican Communion, and over 70 million Lutherans, not even the majority of whom are German. The basic pattern of liturgical worship is very ancient and most probably originated in the unique fusion of synagogue and Church usages in Jerusalem and Palestine which early found expression in the Jerusalem, Syrian, and North African Churches. Far from being "Germanic," our forefathers in Germany, Norway, Sweden, Africa, and elsewhere learned it from those who first brought them the Gospel and the Gospel sacraments in response to the Apostolic Mandate.[37]

That command is to go and make disciples of all nations . . . and the liturgy can be one way to bridge the cultural barriers.

While Lutheran worship is clearly liturgical, it is more than that— it is ecumenically evangelical, with its roots deep in the biblical and catholic tradition. This Christian tradition continues to create a new culture for itself, something which has its own vocabulary and practices that can be passed on to future generations. Included in this culture is the liturgical tradition, which encourages the incorporation of a variety of cultural expressions in response to the Gospel. More than anything else, it is this transcultural gospel which is a key to the Lutheran liturgical emphasis in its worship.

Timothy Maschke is Chair of Theology at
Concordia University Wisconsin.

Bibliography

Allen, Ronald and Gordon Borror. *Worship: Rediscovering the Missing Jewel*. Portland, OR: Multnomah Press, 1982.

Bongard, Rev. Stephen H. Letter in *The Lutheran Witness Reporter* 17:27 (November 11, 1991).

Brunner, Peter. *Worship in the Name of Jesus*, trans. by M. H. Bertram. St. Louis: Concordia, 1968.

Commission on Worship, "What Is Liturgy?" *Lutheran Worship Notes* 24 (Spring 1992).

Cone, James H. *The Spirituals and the Blues.* New York: Maryknoll, 1992.

Dawn, Marva J. *Reaching Out without Dumbing Down: A Theology of Worship for the Turn-of-the Century Culture.* Grand Rapids: William B. Eerdmans Publishing Company, 1995.

Evanson, Charles. "Evangelical Lutheran Worship," *Journal of English District Pastors* 4:1 (November 1991).

Godfrey, W. Robert. "The Reformation of Worship." In *Here We Stand: A Call for Confessing Evangelicals*, edited by James Montgomery Boice and Benjamin E. Sasse. Grand Rapids, MI: Baker Books, 1996.

Harper, John. *The Forms and Orders of Western Liturgy from the Tenth to the Eighteenth Century: A Historical Introduction and Guide for Students and Musicians.* Oxford: Clarendon Press, 1991.

Hippolytus, "Apostolic Tradition." In R. C. D. Jasper and G. J. Cuming, *Prayers of the Eucharist: Early and Reformed* (New York: Pueblo, 1987), 31-38.

Jean-Nesmy, Claude, O.S.B., *Living the Liturgy.* Staten Island, NY: Alba House, 1966.

Kiefert, Patrick. *Worship and Evangelism: A Pastoral Handbook.* Burnsville, MN: Prince of Peace Publishing, 1990.

Klauser, Theodor. *A Short History of the Western Liturgy*, translated by John Halliburton, Second Edition. New York: Oxford University Press, 1979.

Ludwig, Theodore M. *The Sacred Paths: Understanding the Religions of the World.* Second Edition. Upper Saddle River, NJ: Prentice Hall, 1996.

Luther, Martin. "Concerning the Order of Public Worship," in vol. 53 of *Luther's Works.* Philadelphia: Fortress Press, 1965.

_____. "The German Mass," in vol. 53 of *Luther's Works.* Philadelphia: Fortress Press, 1965.

Marquart, Kurt. "Liturgy and Evangelism," *Lutheran Worship: History and Practice*, edited by Fred Precht. St. Louis: Concordia, 1993.

Maschke, Timothy. Review of David Fagerberg's *What Is Liturgical Theory?* (Collegeville, MN: The Liturgical Press, 1992) in *Logia.* V:4 (Reformation 1996), 45-48.

Niebuhr, H. Richard. *Christ and Culture.* New York: Harper and Row, 1956.

Pfatteicher, Philip H. *The Manual on the Liturgy.* Minneapolis: Augsburg, 1979.

Raboteau, Albert J. *Slave Religion: The "Invisible Institution" in the Antebellum South.* New York: Oxford University Press, 1980.

Reed, Luther D. *The Lutheran Liturgy.* Philadelphia: Muehlenberg Press, 1947.

Sample, Tex. *U.S. Lifestyles and Mainline Churches: A Key to Reaching People in the 90's.* Louisville, KY: Westminster/John Knox Press, 1990.

Senn, Frank C. *Christian Worship and Its Cultural Setting.* Philadelphia: Fortress Press, 1983.

_____. "The Spirit of the Liturgy, a Wonderland Revisited," *Liturgy* 5:3 (Winter 1986).

Wainwright, Geoffrey. *Doxology: The Praise of God in Worship, Doctrine and Life—a Systematic Theology.* New York: Oxford University Press, 1980.

Webber, Robert E. *Evangelicals on the Canterbury Trail: Why Evangelicals Are Attracted to the Liturgical Church.* Waco, TX: Word, 1985.

Notes

[1] *The Lutheran Witness Reporter* 17:27 (November 11, 1991), letter by Rev. Stephen H. Bongard, St. Petersburg, FL, raises the issue. Similarly, an article by a seminarian, entitled "Our 'Germanic' Heritage" in the *Spectrum*, 24:12 (April 1992) of Concordia Seminary, St. Louis, addressed the same issue of the supposed German-cultural biases of Lutheran Worship.

[2] Theodore M. Ludwig, *The Sacred Paths: Understanding the Religions of the World.* Second Edition (Upper Saddle River, NJ: Prentice Hall, 1996), 431.

[3] Ap XXIV "The Mass" (Tappert, 249).

[4] Peter Brunner, *Worship in the Name of Jesus*, trans. by M. H. Bertram (St. Louis: Concordia, 1968), 125, illustrates the German term *Gottesdienst*, a word that suggests both God's service to humans and humans' service to God, by saying: "The gift of God evokes man's devotion to God."

[5] Martin Luther, "The German Mass," in vol. 53 of *Luther's Works* (Philadelphia: Fortress Press, 1965), 62.

[6] Commission on Worship, "What Is Liturgy?" *Lutheran Worship Notes* 24 (Spring 1992), 5.

[7] Ronald Allen and Gordon Borror, *Worship: Rediscovering the Missing Jewel* (Portland, OR: Multnomah Press, 1982), 73.

[8] Although slightly later than the Apostolic Fathers, Hippolytus' "Apostolic Tradition" provides a clear perspective on this issue. The text is available in R. C. D. Jasper and G. J. Cuming, *Prayers of the Eucharist: Early and Reformed* (New York: Pueblo, 1987), 31-38.

[9] John Harper, *The Forms and Orders of Western Liturgy from the Tenth to the Eighteenth Century: A Historical Introduction and Guide for Students and Musicians* (Oxford: Clarendon Press, 1991), 11.

[10] Martin Luther, "Concerning the Order of Public Worship," in vol. 53 of *Luther's Works* (Philadelphia: Fortress Press, 1965), 11.

[11] Tex Sample, *U.S. Lifestyles and Mainline Churches: A Key to Reaching People in the 90's* (Louisville, KY: Westminster/John Knox Press, 1990), underscores this reality by designating three cultures—the cultural left, the cultural middle, and the cultural right. Each have their own characteristics

and each needs to be addressed by particular methods in order to transform culture. Yet, he does not see much of the Christian culture as a unique transcultural tool for unity in Christ.

[12] Kurt Marquart, "Liturgy and Evangelism," *Lutheran Worship: History and Practice*, edited by Fred Precht (St. Louis: Concordia, 1993), 68.

[13] This ancient hymn, the *Te Deum Laudamus*, strongly emphasizes the unity between the heavenly and the earthly worshippers in the following lines: "We praise you, O God . . . To you all angels cry aloud, the heavens and all the powers therein; to you cherubim and seraphim continually cry: Holy, holy, holy. . . . The glorious company of the apostles praise you; the goodly fellowship of the prophets praise you; the noble army of martyrs praise you; the holy Church throughout the world does acknowledge you."

[14] H. Richard Niebuhr, *Christ and Culture* (New York: Harper and Row, 1956), 32.

[15] Marva J. Dawn, *Reaching Out without Dumbing Down: A Theology of Worship for the Turn-of-the Century Culture* (Grand Rapids: William B. Eerdmans Publishing Company, 1995), 2-72.

[16] Frank C. Senn, *Christian Worship and Its Cultural Setting* (Philadelphia: Fortress Press, 1983), particularly chapter three, "The Culture of Worship," and chapter six, "The World View of Worship," are helpful discussions on the on-going struggle the church has always faced in this area.

[17] Martin Luther, *Luther's Works*, vol. 53 (Philadelphia: Fortress Press, 1965), 15-40 and 51-90.

[18] Martin Luther, "The German Mass," in vol. 53 of *Luther's Works* (Philadelphia: Fortress Press, 1965), 62.

[19] Luther D. Reed, *The Lutheran Liturgy* (Philadelphia: Muehlenberg Press, 1947), 90, notes liturgies of Bugenhagen, Brenz, Chytraeus, Jonas, Melanchthon, and Osiander, to name a few.

[20] Reed, 182.

[21] Ibid., 195-7.

[22] Patrick Kiefert, *Worship and Evangelism: A Pastoral Handbook* (Burnsville, MN: Prince of Peace Publishing, 1990), 26.

[23] Kiefert, 8, 11, 26, 30.

[24] Robert E. Webber's *Evangelicals on the Canterbury Trail: Why Evangelicals Are Attracted to the Liturgical Church* (Waco, TX: Word, 1985) captures this experience through the testimony of a variety of individuals.

[25] Philip H. Pfatteicher, *The Manual on the Liturgy* (Minneapolis: Augsburg, 1979), 19.

[26] Marva Dawn's book, *Reaching Out without Dumbing Down*, has several chapters which amplify this concept more specifically as the Church confronts contemporary culture through worship.

[27] See volumes 43 and 53 of *Luther's Works* for more details.

[28] W. Robert Godfrey, "The Reformation of Worship," *Here We Stand: A Call for Confessing Evangelicals*, edited by James Montgomery Boice and Benjamin E. Sasse (Grand Rapids, MI: Baker Books, 1996), warns that many evangelicals are teaching theological error through innovative worship practices. He shows that the destructive nature of much of the experimentation which has occurred in evangelical public worship in recent years is a result of cultural conformity.

[29] Claude Jean-Nesmy, O.S.B., *Living the Liturgy* (Staten Island, NY: Alba House, 1966), 7, had entitled a section of the book "The Liturgy as An Apprenticeship."

[30] Peter Brunner, *Worship in the Name of Jesus* (St. Louis: Concordia, 1968), 217.

[31] This is a significant issue and is addressed in recent years by Geoffrey Wainwright in *Doxology: The Praise of God in Worship, Doctrine and Life—a Systematic Theology* (New York: Oxford University Press, 1980), 218-283; and in my review essay of David Fagerberg's, *What is Liturgical Theory?* (Collegeville, MN: The Liturgical Press, 1992) in *Logia*. V:4 (Reformation 1996), 45-48.

[32] Summary from Theodor Klauser's *A Short History of the Western Liturgy*, translated by John Halliburton, Second Edition (New York: Oxford University Press, 1979), 60-68.

[33] Albert J. Raboteau, *Slave Religion: The "Invisible Institution" in the Antebellum South* (New York: Oxford University Press, 1980), 250. James H. Cone, *The Spirituals and the Blues* (New York: Maryknoll, 1992), 129, repeats this idea: "Most blacks do not acknowledge this dualism. They believe that reality is one."

[34] SA iii, IV (Tappert, 310).

[35] Kurt Marquart, "Liturgy and Evangelism," in chapter 2, "Corporate Worship of the Church," in *Lutheran Worship: History and Practice*, edited by Fred L. Precht (St. Louis: Concordia, 1993), 68.

[36] Frank Senn, "The Spirit of the Liturgy, a Wonderland Revisited," *Liturgy* 5:3 (Winter 1986), 25.

[37] Charles Evanson, "Evangelical Lutheran Worship," *Journal of English District Pastors* 4:1 (November 1991), 11.

12

Cultural Obstacles to Evangelism

Joel D. Heck

Introduction.

We "should not make it difficult for the Gentiles who are turning to God" (Acts 15:19 NIV). So stated James, the leader of the early church at the time of the Jerusalem Council. Acts 15 describes a period in the early Christian church when the Christian movement was almost entirely Jewish, followed by a time when the Christian movement crossed cultural barriers and reached Gentiles by the thousands, beginning especially in Antioch. Opposition to Paul arose from among those who taught that all new Christians must observe Jewish customs, special days and festivals, and circumcision. This they insisted upon at the Jerusalem Council in Acts 15 (see v. 5).

After recounting the experience he had with Cornelius, Peter stated, "Why do you try to test God by putting on the necks of the disciples a yoke that neither we nor our fathers have been able to bear?" (Acts 15:10) Finally, James spoke, echoing Peter's observation, "We should not make it difficult for the Gentiles who are turning to God." This major crisis, one of the first for early Christianity, was a cultural clash, but the Judaizers thought that the issues were doctrinal. The issues were in fact a matter of Jewish tradition for the most part, so ingrained in Judaism that some Jews thought all the issues to be doctrinal. They weren't. When we require new believers to take on a new set of customs in order to be part of God's family, we run the risk of confusing Law and Gospel, especially if we insist on these customs as the only proper way for Christians to act. When we require non-Christians to do the same, we run the same risk.

In other words, Christians should not allow tradition, custom, or culture to stand in the way of the communication of the Gospel. But what is culture and what is biblical truth? We need to avoid identifying culture with biblical truth and vice versa, a most difficult task for most. And when does culture stand in the way of the communication of the Gospel? In other words, when are we "teaching as doctrines the commandments of men" (Matt. 15:9)? We have long struggled with those questions and will struggle with them much longer.

We also need to avoid laying aside biblical teaching in the interest of speaking to the modern individual. Attempts to demythologize the New Testament (Rudolf Bultmann), to offer a secular theology (Bonhoeffer, Harvey Cox), to offer a religionless Christianity (Barth, Bonhoeffer), to proclaim the death of God (Altizer, Hamilton), or to explain God as the "ground of our being" (Paul Tillich) have made contributions to Christian theology.[1] They have, however, suffered at times from the same criticism that one scholar offered of Paul Tillich: "He has interpreted the Gospel into a language nobody is speaking."[2] No consensus is in sight on the distinction between culture and biblical truth, so you are about to hear what one student of evangelism believes.

One of the best models with which I have become acquainted is that of the Messianic synagogue movement, a movement that some have estimated to include as many as 100,000 Messianic Jews in the U.S.[3] In an attempt to reach Jewish people with the Gospel, some have established Jewish synagogues that are thoroughly Jewish in every respect, with all the Jewish customs, festivals, and practices, even a Jewish rabbi. They worship on the seventh day, sing hymns that reflect Jewish life, sing the Psalms in a Jewish idiom, follow the Jewish calendar, all the while providing the redemptive fulfillment in Jesus Christ for each of the feasts and holidays.[4] The major distinction between these synagogues and others, however, is that they teach that Jesus is the promised Messiah. These synagogues have reached Jewish people who might not otherwise have been reached. Part of their message has been the fact that Jewish people need not jettison their Jewish cultural background by becoming Christians. These Christians have incarnated, or contextualized, the Christian message within Jewish culture.[5] Indeed, this is only what the first Christians, all of them Jews, did when they proclaimed the Messiahship of Jesus to their fellow Jews and continued to worship in the temple.[6] Even Paul, the greatest missionary of the Christian church, affirmed, "I am an Israelite myself, a descendant of Abraham, from the tribe of Benjamin" (Rom. 11:1).

Victor Smadja, a Messianic Jew, has written of the importance of this contextualization: "Unfortunately in the so-called Christian countries of the world the Jews who have accepted Jesus as their Savior have often made the attempt to forego their Jewish identity, and this places a further stumbling block before their fellow Jews who might otherwise be open to the Gospel of our Messiah."[7]

The application of this principle of contextualization is in dispute in the church today. The major reason for this is that we have lost the missionary impulse of the church in America, thinking that we still live in a Christian nation without need of a missionary attitude toward ministry. While this chapter will focus later upon the obstacles resident in our culture, many other obstacles exist within our own minds. The loss of the missionary impulse is one of them.

We should never have abandoned the missionary attitude, but most churches in America have long since exchanged a missionary attitude for a maintenance stance. A truly missionary attitude would try to understand the world, the problems of daily life, and the nature of the work of the church from the non-Christian's point of view. That attitude would take the Gospel into people's homes instead of expecting them to take the first step and come to the church. Along with its traditional manner of worship, it would offer worship services in a style that the non-Christian understood, without changing the biblical content of the services themselves. It would "find a need and fill it," as Robert Schuller once said. It would become a legend on the community grapevine for a ministry that meets the needs of the community, as Kennon Callahan has stated. This attitude would also motivate some pastors to ask a non-Christian to read one of his sermons and underline every word and phrase that appears unintelligible to him, and to strive to deliver sermons in the actual language of the audience.[8]

The incarnation of Jesus Christ sets the standard for this approach to evangelism. God did not wait for us to arrive at a certain point, either spiritually, socially, or in any other way, before He sent His Son. He did not expect us to step into His world; He chose to step into ours. He adopted our culture, our customs, our language and dress. He did not expect us to adopt His. If we are to reach others, we must become naturalized citizens of the world of people whom we would reach for Jesus Christ. We must understand them well enough to speak their language, as do the missionaries on the mission fields with the missionary attitude and impulse. Indeed, this is Christ and culture in paradox. By visiting a non-Christian in his living room, we do not condone the lies he tells, the foul language he may use, or the petty theft in which he engages. But we approach him on his turf to proclaim the Gospel. By incorporating an upbeat style of music in our worship, we do not use the words of the latest, sleazy love song, but we use the music style of the culture and the biblical concepts for the lyrics. The two kingdoms overlap. They always have. If they didn't, Christians would not be able to wear clothes, eat most foods, watch television, or listen to the radio. If they didn't, churches would not be able to build buildings, use electricity, lay carpet, or install a sound system.

But thus far I have been talking about cultural obstacles which Christians erect for the non-Christian inquirer. What about the cultural obstacles inherent in our country, which our entire society has erected, some of them blatant attempts to hinder the proclamation of the Gospel? I read recently that "those trained in seminary before 1988 were trained to minister to a culture that no longer exists."[9] That suggests the value of this topic. But before I proceed to that topic, let me offer three caveats.

Three Caveats

First, as I looked at obstacles in our American culture to evangelism, I realized more completely the difficulty of distinguishing between a cultural obstacle and a theological obstacle. Every aspect of American culture has a relationship to theology. The two kingdoms do overlap. What one person thinks is purely cultural is simultaneously theological or at least closely connected to theology. This chapter, therefore, will look at those aspects of American culture that stand in the way of our proclamation of the Gospel, but aspects that most often carry a set of clothing other than a theological one in our society. However, even those obstacles which all might agree are cultural have a theological solution. It's no surprise, then, that T. S. Eliot said, "No culture has appeared or developed except together with a religion."[10] He also said, "Culture [is], essentially, the incarnation (so to speak) of the religion of a people," and therefore culture and religion are "different aspects of the same thing."[11]

Secondly, everyone's list of cultural obstacles to evangelism will be different. Your list may contain some I omit and omit some I include. I do not pretend to give you an exhaustive list, nor do I pretend to offer them in an infallible sequence.

Thirdly, we must be careful not to think of culture as the real enemy. In the list of our three great enemies—the devil, the world, and our flesh—culture, I suppose, or at least certain aspects of culture, is only one enemy, that is, the world, or at least part of it. But the church will not reach more people simply by attempting to remove these cultural obstacles if it ignores the other two enemies. The greater obstacle is the unbelief of the human heart, caused by pride and self-centeredness, and a greater obstacle still is Satan. Solomon writes in Ecclesiastes that God has "set eternity in the hearts of men; yet they cannot fathom what God has done from beginning to end" (Eccl. 3:11). The real obstacles are spiritual; in this chapter I write only of those obstacles that often blind us to the real enemies. We wrestle not against flesh and blood.

Cultural Obstacles

1. The first cultural obstacle is the hostility of *the media*[12] to Christianity. In 1996, the Freedom Forum and the Roper Center published the results of their survey of 139 Washington Bureau chiefs and congressional correspondents. In 1992, 89% voted for Bill Clinton, 7% for George Bush, and 2% for Ross Perot. Wrote Michael Barone of *U.S. News and World Report*, "Today the claims of objectivity of the mainline press are laughable." Evan Thomas added, "They blame us, but this is true. There is a liberal bias. It's demonstrable. . . . There is a liberal bias at *Newsweek*, the magazine I work for."[13]

This media bias, I believe, has had two major effects. *First*, Christians subconsciously believe that to talk about their faith is strange, inappropriate, and subject to ridicule, if not abuse; *secondly*, non-Christians are afraid of entering a church lest they be poorly received. On the first point, Christians have allowed the media portrayal to seep into their consciousness without realizing it. There is a theological solution to this cultural problem, and Peter says it well,

"'Do not fear what they fear; do not be frightened.' But in your hearts set apart Christ as Lord. Always be prepared to give an answer to everyone who asks you to give the reason for the hope that you have. But do this with gentleness and respect" (1 Pet. 3:14-15 NIV). The solution is not to fear the reactions of other people, who often simply parrot what they see on television, but to set apart Christ as Lord in your hearts. To adapt a famous saying of G. K. Chesterton, evangelism "has not been tried and found wanting." Rather, "[i]t has been found difficult; and left untried."[14]

2. Americans are known for their *individualism*. William Dyrness writes, "Whatever the roots, individualism has come to define American culture."[15] In his book, *How Does America Hear the Gospel?*, he finds the source of this individualism in the Puritans, Thomas Paine, Adam Smith, Ralph Waldo Emerson, John Dewey, and others. Some believe that it has a lot to do with our history, with the kind of person that immigrated to our shores, with our emphasis upon freedom and independence. However, we have taken our Declaration of Independence too far. We love to tell people, "I did it my way." George Barna writes, "In our culture, the thrust is to enhance self-esteem, self-preservation, self-protection, self-fulfillment, self-promotion and self-development. Involvement with a church is based on what the church can do for the person, not what the person can do for the church."[16] Men do this more than women perhaps, but neither gender is immune to individualism. Indeed, individualism is usually only a euphemism for selfishness. It manifests itself in the hesitance of many unchurched to come into contact with the body of Christ. In fact, George Barna tells us that 17 percent of the unchurched are Christians, but Christians who do not wish to associate with the church.[17] They place a high importance on Jesus Christ, but a much lower importance on the church. This issue cuts both ways. Individualism may enable a Christian to reach a Muslim for Christ because that Muslim has broken solidarity with family. On the other hand, some individuals are so individualistic that the idea of being dependent upon anyone, let alone God, is repulsive to them.

Individualism strikes the Christian too, especially when the Christian has few non-Christian friends. When friends are the people among whom my witness is most likely to be heard and I have few non-Christian friends, I limit my audience.

Another problem with our individualism is our pride, a corollary to individualism, which makes us think we need to look good. In reality, that is a form of triumphalism, and triumphalism feeds on cheap grace, as Dietrich Bonhoeffer states.[18] We need to understand the cross, the price Christ paid for our redemption, and to stand ready to admit our shortcomings, even to those outside of Christ. Indeed, every person on this earth is a broken person, a person broken by sin. Christians, however, know what to do with their sin and need not be afraid to admit their brokenness, even to non-Christians. Don't think you need to witness from above the fray, when in fact you are a part of it.

3. A third obstacle is that America is *over-evangelized*, at least in one sense of the term (Barna to the contrary),[19] but ignorant of the Bible, i.e., America is post-Christian, postmodern, nine out of ten unable to define the Great Commission and seven out of ten with no clue to the meaning of John 3:16.[20] Many Americans think that they understand the Christian Gospel, but in reality they understand only a caricature of the Gospel, and we all know what Paul said about another Gospel in Galatians 1. This is not to say that mere understanding of the Gospel will result in conversion. I am far too conscious of the wickedness of the human heart, which does not want to admit error, sin, or shortcoming. But with the number of churches we have in America (350,000), the number of Christian television and radio stations, the number of high visibility evangelistic crusades and other outreaches (such as "Here's Life, America" from the 1970s), the number of people who go door-to-door (both among the cults and among Christians), the amount of Christian literature published each year (although, admittedly, most of it appears in Christian bookstores, which the non-Christian never visits), and the number of parachurch organizations such as the Navigators, Campus Crusade for Christ, InterVarsity Christian Fellowship, Fellowship of Christian Athletes, and many others, nearly every American has had a chance to hear the Gospel, and most have heard the Gospel (especially if we look at the number of unchurched people who used to attend church). A little knowledge is a dangerous thing. Well we know the dangers of the little child who thinks he knows how to shave, after he has seen Dad do it, and then cuts himself with Dad's razor. The boomers learned just enough about the church to think they understand the church and the

Gospel, to reject it, and to begin their massive retreat starting in 1991.[21]

4. My next two obstacles are well known to nearly everyone. The fourth obstacle is *relativism*—the idea that there are no absolute truths, especially popular among young people. More than four out of every five Americans under the age of thirty claim that there is no such thing as absolute moral truth.[22] There comes with this idea a concomitant lack of concern for truth and a far greater concern for something that works. This surface pragmatism makes evangelism in the narrow sense of the term more difficult. The Christian may well proclaim the message of the Gospel, but the relativist may well reply, "Well, what works for you may not work for me."

"As she sets out in her car, Anne imagines a blue light circling her vehicle clockwise three times, then silently chants, 'Three times around, three times about/A world within, a world without.' Then she adds a silent prayer to Artemis, goddess of the hunt, 'to protect the deer and tell them I'm coming. I imagine this as a psychic warning system.' Anne believes wholeheartedly in this practice. 'It works!' she says. 'I have a friend who's hit twelve deer in five years. I've never hit one.'"[23] By that logic, a daily recitation of "Mary had a little lamb" would most likely prevent hepatitis.

Nevertheless, that's the playing field. The Christian witness must not only proclaim the Gospel to many of these people, but also demonstrate, in a sort of pre-evangelism, that Christianity does indeed work. As a matter of fact, if it doesn't work, then Christianity is truly a pie-in-the-sky religion. But every New Testament writer demonstrated that the Christian faith is a faith *that* works. Martin Luther once said that it's not faith plus works that saves, but a faith that works. And so it is. We ought not to allow the community to proclaim the irrelevance of the church without an attempt to show the relevance of the church to daily life. The fact is that our culture used to support the church with an assumption that the church proclaims a meaningful message, meaningful both now and in eternity. Our culture no longer does that, so we must demonstrate it.

Alongside this relativism is a love affair with the superficial. Everyone seems to want a quick fix—a quick solution to a headache, a quick solution to learning a particular subject in college without putting in the necessary effort (How many of our students spend two hours outside of class for every hour in class? I once asked a few students who were struggling in a class I was teaching how many of them put in two hours outside of class for every hour in class and not one raised a hand), a quick solution to an unwanted pregnancy, a quick solution to those few extra pounds, and all of this without the long-term commitment to a God-given solution. Politics has been beset for decades in America with an obsession with appearance far above that of content, and the examples could be multiplied.

For many people, Christianity, therefore, is relatively true. It's true for some, but not for others. James Barr sounds the note of modern relativism:

> Any work or text composed in an ancient time and in an ancient culture has its meaning in that time and culture, and in our time and culture may have a different meaning or indeed no meaning at all.[24]

By losing our doctrine of the inspiration of Scripture, we have lost the transcendence of our values and need to recover that. N. P. Andersen argues, "The marked change in behavior patterns of the last fifty years can be traced back to the movements of thought which have reduced the Word of God to an outmoded piece of literature, to theories which have put man at the center of religion and ethics."[25] At the same time that we stress the immanence of God in our daily lives, we must also stress the transcendence, the Creator of the law above all laws. It was that transcendence that enabled the Nuremberg trials to find Nazi war criminals guilty, when the Nazis argued that no other country had the right to impose their ethic upon Germany. As the song goes, "Our God is an Awesome God," and few truths are more important than that one.

This obstacle, in slightly different dress, contains a self-evident irony. In our country where we practice the freedom of religion, some have taken that conclusion to an illogical conclusion. For them the freedom of religion means the equal validity of all religions. I'm talking about a *pluralism*, fed by the rapidly growing world population, especially in the cities,[26] that often includes *universalism*.[27] Indeed, if there are no absolute truths, then one set of truths is as valid as any other. The only problem is that what masquerades as a set of truths may actually be a set of falsehoods. If there is no transcendent God, then any local deity will do, and we soon find ourselves back in the days of the Old Testament when every tribe or nation had its own deities. Whichever nation won in battle was the nation with the more powerful god. It is a measure of our culture's illogicality to believe that mutually contradictory religions can be equally valid. Christianity teaches that the way to God is through faith in a person who was Himself God. All other religions teach that the way to God is through our own effort, whether that be meditation, hard work, submission to some *karma*, or the loss of oneself to the world soul. You can't have it both ways.

5. and 6. The fifth obstacle is really two obstacles, or perhaps four or six or eight—*secularization*[28] and *materialism*. Secularization and materialism, and their ancient cousin *hedonism* and younger cousin *nihilism*, are forces that coincide with many of those that have preceded. Our deification of science and technology has taught that "seeing is believing." It feeds both secularization, the idea that we can get along nicely without God, thank you, and materialism, the idea that only that which we can see is real. Many believe Carl Sagan, who says that "the Cosmos is all there is or ever will be."[29] When you're dead, you're done. There is no day of reckoning. Paul Davis, an English-born physicist and a modern-day Deist, is well known for his thesis that the nature of the universe and our ability to observe it suggests a deliberate purpose and design in existence. One of his major themes is that science offers a surer path than religion in the search for God.[30] These views feed secularization and materialism, whether that is his intention or not. However, our existential and hedonistic living for the moment, since there is nothing certain to live for in eternity, fails to see the higher purpose for which we have been created. When there is no God or when we aren't sure there is, we worship ourselves. And so, some turn to drugs and alcohol, others to sex and money, still others to all these and more.

Dorothy Sayers, a contemporary of C. S. Lewis, once said that the sin of our times is "the sin that believes in nothing, cares for nothing, seeks to know nothing, interferes with nothing, enjoys nothing, hates nothing, finds purpose in nothing, lives for nothing, and remains alive because there is nothing for which it will die."[31] That is the natural consequence of a society that elevates itself in the place of God.

7. I would be remiss if I failed to mention one of the cross-cultural obstacles to the proclamation of the Gospel, and that is the mistaken perception in some circles *that Christianity is a white man's religion or that it is a Western religion.* This view is fueled by the many subtle and overt instances of racism in our country today. While it is true that Anglos have come into the Christian church in large numbers and comprise the vast majority of Christians in the West, the perception that Christianity is a white man's religion fails to perceive either the origin of Christianity or the recent and rapid growth of Christianity in Africa and Asia. Christianity originated in Asia, the land of Israel, that portion of this world where three continents come close together. Jesus was a Jew, and all of the first Christians were Jews. As to the growth of Christianity in Africa and Asia, Dr. Martindale's chapter mentions the estimated 80,000,000 Christians in mainland China today. Africa is now approximately 50 percent Christian, Singapore is approximately 20 percent Christian, Korea is rapidly becoming Christian, and many other success stories could be cited from New Guinea to Indonesia to Nigeria, Ghana, and Botswana. Within ten to twenty years, the center of Christianity will no doubt shift from North America to Africa and Asia. This view that Christianity is a white man's religion is another part of the curse of superficiality which we must face. However, as long as our culture mistakenly believes that Christianity is a white man's religion, we will find it hard to reach many of our black brothers, especially those who are attracted to the Nation of Islam and other Muslim offshoots.

Billy Graham argues that one of the four trends that will pose a serious challenge to Christian evangelism in the years leading up to 2000 and beyond is the expansion of non-Christian religions.[32] The growth of Islam, the militancy of Judaism in Israel, and the continued success of many cults are fueled by this mistaken impression regarding the Western nature of Christianity.

While it is important to understand the enemy in order to be prepared to do battle (hence the inclusion of this chapter), it is even more important that we understand the power of the Gospel, involve every willing Christian, explore new methods and new fields, and trust in the God who has redeemed us in Jesus Christ.[33] We must not merely understand the enemy, but we must truly understand the enemy. We must think through the obstacles to evangelism, and we must understand the biblical antidote.

The hostility of the media, individualism, the idea that America is over-evangelized, relativism, secularization, materialism, and the idea that Christianity is a white man's religion are seven of the major obstacles that the world has erected against Christianity. Our understanding of the enemy and our conviction that the Gospel meets each of these obstacles head-on will equip us to dialogue with those who do not share that faith today. May God grant that we not add to the list by erecting barriers to the Gospel, for we may not have a Jerusalem Council to set us straight.

Joel Heck is Academic Dean at Concordia Austin and former Professor of Theology at Concordia University Wisconsin

Bibliography

Andersen, N. P. "Biblical Theology and Cultural Identity in the Anglo-Saxon World," *Let the Earth Hear His Voice*, edited by J. D. Douglas. Minneapolis: World Wide Publications, pp. 1278-1293.

Barna, George. "What Evangelistic Churches Do." Ventura, CA: Gospel Light videotape, 1996.

_____. *Evangelism That Works*. Ventura, CA: Regal Books, 1995.

Bell, James. "Engaging the Scientific Worldview." Unpublished article.*Christian Witness to the Jewish People*. Lausanne Occasional Paper No. 7. Wheaton: Lausanne Committee for World Evangelization, 1980.

Chesterton, G. K. *What's Wrong with the World*. San Francisco, CA: Ignatius Press, 1994.

Colson, Charles. *Presenting Belief in an Age of Unbelief*. Wheaton: Victor Books, 1984.

Dyrness, William. *How Does America Hear the Gospel?* Grand Rapids: Eerdmans, 1989.

Eliot, T. S. *Christianity and Culture*. New York: Harcourt Brave Jovanovich, 1968.

Graham, Billy. "Recovering the Primacy of Evangelism." *Christianty Today* Vol. 41, No. 14 (December 8, 1997): 27-30.

Hunter, George. *How to Reach Secular People*. Nashville: Abingdon, 1992.

Lichter, Robert and Stanley Rothman, *The Media Elite*, 1980.

Smadja, Victor. "Evangelization Among Jews," *Let the Earth Hear His Voice*, edited by J. D. Douglas. Minneapolis: World Wide Publications, pp. 808-815.

Strobel, Lee. *Inside the Mind of Unchurched Harry and Mary*. Grand Rapids: Zondervan, 1993."What Is Messianic Judaism?" Web site: www.cby.org/MJ.htm. Philadelphia, Pennsylvania: Congregation Beth Yeshua, 1997.

Notes

[1] The contributions of these theologians will be assessed differently. Certainly many of their writings offer valid and useful insights, and this chapter does not attempt to throw the baby out with the bath water. Many critics, including N. P. Andersen, listed below, question portions of their scholarship, including the point made here—their ability to translate theology both faithfully and in a way that makes sense to the Christian and non-Christian world.

[2] N. P. Andersen, "Biblical Theology and Cultural Identity in the Anglo-Saxon World," *Let the Earth Hear His Voice*, edited by J. D. Douglas. (Minneapolis: World Wide Publications), pp. 1278-1286.

[3] "What is Messianic Judaism?" Web site: www.cby.org/MJ.htm, the Web site of Congregation Beth Yeshua, Philadelphia, Pennsylvania, 1997. See also Menorah Ministries at www.best.com/~ray673/search/database/is9.3.html.

[4] Victor Smadja, "Evangelization Among Jews," *Let the Earth Hear His Voice*, edited by J. D. Douglas. (Minneapolis: World Wide Publications), p. 810.

[5]Lausanne Occasional Paper No. 7, "Christian Witness to the Jewish People," recommends contextualization "by fostering and encouraging Jewish Christians to continue to enjoy their heritage and to enhance the life of the church through elements of Jewish culture such as music, drama, dance, art, literature, and humor" and "by identifying with the Jewish community through adaptation of a Jewish lifestyle, e.g., observing of religious and national festivals, traditions and events of life (Jewish-style weddings, funerals, etc.)" (p. 18). It further states that the Jewish Christian "must be accorded the freedom in Christ to observe religious elements appropriate to him as an Israelite (e.g., Jewish religious festivals). . . . "

6 For example, Acts 3:1, 21:26.

7 Victor Smadja, "Evangelization Among Jews," *Let the Earth hear His Voice*, edited by J. D. Douglas. (Minneapolis: World Wide Publications), p. 809.

8 Strobel, *Inside the Mind of Unchurched Harry & Mary*, pp. 217-218.

9Doug Anderson, "When the Sodalic Voice Is Gone . . . ," *Changing Church Perspectives*, Vol. 19 (July-August 1996), p. 1.

10 T. S. Eliot, *Christianity and Culture* (New York: Harcourt Brave Jovanovich, 1968), p. 87.

11 Ibid., p. 101.

12 This matter of media bias was the subject of a 1980 study entitled *The Media Elite*, by Robert Lichter and Stanley Rothman.

13 Robert P. Dugan, Jr., *NAE Washington Insight*, Washington, DC: August, 1996 (Vol. XVIII, No. 8), p. 1.

14 G. K. Chesterton, *What's Wrong with the World* (San Francisco, CA: Ignatius, 1994), p.37.

15 William Dyrness, *How Does America Hear the Gospel?*, (Grand Rapids: Eerdmans, 1989), p. 96. For an account of the various origins of American individualism, see William Cario's chapter in this volume.

16 George Barna, *Evangelism That Works*, (Ventura, CA: Regal Books), p. 51.

17 Ibid., p. 53.

18 Charles Colson, *Presenting Belief in an Age of Unbelief*, (Wheaton: Victor Books, 1984), p. 6.

19 Barna, op. cit., p. 44.

20 Ibid., p. 35.

21 Ibid., p. 48.

22 Ibid., p. 108.

23 Quoted in Lee Strobel, *Inside the Mind of Unchurched Harry and Mary*, (Grand Rapids: Zondervan, 1993), p. 58.

24 N. P. Andersen, "Biblical Theology and Cultural Identity in the Anglo-Saxon World," *Let the Earth Hear His Voice*, edited by J. D. Douglas, (Minneapolis: World Wide Publications), p. 1283.

25 Ibid., p. 1289.

26 Billy Graham lists four trends that pose a special challenge to Christian evangelism: uncontrolled urbanization, unrelenting aggressive secularism,

expanding non-Christian religions, and shifting frontiers and emerging fields. Graham, Billy. "Recovering the Primacy of Evangelism." *Christianity Today* 41, no. 14 (December 8, 1997): 27-30.

[27] George Barna, "What Evangelistic Churches Do," Glendale, CA: Gospel Light videotape, 1996.

[28] Graham, op. Cit., p. 28.

[29] Colson, op. cit., p. 19.

[30] James Bell, "Engaging the Scientific Worldview," unpublished article, p. 3.

[31] Colson, op. cit., p. 12.

[32] Graham, op. cit., p. 28.

[33] These are Graham's four major keys to effective evangelism in the years ahead. Graham, op. cit., p. 30.

13

Discriminating Multiculturalism

Patrick G. D. Riley

In the early '90s you could hardly pick up a newspaper without reading about "multiculturalism." Nowadays the word may not be quite so ubiquitous as it was during the debate over Columbus and the importation of Western culture into this continent—or the imposition of Western culture on this continent, as the multiculturalists would have it. Yet it remains important. *Multiculturalism* is a salient term in current educationist chatter.

A term, yes; but a theory, hardly. Multiculturalism is too plastic and ambiguous for that. It hasn't yet been raised above the realm of rhetoric, or cleansed of the taint of ideology. Maybe those who wield the word as a weapon have strong convictions about what they mean by it, but more likely they've taken Lady Macbeth's advice and not considered the matter so deeply. Nonetheless our multicultural friends don't hesitate to demand that the curricula of American education become "multicultural" and represent "diversity."

In due course we'll examine their efforts and the pressures they bring to bear. We'll enquire whether or to what degree a religion-based, church-sponsored university should adapt itself to current notions of what a university should be. But first—while never forgetting that if the church marries herself to any age she'll soon find herself a widow—we must do some spadework. We must attempt to clarify why multiculturalism constitutes such a lethal threat to higher education of any kind, religious or otherwise. And to get a firm grasp on the necessary tools, we shall examine the nature of culture, some characteristics of a Christian culture, and some differences between ideology on the one hand and philosophy and religion on the other. We must, in accordance with the classic method, attempt some definitions.[1]

That isn't easy with the key term *multiculturalism*. It can't be found in dictionaries published as recently as a dozen years ago, even if the latest Merriam-Webster's Collegiate Dictionary says it goes back half a century. Every time I type the word, my advanced word-processing program warns that no such term exists. Most of us began to hear it only when the country began to prepare for the 500th anniversary of the arrival of Columbus on these shores. Then "multiculturalism" became a battle-cry against any supposed superiority of the culture—Western culture—that Columbus and his successors thrust on this land and its natives. The implication was that all cultures are somehow equal, that no one culture has the right, so to speak, to predominate over others.

If few of the folks arguing against Western culture evince a very clear idea of what culture itself is, we must be fair and admit that most of us are in the same boat. We find ourselves with regard to culture as St. Augustine did with regard to time: we know what culture is until somebody asks us to define it.[2]

The real quarrel with multiculturalists is less that they are confused about the nature of culture, less even that they are hostile to Western culture (about which, in its present state especially, we ourselves may have reason for reserve), than that they show no awareness of the eclecticism, the openness to excellence of all kinds, wherever it is found, that characterizes Western culture.

Since we're practically constrained at this point to supply a definition of culture, let's make a stab at it. Any culture worthy of the name is at base a societal consensus about justice in its many mansions. This may seem an impoverished definition, an outlandishly Laconic definition.[3] Yet it goes, I think, to the root.

Obviously culture implies a society and a consensus. That particular consensus without which there is no society concerns, first, the common good, the consensual goal that turns a mere assembly into a society. Dependent in large part (but not exclusively) on that common goal is a consensus concerning what the members of the society owe each other, otherwise known as justice.[4] Beyond that are other species of justice, but what concerns us most here is the kind called piety or, somewhat less confusingly, *pietas*, whereby we attempt to render the justice of gratitude to those we can never fully repay, namely God, our parents, and our country.[5] Hence if we conceive justice as the foundation of culture, it seems to follow that the four corners of culture would be, first, elemental justice to one another (civic justice, embodied partly in law and partly in customs, and enforced by the state insofar as it is able prudently to do so), then justice to God (or religion), justice to parents (and by inference to children), and finally justice to the country (patriotism).

What has this to do with that flowering of the fine arts which we ordinarily identify with high culture? Can they be fitted into this austere scheme?[6] If they can't, the thesis presented here collapses. But a case can be made that the arts of the word, of sight, and even of music contribute to a societal sense of justice, signify it, and even flow from it if only in the narrow sense that a truly just society abhors obstacles to the free expression of human genius.

Among all cultural symbols, works of literature most perspicuously embody culture conceived as the explicator and fortifier of justice both in its primary sense of due reciprocity and in its further function of directing all virtues to the common good, hence becoming as it were the sovereign and compendious virtue, subsuming all virtues within itself.[7] Transcendental writers in every language of Western culture exemplify this, if not always in the morality they expressly teach then in the morality they take for granted.[8] To name some: Sophocles, Cicero, Livy, Shakespeare, Goethe, Cervantes, Calderon de la Barca, Pascal, Mickiewicz, Dostoevski, and, perhaps above all, Dante. Nor need we confine ourselves to the West: Confucius offers a good example.

As for the visual arts, in modern times we have witnessed their destabilizing potential, especially through obscenity but also more subtly through, for example, nihilism.[9] From such abuse we can the more easily, perhaps, deduce their role in maintaining a culture. In this light the visual arts may appear to play a chiefly negative role, through abstention from portrayals that induce to vices whether moral or intellectual, such as relativism or nihilism.[10] But anyone who has felt the elevating power of, say, great sculpture or lofty architecture, will know otherwise. The same holds for music.

Just how progress in the physical sciences—doubtless a constituent if subordinate part of culture—can be connected with the four corners of justice, as delineated above, is problematic. The inherent rationality of life in a just society may inspire confidence in the inherent rationality of the physical world, confidence that is a *conditio sine qua non* for the advance of physical science. Cicero linked both law and justice proximately with right reason, and ultimately with the mind of God.[11] Alfred North Whitehead expounded a link between the advance of science and a rational belief in the existence of God: he claimed that "medieval theology," with its "insistence on the rationality of God," had generated "faith in the possibility of science."[12] As if to confirm this view, some scholars attribute the baffling halt, or regression, of Chinese science to loss of a primal belief in God, and its substitution by a species of pantheism and a cyclical notion of history.[13]

Western Culture as Multiculture

In any case, our own culture has refused to content itself with notions native to itself, with advances that it itself has realized. Beyond them, our culture has drawn from the achievements and the tested wisdom of so many other civilizations that on that count it can be called a multiculture, or better, a universal culture. Hence the salient note of the West is its *discriminating* multiculturalism. We have taken the best.

To see that, we have only to look at the classical curricula of our universities, the so-called academic canon. Our mathematics began, we're told, with the very practical geometers, or land-measurers, of Egypt. The Greeks took those methods and tore the guts out of them, gave us meticulous, rigorous proofs, and thus showed us, as Lincoln observed, how an argument is made. The Greeks also gave us the foundations of philosophy. This is summed up in Whitehead's oft-quoted observation that the Western philosophical tradition is "a series of footnotes to Plato."[14] By the time we reach the thirteenth century, we find theologians reaching out to all the cultures they knew for natural wisdom, to cast light on the supernatural wisdom of Divine Revelation. Thomas Aquinas, for example, constantly refers to a pagan Greek, Aristotle, as "the philosopher." The pages of St. Thomas's *Summa Theologiae* are strewn with references to "Rabbi Moses," the name of honor he gives Maimonides, a Spanish-born Jew who worked as a physician in Egypt. He draws upon Islam, and it is widely held that he borrowed at least one of his five "ways" to the existence of

God, the third (based on the contingency of limited being), from the Persian thinker Avicenna.[15]

The point is not only that we are a multiculture. There is far more. A mere multiculture is cultural chaos. Unless we remain a *discriminating* multiculture, a multiculture ready, willing, and able to sort out the good from the bad of other cultures, we shall soon sink into mediocrity or worse.

Perhaps the most basic reason for this is that principles are literally starting-points: if we abandon them we have no place to start from, hence no place to go to. Most especially must we cling to the principles of justice: the principle that justice must be done even—to recall the Roman maxim—if the heavens fall; the principle that right is right even—to recall the Chestertonian maxim—if nobody is right, and wrong is wrong even if everybody is wrong. Yet moral relativism is the theme that an undiscriminating multiculturalism, a muddle-minded multiculturalism, seems to harp on most insistently.

Not even the most ideological multiculturalist, however, can speak of technological relativism. Here no one dare claim that any other culture is the equal of the West. Even prescinding from the flowerage of philosophy and theology in the High Middle Ages, prescinding too from the unexcelled poetry, visual arts, and music of more recent times, and confining ourselves instead to the mathematics and physical science the West produced during a mere two centuries starting from the late sixteenth, we must aver that the progress in physical science was unprecedented, and the progress in mathematics never excelled. Nor is the luster of that achievement dimmed by the fact that it was achieved with the indispensable help of Greek and Arabic mathematics, and with the use of a number-system taken from India. In those twenty or so decades the foundations of modern technological advance were laid. The rest of the world has been racing to catch up.

If we must conclude that no culture can compete with ours for scientific progress, if we believe that no culture has reached the philosophical profundity of the West, or the theological heights, if we dare think that no art anywhere is more beautiful, no literature more delightful or profound, no music quite so sublime or moving, no legal system more firmly aimed at justice or more relentless in its achievement, no political system more solicitous for the rights of persons and free societies, we must nonetheless hold that little of this would have been possible had we not borrowed liberally from a multitude of cultures.

We are a multiculture. And because we have borrowed the best, we have proved ourselves a discriminating multiculture.

Yet of what we've taken from other societies, we could dispense with any and all except one and still remain apart. That indispensable element of our society is what we have taken from the Hebrews. Indeed insofar as Western civilization is catholic in the sense that I understand Martin Marty to use the term, namely that submission to God has a net tendency to permeate the whole, we are a new Israel, a mystical Israel consecrated to God as His people by dedicating ourselves to the Covenant that the Hebrews made with Him three millennia and more ago. We have done that by adopting the stipulations of that Covenant: the Ten Commandments. The West became what it has been at its best by adopting the law of God, the divine concept of justice, and by accepting the Hebrew prophecies and their fulfillment in Christ.

Readers may well wonder how this can be so. Not, I suppose, that anybody blessed with faith in Our Lord Jesus Christ is likely to deny that in His Person He has fulfilled the promises made to the Jews; nor is any believing Christian likely to doubt that the church in the sense that Dr. Marty has employed is the fulfillment of the promises of a Redeemer, an Anointed One. It is rather that most of us are likely to wonder in what sense our society was built around Christian teachings. Where can we see that our civilization, Western civilization, is a Christian civilization?

Distinctive Notes of Christian Culture

I can't claim to be a social scientist or an historian, but looking at the differences among historical societies, and at the teachings of the Gospel, it seems to me we can distinguish at least three salient and even unique characteristics of a Christian society. One, perhaps the most perspicuous, is the absence of slavery.

While some readers may think this plain enough, others will bridle at the claim, and for a number of formidable reasons. Christian theologians long attempted to justify slavery albeit with severe restrictions, persisting in this attempt despite centuries of experience showing that slavery itself was inherently hostile to decent treatment, whatever safeguards might be ensconced in law. The Eastern Roman Empire, Christian from its beginnings in Byzantium, retained slavery in one form or another until overrun by the Turks twelve centuries later. A flourishing trade in Muslim and also in Slavic slaves, some of them Christian, was pursued by Italians on the Eastern fringes of Europe, while Portuguese worked the slave-markets of West Africa; during seven centuries of struggle with Saracen invaders, Spaniards continued to enslave prisoners of war.[16] Papal history itself is chequered.[17] Christians from Western Europe, once they arrived in the New World, tried to enslave the natives; eventually they imported hardier slaves from West Africa, and the stage was set for the unspeakable tragedy of our Civil War.

The chronicle could go on, yet a broad survey of history would be dominated by one unassailable fact: *Until this century, when Western customs and Western notions—in a word, Western culture—became a standard to which nations throughout the world aspired, the only free societies have been Christian societies.*

Although in itself the absence of slavery can be seen as a practical respect for basic human rights, hence a kind of elemental justice, nonetheless in the perspective of history this is a wholly new phenomenon. It stands as a momentous, monumental achievement.

Slavery as a Universal Institution

All the peoples of antiquity, including the Hebrews, had slaves. Western society, as the heir of Rome, has been affected most by the slavery known in the Roman Empire. Particulars of the history of slavery in Rome are disputed, but it seems established that the wars with Carthage resulted in vast additions to the numbers of Roman slaves. Moreover the family farms of Italy, whose owner-workers were long the backbone of Rome's economic and military strength, not to speak of her much-prized homespun virtues, were practically swallowed up by the cataclysm of the Second Punic War; small farmers fled to the cities where they vanished into a proletarian client-class, while the lands they had tilled as their own were amalgamated into vast tracts worked by slaves. The Roman economy, thus debased, grew heavily dependent on slavery, and the land reforms of the

Gracchi (to mention only them) were in large part an attempt to rectify that imbalance. But so deeply entrenched did the servile institution prove that Roman thinkers and literary figures such as Seneca who decried the intrinsic injustice and incidental abuses of slavery suggested no way that slavery might be uprooted.[18]

This apparently insoluble problem faced the church when she entered the Roman world. She counseled no revolution, but only urged that everyone involved in the institution of slavery behave according to Christian teachings. Eventually she even inherited slaves from rich benefactors. But on the issue of family life, certainly not excluding that of slaves, just as on the issue of worship, the church showed herself willing to brave the Roman state and Roman custom.

This was an especially bold stance in an age when those who held the reins of state were convinced that civic life depended heavily on family life and on worship, hence that they were the special province of the state.[19] Augustus, in founding the Empire, had given these matters his special attention. But purity of worship and purity of family life, as defined by the church, were also the concern of the church. Indeed they were to be her two preeminent concerns throughout history.

Hence conflict with the Roman state was inevitable. It came soon enough, and not only in matters of worship, where Christian martyrs gave deathless witness, but in matters of marriage as well. In the first quarter of the third century Pope Callistus, opposing rooted Roman custom and Roman law itself, declared that free women of position in society could marry freedmen or even slaves.[20] Here, in accordance with a principle that has become one of the most contentious features of the Christian tradition, church authority stood up to unjust civil law.

The frequent collisions of church and state ceased early in the reign of the first Christian emperor (yet the two soon veered back toward collision, as the history of the councils, of caesaropapism, and of the investiture of ecclesiastical authorities by lay authorities attests). Like the conduits and other artifacts remaining from the reign of Constantine, which bore the Christian Chi-Rho symbol, the laws of Constantine had a distinctive Christian stamp. He not only ameliorated the lot of slaves, but the very first relief he gave them was— significantly, we must think—to safeguard the integrity of their families.[21] Amelioration was the only practical means available to

Roman civil authorities, despite the radical injustice of slavery itself (injustice obscured by centuries of tradition and rationalization), and despite what might be called the incidental injustices, often hideous, that proved endemic to the institution and which were manifest to everyone.[22]

Why Slavery Declined

For centuries, then, contrasting forces were at work. One was the drive to ease the lot of slaves, or even abolish the institution. Another was the perceived economic advantage attached to slavery and entrenched in society. A third was the seemingly universal libido for domination, combined with the corruption that inevitably accompanies the near-absolute power of one man over another, or—very significantly indeed—over a woman, or even of a woman over a man.

The Roman state, solicitous for order in society and for stability in the economy, exercised its authority to maintain the servile institution. But under the Christian emperors it outlawed or tempered the outrages endemic to slavery while restraining—hence holding in equilibrium, however fragile—other forces at play, namely the lust for exploitation and the drive for human dignity. But from the sixth century, when in the West the centralized Roman authority broke down, these opposing forces were freed to work against one another. In the ensuing struggle, Christian principles and Christian compassion eventually prevailed.

There was a lot more in play. The extensive economic undergirding of slavery was for the most part dismantled, and its place taken by the new and largely local economies that had inherited slavery. Then another momentous event overtook the West: the westward thrust of Islam. By the eighth century Islamic navies consolidated control of the Western Mediterranean, bringing commerce in the West to a standstill. Most of the cities of Europe with the major exception of those trafficking with the Byzantines, such as Venice and some in southern Italy, stagnated or shriveled, losing all but ecclesiastical authority (which however, in some cases simultaneously constituted civil authority).[23] The Roman villa, smallest of civil circumscriptions, in most places became the chief or even the sole political and economic unit, its slaves responsible only to the lord of the manor. Politics became focussed on interpersonal relations (to employ a hackneyed phrase in a richer and more precise sense), and so-called reasons of state all but vanished, to be replaced by personal ethos, private ethics, and religious principle. It was within this microeconomic and micropolitical setting that slavery was transformed into serfdom, a radically different institution.

In this transmutation, the question of whether the political and economic elements of the historical scene were true causes or merely *conditiones sine quibus non* is hard to determine, given the scarce documentation of those centuries. For when political authority and economic life retreated to the villa, letters retreated into the monasteries; hence secular history went largely unrecorded during the critical centuries from the eighth to the eleventh, and for our understanding of that period we are reduced to deduction and speculation.

This much however can be held with confidence: *In those same centuries, when culture was suffused with Christian belief, and when the episcopal and monastic institutions exercised powerful social or even civil authority, Christian principles were powerfully at work.*[24] *Moreover—and this is critical—the Christian principles at work were indubitably causes.*

Unlike the *conditio*, principle has nothing of the passive about it. Thus Christian principles remain dynamic even though they can exercise their full powers only when allowed free rein by economic and political conditions. Throughout history they have acted as the most revolutionary ferment in society, or as a counterrevolutionary ferment. (We have witnessed that in the destruction of communism in Europe.) They can be seen at work in the apparently unending struggle against the servile institution, embodied in modern times in the great antislavery figures of the eighteenth and nineteenth centuries, such as William Wilberforce, Samuel Romilly, William Lloyd Garrison, Abraham Lincoln, David Livingston, and Charles-Martial Lavigerie.

The Two Sovereignties

Partisanship, which has muddled our understanding of slavery in the Christian West, probably has also obscured our view of the second characteristic of a Christian society I want to cite. It is the subjection of society to two sovereignties, that of God and that of the civil ruler.

Rendering to Caesar only what is Caesar's, and to God all that is God's, is a distinctly Christian principle unknown to the ancient world, where the civil and the religious were inextricably intermingled.[25]

One of the misfortunes of history is that the application of this principle has been anything but uniformly faithful. Every generation hears the cry, "We have no king but Caesar!" Moreover the same lust for domination that we saw at work in the preservation of slavery can play its part in conflicts between church and state, even where principle is at stake; they can become mere struggles for power, and the worst offenders may be the very men dedicated by their calling to the sovereignty of God. That however is a topic for another essay, even for volumes. Here I merely recall that the civil authority exercised by bishops, which during the decline of Roman authority in the West was in places a practical necessity, often continued long after the conditions that necessitated it had ceased. A further point to be made here is that the distinctive Christian division between church and state is but one of the Christian principles that modern liberalism has appropriated.

Or, rather than appropriated, one might think highjacked. In the hands of modern liberalism that unique Christian teaching has undergone a stunning inversion. Where the principle, first uttered by Our Lord Jesus Christ Himself, once gave us courage to tell our civil rulers they had no right to impose unjust laws, to violate consciences, to trample on religious conviction and on free worship, the same principle in the profane hands of our new masters is made to tell us we have no right to bring our worship, our convictions, even our consciences, into public life. Never mind how firmly founded in reason this right may be, never mind how long before the Christian era this right, or rather this duty, was articulated,[26] or how long before the birth of Christ it was the common property of philosophy and good citizenship.[27] Religion has tainted it, and we who won't surrender it are condemned to wear the scarlet letter of our times: R for religious. The will of the lawmaker runs amuck, itself becoming law, while legal positivism inevitably rules our law schools, dangerously debasing the conception of law in the minds of our lawyers.

Our task of the moment is to examine the things that are Caesar's and the things that are God's, not to frame an indictment of modern liberalism, either in its starting points or in its wanderings. But it is important to note, if only in passing, that what has gone under the name of liberalism during the twentieth century has shown itself, by its claim both to exclusive possession of reason and to exclusive presence in the public domain, to be a scion of that eighteenth-century drive for the secularization of society which called itself Enlightenment.

Of itself, the distinction voiced by Jesus Christ between what is Caesar's and what is God's could be taken in the Sophoclean sense of the precedence due religious piety over civil law. However, His proclamation of the kingdom of God, His refusal to deny that He is a king, indeed His affirmation when questioned by Pilate about His kingship, make it clear that He is referring to the two sovereignties of church and state, as subsequent tradition has understood. This view is confirmed by the achievement of the Apostles, who created a society subject directly to God. But within this new society, unlike every society known till then, there was no distinction of class, of sex, or of nation.[28]

Paradoxically, one might think, loyalty to the nation and willing subjection to its authorities were to become hallmarks of the members of this new society. On the other hand, many adherents of modern liberalism were to distinguish themselves by rising above such subjection and such loyalty; this phenomenon, which we have seen in our own times, may have derived from modern liberalism's own refusal—in another appropriation by liberalism, on its own terms, of a Christian principle—to allow distinctions of nation, class, or sex.

At the outset of this section on the two sovereignties, that of God and that of the civil ruler, the widely-held claim was echoed that until the Christian epoch these two sovereignties were inextricably intermingled. I believe the claim to be true, but it requires a qualification. In all ancient societies but one, civil rule ruled over religious rule. That unique exception was primeval Israel, where Yahweh Himself was the ruler, and the Covenant the organic law of the nation.[29]

Marriage as a Political Institution

If our enlightened multiculturalists are unwilling to accept the Christian distinction between church and state in Christian terms, equally unacceptable to them on Christian terms is the third characteristic of a Christian society that I'll single out. It is the understanding that marriage is a lifelong union between equals.[30] This strikes me as the most basic of the three, if only because the family is the most basic institution of political society.

We have already seen the early church standing against the law and settled custom of Rome in the matter of marriage between slaves and free persons of position. Still earlier, in the mid-second century, Justin Martyr confronted the Emperor Antoninus Pius over the sexual immorality rampant in the empire. He cited, among other institutionalized iniquities, the exposition of newborns and their "rescue" by an infamous class of pedagogues (Justin's term) dedicated to rearing them to prostitution, male and female. "You take their taxes," he tells the emperor, "but you ought to extirpate them from your realm."[31]

The very first teaching assembly of the church, conventionally called the Council of Jerusalem, laid down four rules for Gentiles who wanted to become Christians. Among them is one that concerns us especially here: that they abstain from fornication.[32] Such a requirement, comments the Cambridge philosopher Elizabeth Anscombe, "must have meant a very serious change of life to many, as it would today."[33] It casts a searching light on the customs outside Israel in those days, and not least on Rome.

But with the accession of Constantine, the first Christian emperor, a change is manifest. Even the seemingly all-powerful institution of slavery, a foundation of the Roman economy, now takes second place behind marriage in Roman law. As we have seen, Constantine forbade the sundering of slave-families through sale of the members. No longer property first of all, women now first were wives and mothers, men husbands and fathers, children sons and daughters and brothers and sisters.[34]

The Christian conception of marriage was bound to take a further toll on Roman slavery, and its effects within the Roman Empire were to be more far-reaching still. Constantine did not content himself with giving precedence to marriage and the family over the long-established rights of slaveowners, but with the same measured gradualism made unilateral divorce more difficult, prohibited the keeping of concubines by married men, and forbade tax officials to drag mothers from their children.[35]

In this regard I take the liberty of quoting the opening lines of George Hayward Joyce's classic work, *Christian Marriage: An Historical and Doctrinal Study*.

> The civilization of Christendom—the civilization of which we are the heirs—was founded on Christian Marriage. The religion of Christ had lifted family life on to a new plane. It taught that marriage is sacred, God being the agent Who establishes and ratifies the union between husband and wife: that the bond thus divinely blessed is indissoluble until death; that the wife is no mere chattel, but a party to a contract between equals; and that all sexual relations outside marriage, whether on the part of the husband or the wife, are grievously sinful. These truths gave to the union a dignity, a purity, and a sanctity hitherto undreamed of. Where they held sway in men's minds the foundations of society were secure: it could never suffer complete ruin. For in the social organism the true units are not isolated individuals, but families. And where the Christian ideal of marriage prevails, the family, strengthened by supernatural sanctions, will hold good through every crisis, and even in the greatest political convulsions provides the principle of eventual recovery.[36]

Joyce points out that when Roman authority disintegrated in the West, and the barbarians from which most of us are descended moved into the void and, about that time, accepted the faith of Christ, the church then strove by exhortation and a rigid ecclesiastical discipline to bring the lives of our newly-converted ancestors into conformity with the Gospel. He proceeds:

> But her efforts for that end were directed in large measure to enforcing the law of Christian Marriage. . . . And though her aims were primarily spiritual, they were also fruitful . . . in the temporal sphere. By giving to the world the Christian family, she provided the basis of a new and better social order. She rebuilt society from its foundations. Indeed she did more than rebuild: she re-fashioned the very material of its construction.[37]

From this it is clear that the writer, in referring earlier to "the Christian ideal of marriage," is not speaking of some beautiful if humanly unattainable ideal, but rather of a standard to be lived, a standard moreover to be sustained by law and by its tireless enforcement. He drives the point home with particulars of the penitentials—rules of penance stipulated for the violation of laws—and with decrees of local councils.

None of this constituted the imposition of a merely ecclesiastical discipline. Nor was it merely—if we can speak in such terms—the law of Our Lord Jesus Christ. His teaching on marriage is, according to His own account, a restoration of the original institution.[38] He restored marriage as it came from the hand of God.

Modern Marriage

That can be perceived if only dimly, as if reflected by a dirty and distorted mirror, in the societal and personal havoc that our modern Enlightenment-style marriage has wreaked. Modern marriage is centered on the fulfillment of the spouses, to the neglect if not exclusion of the further intrinsic purposes of marriage, especially offspring and their education. This was already clear more than half a century ago when Joyce observed:

> . . . the idea that the family is the basis of social order, and that, in consequence, those who enter on marriage are assuming grave responsibilities to society as a whole, which society has the right to safeguard, and, if need be, to enforce, has practically disappeared. . . . A most grave result of this new conception of marriage is the altered attitude of public opinion as regards conjugal unfaithfulness. Formerly adultery was reprobated not merely as a heinous breach of God's moral law, but as an offence against the very foundations of social order. Society struck back and inflicted correspondingly severe penalties.[39]

It is no accident that the most corrosive attack on Christian principles in our lifetime turns out to have been an attack on the family. Obviously I refer not to the Marxian revolution, now sunk in defeat and disrepute, its only remaining partisans clinging either to chairs in academe or to power in countries ruined economically, academically, and politically by the ideology of Marx and Lenin. Rather I refer to the sexual revolution of the '60s and '70s, still in full cry and still inflicting casualties, not least on children both born and unborn. I dare say that there isn't a reader of these lines who has not suffered from it, if not in his own person then in that of someone he loves. When we hear denunciations of the term "culture wars" on grounds of shrillness and divisiveness, we need only look around us at the walking wounded.

We could cite other characteristics that tend to set a Christian society apart, such as respect for the moral unassailability of innocent human life, and the tempering of justice with mercy, the latter exemplified in Italy's "Ministry of Mercy and Justice" with mercy taking pride of place. By contrast, the vagaries of an untethered liberalism are exemplified in its drive for universal mercy coupled with death for the most innocent.

Before proceeding to the core of this essay, namely the effect on education of that gross misconception of culture which goes under the names of "multiculturalism" and "diversity," we might pause to take our bearings. We've dealt with our common culture and our common faith, and tried to show that the culture that nourishes us has in large measure been derived from many cultures, but in an essential way from the faith that nourishes us. The big question is whether culture can stand if faith fails.

Education in a Faithless World

An integral part of that question, and the one that most concerns us here, is this: If faith fails, what kind of education would survive? That looms over the more particular problem we'll touch on, namely the threat posed by college accreditation to classical, faith-based education, the education that has sustained our culture. To put the matter plainly, college accreditation has been turned into a tool to cram higher education into a uniform mould, thus destroying diversity *among* institutions of higher education in the name of creating diversity *within* them.

If the reader thinks this attempt to create somebody's idea of diversity within our institutions of learning threatens their religious character, I agree. If the reader thinks that making all our colleges and universities alike—ironically in the name of diversity—would affect the future of the nation, I agree. If this drive to enforce diversity and multiculturalism in higher education reeks in the reader's nostrils of ideology, so it does in mine.

In employing the term *ideology*, I don't mean it as a mere smear-word for a philosophy I happen to find inadequate or misleading. An ideology in the strictest sense, the pejorative sense, is not a philosophy. An ideology rather is a very limited thesis, usually far outside the ambit of any perennial philosophy, characteristically presented as a panacea. In ideology, theory seems to be inevitably conjoined to a social movement. Both the movement and the theory are explained by the phenomenon noted by Aristotle, that men tend to think happiness lies in the possession of whatever good they happen to lack most.[40]

Thus Marx was able to persuade exploited and impoverished workers that his materialistic vision of reality would banish poverty. Feminists of an extreme stamp see in the abolition of "patriarchy" an end to all that women have suffered from men. As for the problems of philosophy proven insoluble by centuries of failed effort, Marx's ideology would, he held, banish them forever. Antoine Destutt de Tracy, founder of a forgotten philosophy he called *Idéologie*, and moreover coiner of the term, thought like most secularizing *philosophes* of the French Enlightenment that getting rid of religion would create a kind of utopia. Reason itself would persuade men to be good, but only on condition that priests were forbidden to "interfere in education." (The phrase is his.) That happy priest-free day came about, but it didn't keep Destutt out of the shadow of the guillotine, as we'll see.[41]

Among the benchmarks of ideology is narrowness of mind, an almost necessary consequence of its focus on one good to the exclusion of other necessary goods. Because of that same focus on one good, an ideology that strives to change society will inevitably demand radical changes in the institutions of society. Hence if an ideology triumphs in a society, it will almost certainly cause great dislocations, sufferings, and injustices, and even widespread death. The demise of the Marxist former dictator of Cambodia, Pol Pot, brought renewed attention to the death of more than a million Cambodians during his rule from 1975 to 1979.

Moreover the ideologue is so wedded to theory that he tends to be impervious to facts. Neo-Malthusianism offers an example. Predictions in the '60s of global famine were soon followed by a glut of food, but the new Malthusians didn't budge from their positions. Professional prophets of doom such as Paul Ehrlich and Lester Brown offer clarion examples. By the mid-'70s the Carter Administration had dropped worries about famine but was predicting, in Global 2000, that "the world in 2000 will be more crowded, more polluted, less stable ecologically," while "the world's people will be poorer in many ways than they are today." There was a humorous touch: Dr. Ehrlich's $1,000 bet with the late Julian Simon that five natural resources of Ehrlich's choosing would be costlier within a decade cost the doomsayer his thousand bucks in 1980.[42] Despite their wretched record, Neo-Malthusians are still taken seriously in academe.

A characteristic of ideology that inevitably sets it on a collision course with reality is its lack of *pietas*. Gratitude and awe for the great philosophers who have helped shape our culture is alien to it.[43] One reason for this is the innate hostility of ideology to tradition. Another may be that an ideologue is unlikely to have a broad education in philosophy, or for that matter in history or literature. Such an education, a liberal education, is an excellent inoculation against ideological infection.

Yet no characteristic of an ideology is more striking than antipathy toward religion. This is a species of jealousy. Religion offers the kind of passe-partout that an ideology pretends to give us. We might even see ideology as a surrogate religion. But where ideology narrows its focus, tends to dismiss the moral, and depends largely on theory, religion explains reality in a global and one might say existential way. Hence comes ideology's tendency to deny that problems confronted by religion really exist.[44]

Leafing through the proceedings of the 1995 convention of the Fellowship of Catholic Scholars,[45] which met on the problem of keeping Catholic higher education faithful to its original purposes, I find a curious omission. All the speakers recognize that what threatens the religious character of a religion-sponsored college or university is secularization, the spread of the notion that only a "neutral" education—that is, a secularist education—can be scholarly. This of course is the basis of the so-called Enlightenment university. While the speakers seemed to recognize Enlightenment ideas as the enemy, little if any mention was made of the driving force behind the Enlightenment. That was, and to some extent remains, antagonism toward religion, toward Revelation-based religion. To talk of the Enlightenment without speaking of hostility to Revelation is historically naive, certainly in the context of threats to religiously-sponsored higher education.

What makes this omission especially curious is that the great eruption of Enlightenment ideology, the French Revolution, was characterized not only by an attempt to wrest education from religious sponsorship, which set back education on every level, but by a literally lethal hatred of religion. The children of Enlightenment actually killed people out of hatred for their religion, which in an almost incredible example of unconscious irony they kept calling fanaticism.

Of course Enlightenment politicians, like Enlightenment philosophers, were not necessarily atheists. True, Voltaire's notion of God as a sort of cosmic clockmaker was worlds removed from St. Thomas's notion of God as pure act and subsisting intellect, but the hostility of the Enlightenment to traditional religion had little to do with any metaphysical notion of God. It had everything, or almost everything, to do with hostility to revealed religion, to organized religion.

In France, naturally, that meant hostility to the Church of Rome. Just consider how often the phrase "Ecrasez l'infame!"—Crush the wretch!—flowed from the pen of Voltaire. He even had a coded abbreviation for it: "Ecr. l'inf." It was his mantra. The man was consumed by lust for the destruction of institutional religion, of religion based on revelation.

There are literally countless examples of this from the French Revolution. The confiscation of ecclesiastical property is one, the dissolution of the religious orders is another. But the clearest and most striking example of hatred for the church, in my view, was the judicial murder of nuns, as enemies of the nation. Readers may be familiar with this through the opera of Francis Poulenc, *Dialogues of the Carmelites*, a fictionalized version of the martyrdom of Carmelite nuns in Paris, but it wasn't only in Paris that nuns were guillotined. About the time that the sixteen Carmelites were executed in the capital, sixteen Ursulines were executed publicly in the south of France at Orange, along with an equal number of nuns from other orders.

I don't want to linger too long here, but there are significant lessons to be drawn from these episodes. Poulenc's opera, presented in major opera houses throughout the world, and on television, has brought this drama to the attention of people everywhere, yet omits or distorts some of the most interesting and significant facts. For instance, when the Carmelites were being led before the tribunal, one of them overheard the prosecutor explain to his aides that they were about to deal with a group of fanatics. "What do you mean by fanatics," she demanded. He tried to brush her off, but the spunky young nun demanded a citizen's right to know what was this fanaticism she and her fellow Carmelites were being tried for. "I mean by it," the sinister Antoine Fouquier-Tinville finally responded, "your attachment to childish beliefs and your silly religious practices." "You see," she cried triumphantly to her fellow nuns, "we are being tried for holding to our holy religion. We have the happiness to die for God."[46]

Martyrdom as Enlightenment

Now it has often been remarked that nothing reveals the truly important realities quite so clearly as martyrdom. We find ourselves saying, Why yes, God is worth dying for. Yes, He really exists. Yes, the spiritual holds absolute primacy. The martyrdom of these sixteen very obviously innocent women reveals that politics wasn't the only question, not even the basic question, but that something deeper was at stake. It was religious belief, the sovereignty of God and of His Law.

Did the crowd sense this, that unruly, thrill-seeking crowd which gathered round the guillotine to watch heads fall? When the nuns in their white Carmelite mantles mounted the guillotine one by one, the youngest first as if in liturgical procession, the turbulent crowd, the sensation-seeking crowd, was struck dumb. We are told that never before in the two years of the Terror had this happened. Quiet as if in a cathedral, all the customary catcalls awed into silence, the crowd could hear this young woman, not yet thirty years of age, intone the psalm, *Laudate Dominum omnes gentes, laudate Eum omnes populi*—Praise the Lord all ye nations, all ye peoples praise Him—and could hear her sister nuns take up the song while she waved away the executioners and, with a bearing that witnesses called queenly, advanced to the blade.

Someone in the crowd was moved—or inspired—to make a remark that through two centuries has retained all the freshness of truth: If they don't go straight to Heaven, there's no such place.[47]

As it happens, at that very moment, waiting in prison in full expectation of his own execution, was our friend, the Enlightenment philosopher and historical founder of ideology, Antoine Destutt de Tracy. A mere ten days after the execution of the Carmelites, a woman wearing a robe and holding a stone appeared outside the prison where Destutt awaited the inevitable. She tugged at the robe and held up the stone, then made chopping motions on her neck. Robespierre, the monster, was himself on his way to the guillotine.[48] The Terror, the long reign of mortal fear, was over. Destutt would be spared, but never would he dream—never within the narrow confines of his ideology could he dream—that these sixteen Carmelite nuns, long before danger seemed imminent, had solemnly offered to God their own lives for an end to the Terror.[49]

Ideological Harassment of Higher Education

Destutt is long forgotten. Ideology thrives. Some of those who find themselves with a certain power over institutions of higher learning through their authority to withhold accreditation have mandated ideologically-oriented changes: in curricula, in faculty, in administrative personnel, in the student body, and even in the governing board. Let's recall some cases.

Only three such are publicly known, so far as I can determine, but the U.S. Department of Education has made it clear that there have been many, many more, and educators I have consulted maintain that the ideological pressures from accrediting agencies are continuing.

The first case to come to public attention was that of Baruch College of the City University of New York. When a team of visitors representing the accrediting association found that the school was lacking in "diversity"—a subcategory of *multiculturalism*—the story made the *New York Times*. The accrediting agency had held up accreditation. Immediately the college was besieged by phone calls from alumni, wanting to know whether their degrees meant anything, and from students, wanting to know if they could still get government loans despite the delay in accreditation. Prospective donors canceled appointments with the college. The college president "caved in"—his term—and eventually resigned.[50]

Without deprecating the importance of this case, which drew attention to the immense power wielded by accrediting agencies, we won't go any deeper into it. The reason is that it dealt with diversity of race, not diversity of curriculum, our own focus here. For our purposes, the principal lesson to be drawn from the Baruch College case is that publicity about criticisms of a college by accreditors can damage the college, its reputation, its fund-raising ability, and especially the number of students applying for admission. This is one of the reasons why college administrators cave in, and make no public fuss. Another is that hardly any college or university in the country can do without the governmental funds that, either by direct grant or through aid to students, for better or for worse, have come to keep higher education afloat.

The two other cases that have come to public knowledge are those of Westminister Theological Seminary in Philadelphia, and of Thomas Aquinas College in Santa Paula, California.   These two institutions hung tough, no matter what. If you're looking for the reason why, it's probably religious conviction.

The Middle States accrediting association, the same body that forced the "cave-in" of Baruch College, demanded of Westminster Theological Seminary that it include women on its governing board. The Presbyterian seminary responded that its by-laws stipulated that all members of the board be ordained elders of the church, and that as a matter of church teaching, only men could be ordained. But the accreditors ignored doctrine, the very reason for the seminary's existence. Declaring they would not "compromise" on "principles," they ordered Westminister to show cause why its accreditation should not be removed.[51]

But by this time, the new U.S. Secretary of Education, Lamar Alexander, had been alerted to the behavior of Middle States, and announced that he was delaying the renewal of its authority as an accreditor. To make a long story short, Middle States moved to save face yet save its skin through an arrangement with Westminister that did not compromise the doctrinal principles of the seminary.[52] The board of Middle States voted that diversity would not be a condition of accreditation. The executive director of Middle States resigned.

One would think that this defeat would have chastened any other accreditor with diversity on the brain. (I should say that not all six regional accrediting agencies have been so aggressive.) Yet on the opposite coast, the accrediting agency known as Western Association of Schools and Colleges, or WASC, kept pushing a document on "diversity." In doing so it ran up against tiny Thomas Aquinas College, then scarcely twenty years old and with graduating classes measured in dozens of graduates.

This is an epic awaiting its Homer. To give a few incidents: Under pressure to teach African philosophy, the college president offered to comply if WASC proposed an African philosopher up to the level of the philosophers that his school taught; no candidate was forthcoming. Another visiting accreditor demanded to meet with minority students; the president told him the college didn't classify its students that way, though the team was free to buttonhole any students anywhere on campus, and provisions for private interviews would be made.

As for WASC's statement on diversity, Thomas Aquinas College sent its critique to the top administrators of every institution of higher education in California. Among its comments:

- *One would expect the statement to begin with recognizing this obvious truth—that "diversity" of itself is an empty word, and signifies no principle whereby a given course of action might be justified or condemned. But there is no such recognition.*

- *. . . when an institution pursues diversity as an end, it loses its original purpose and coherence, and becomes quite literally indefinable.*

- *Here it is assumed without argument that one cannot reasonably evaluate different views and perspectives unless one is surrounded by those who exhibit them in their life and thought. Thus, for example, to understand Marxism rightly, one must (for it is "essential") live and converse with Marxists. Accordingly, the faculty, student body, and staff should include Marxists.*

- *If this ['appreciation of cultural diversity'] means the sober and attainable goal of breadth of mind achieved by a wide range of studies, we have no difficulty with it. If it means historicism or cultural relativism, or an immersion in the ephemeral cultures of the present, our program excludes it.*

Argumentation of this sort convinced some of the most powerful educators in California.[53] The president of Stanford threatened to take his institution out of WASC. In a striking parallel to Middle States, the executive secretary of WASC resigned, and the remaining officers made pacific noises all around.

Happy endings, we may say, yet the drama goes on. The public remains largely unaware of it because colleges and universities go to great lengths to avoid publicity about problems with accreditors. All but the most prestigious would suffer. Some, if their accreditation were perceived as shaky, could go under. Hence the punitive power of accreditors is virtually limitless, and there is little to curb their hubris. Acton's dictum about absolute power must come to mind.

Yet our institutions must stand ready to abandon everything but that priceless pearl which is the very reason for their existence. Stately campuses may calm the mind, fine academic buildings may delight the eye and lift the spirit, but if through our callowness true education is banished, they become ruined shells and noxious deserts. Hence the most splendid academic architecture can never obstruct our vision of just what education is, and what our lifelong enterprise is about.

Did not the founder of academe himself tell us that heaven descended on the low-roofed cottage of Socrates?

Patrick Riley teaches Classical Antiquity at Concordia University Wisconsin. A journalist by trade, he covered all four sessions of the Second Vatican Council, and has reported and broadcast from two dozen countries of Africa, Asia, Europe, and North America.

Bibliography

Alfoldi, Andrew. *The Conversion of Constantine and Pagan Rome*, trans. Harold Mattingly. Oxford: The Clarendon Press, 1948.

Anscombe, Elizabeth. *Contraception and Chastity.* London: The
    Catholic Truth Society, n.d.

Brett, Stephen F. *Slavery and the Catholic Tradition.* New York: Peter
    Lang, 1994.

Bush, William, ed. "Literature and Martyrdom." *Renascence,* Vol.
    XLVIII, no. 1 (Fall 1995).

Chesterton, G.K. *Collected Works.* San Francisco: Ignatius Press,
    1986.

Davis, David Brion. *The Problem of Slavery in Western Culture.*
    Ithaca, NY: Cornell University Press, 1966.

_____. *The Problem of Slavery in the Age of Revolution, 1770-
    1823.* Ithaca, NY: Cornell University Press, 1975.

_____. *Slavery and Human Progress.* New York: Oxford
    University Press, 1984.

Fortin, Ernest L. *Collected Essays.* Lanham, Md., et alibi: Rowman &
    Littlefield, 1996.

Joyce, G. H. *Christian Marriage: An Historical and Doctrinal Study,*
    2nd. ed. London: Sheed and Ward, 1948.

Gardiner, Robert, ed., with John Morrison. *The Age of the Galley.*
    London: Conway Maritime Press, 1995.

Goodman, L.E. *Avicenna.* London: Routledge, 1992.

Jaki, Stanley. *Science and Creation: From Eternal Cycles to an
    Oscillating Universe.* Edinburgh and London: Scottish Academic
    Press: 1974.

Kennedy, Emmet. *Destutt de Tracy and the Origins of 'Ideology'.*
    Philadelphia: American Philosophical Society, 1978.

_____. *A Cultural History of the French Revolution.* New Haven:
    Yale University Press, 1989.

Kimball, Roger. "My Darling Clement: The Art of Writing about Art,"
    The Weekly Standard, Vol. 3, No. 35 (May 18, 1998), pp. 45-47.

Mendelsohn, Isaac. "The Family in the Ancient Near East," *The
    Biblical Archeologist,* Vol. 11, No. 2 (May 1948). Reprinted in *The
    Biblical Archeologist Reader* 3 (Garden City: Anchor Books,
    1970).

Owens, Joseph. *St. Thomas Aquinas on the Existence of God.* Albany,
    NY: State University of New York Press, 1980.

The Oxford Companion to Philosophy. Oxford: Oxford University
    Press, 1995.

Mastroeni, Anthony J., ed. *The Nature of Catholic Higher Education,
Proceedings from the Eighteenth Convention of the Fellowship of
Catholic Scholars*, Minneapolis, Minnesota, 1995 (Steubenville:
Franciscan University Press, 1996).

Pirenne, Henri. *Economic and Social History of Medieval Europe.*
New York: Harcourt Brace, n.d.

Riley, Patrick G.D. *Chastity and the Common Good* (forthcoming).

_____. "Medicine as a Moral Art," *The Linacre Quarterly*, August
1998.

Segal, Joel. "When Academic Quality Is Beside the Point," *The Wall
Street Journal*, Oct. 29, 1990, op-ed page.

Vogt, Joseph. *The Decline of Rome*, trans. Janet Sondheimer. London:
Weidenfield and Nicolson, 1967.

Simon, Yves. *The Tradition of Natural Law.* New York: Fordham
University Press, 1965, 1992.

Whitehead, A.N. *Process and Reality.* New York: Macmillan, 1929.

_____. Science and the Modern World: Lowell Lectures, 1925
New York: Macmillan, 1925.

Notes

[1] It will soon enough become clear to the reader that the present essay is written from a specifically Thomistic perspective. Until recently, most readers would have concluded from this that the writer is a Roman Catholic, which in fact he is. But as *The Oxford Companion to Philosophy* (Oxford and New York: Oxford University Press, 1995) observes s. v. "Aquinas, St. Thomas":

> "After centuries of neglect by thinkers outside the Catholic Church, his writings are increasingly studied by members of the wider philosophical community and his insights put to work in present-day philosophical debates in the fields of philosophical logic, metaphysics, epistemology, philosophy of mind, moral philosophy, and the philosophy of religion."

That long list is far from exhaustive. One might add, for example, political philosophy, a special interest of the present writer.

[2] *Confessions*, XI, 14. St. Augustine's words: *Quid est ergo tempus? Si nemo ex me quaerat, scio; si quaerenti explicare velim, nescio.*

[3] And even if I derive it from a great Athenian, in founding culture on the paradigmatic virtue of justice I follow what I take to be the drift of Plato in *The Republic*. Hence I construe culture as an essential part of the life of the city, that is of politics. It may be significant that Aquinas, the foremost

Aristotelian of the Middle Ages, does not take Aristotle's cue and move direct from private ethics into politics conceived as public ethics, but rather bases himself on Plato and the Roman jurists, who made justice the key to politics. Cf. Ernest L. Fortin, "The Political Thought of Thomas Aquinas," chap. 8 of vol. 2 of his *Collected Essays* (Lanham et alibi: Rowman & Littlefield, 1996), reprinted from Leo Strauss and Joseph Cropsey, eds., *History of Political Philosophy*, 3d edition (Chicago: University of Chicago Press, 1987).

[4] A distinction can and perhaps should be drawn between the act of justice, which is to render another his due, and the virtue of justice, which is the *habit* of rendering everyone his due. Societal consensus would concern the nature of the act, and its desirability; custom would include the virtue and its enforcement.

[5] See Thomas Aquinas, *Summa Theologiae* IIa-IIae, Question 101, Article 1, body and response to the first objection; cf. Article 3, body and response to the second objection.

[6] For the classical understanding of the arts, and their relation to the fine arts, see the present writer's "Medicine as a Moral Art" which is to be published in the future.

[7] Op. cit., IIa-IIae, Q. 58, Art. 3. Cf. Ia-IIae, Q. 60, Art. 3.

[8] The qualification is G.K. Chesterton's: "The morality of a great writer is not the morality he teaches but the morality he takes for granted." *(The Superstition of Divorce*, in *The Collected Works of G. K. Chesterton* [San Francisco: Ignatius Press, 1987], vol. 4, p. 243.)

[9] High moral significance is almost customarily accorded to nihilistic, pornographic, or blasphemous art by a school of criticism characterized by indecipherable gobbledygook. For some striking if shocking examples, see Roger Kimball's "My Darling Clement: The Art of Writing about Art" in *The Weekly Standard*, Vol. 3, No. 35 (May 18, 1998), pp. 45-47.

[10] The liberal shibboleth against any restrictions savoring of censorship has reached the extremes to which its inner logic long drove it. Thus it has become highly vulnerable to criticism from so influential a thinker as Robert Bork, and others.

Here too, however, the principle that the state is not omnicompetent demands respect. The subtleties of art ordinarily lie beyond the capacities of the state, as to a lesser extent do the subtleties of intellect. Only with reluctance, caution, and a certain humility should the state venture into such domains, whether in promoting them or in protecting the public from their abuse. Nonetheless where public opinion cannot maintain public propriety, and where religious institutions (including universities) are too timid, divided, or tainted to be effective, the state may find itself constrained to intervene.

For the establishment of justice as the proper object of the state, see the Preamble to the U.S. Constitution, bearing in mind the historical conditions that prompted the Framers to put "form a more perfect union" ahead of "establish justice." For the confinement of civil law to matters of justice conceived narrowly, see Aquinas, *Summa Theologiae* Ia-IIae, Q. 100, Art. 2.

[11] Of the Ciceronian passages dealing with this, the clearest I know is *Laws*, II, iv, 8, quoted in note 27 infra.

[12] *Science and the Modern World: Lowell Lectures, 1925* (New York: Macmillan, 1925), pp. 17-18.

[13] Stanley Jaki treats this particular question extensively in his *Science and Creation: From Eternal Cycles to an Oscillating Universe* (Edinburgh and London: Scottish Academic Press: 1974). He points out that even a Marxist Sinologist, Joseph Needham, holds this view.

Jaki's work also expands and documents Whitehead's thesis considerably, drawing largely upon the work of Pierre Duhem.

[14] *Process and Reality*, II, 1, 1, where Whitehead describes this metaphor as "the safest general characterization of the European philosophical tradition." In section 3 Whitehead appears to explain his famous metaphor:

"In its turn every philosophy will suffer a deposition. But the bundle of philosophical systems expresses a variety of general truths about the universe, awaiting coordination and assignment to their various spheres of validity. Such progress in coordination is provided by the advance of philosophy; and in this sense philosophy has advanced from Plato onwards."

[15] See L. E. Goodman, *Avicenna* (London: Routledge, 1992), pp. 97 and 109. Joseph Owens, in a much broader study of Thomistic proofs that includes Thomas's commentaries on Aristotle (*St. Thomas Aquinas on the Existence of God* [Albany: State University of New York Press, 1980]), also sees the influence of Avicenna in what St. Thomas calls "the first and more manifest way" to the existence of God, namely from motion.

The five "ways" of St. Thomas are found in the *Summa Theologiae* Ia, Q. 2, Art. 3.

[16] For these and other cases of slavery in Christian societies, see David Brion Davis, *The Problem of Slavery in Western Culture* (Ithaca, NY: Cornell University Press, 1966), chapt. 2.

[17] Pope Leo XIII is only echoing historians of the nineteenth century, notably Henri Wallon, in claiming (Encyclical of 20 November 1890) that the Church "from the beginning sought the complete elimination of slavery." Despite Wallon's voluminous labors, the claim can hardly be justified. From earliest Christian times, ecclesiastical authorities and representative Christian thinkers had defended the intrinsic justice of slavery, though under specified conditions designed to ensure human and Christian dignity. Because such restrictions proved incapable of rendering slavery less than odious, they seem in retrospect to indicate the intrinsic injustice of the institution, yet Christian thinkers and authorities maintained a consensus that slavery was just in itself.

Zeal for the spread of the Christian faith may have been at work here. There was fear that agitation against slavery would hinder the acceptance of the Christian faith, which wherever slavery prevailed—and that was everywhere—would have been seen as politically subversive. John Chrysostom voices this prudential reason early in the fifth century when introducing his homilies on Philemon (J. P. Migne, *Patrologiae cursus completus: Series graeca*, 62, 703-4). Thomas Aquinas offers a variation on this argument, asserting that the church refrains from demanding the manumission of newly-baptized slaves in non-Christian countries "in order to avoid scandal" (*Summa Theologiae*, IIa-IIae, Q. 10, Art.10).

Yet a contemporary of Chrysostom, Gregory of Nyssa, raised a strong protest against slavery (Migne, op. cit., 4, 549-550). This was rare. One exception in the Middle Ages was John Duns Scotus, the Franciscan theologian who seems to have achieved greater fame than any teacher at the University of Paris, even his near predecessor Aquinas. Scotus rejected all the traditional justifications for servitude except voluntary self-sale and punishment by the state (*Commentary on the Second Book of the Sentences*, Distinction 44, Question 1).

One of the traditional justifications for slavery, reaching back to ancient times, was that it was a merciful alternative to killing prisoners of war, especially aggressors; the Latin word for slave, *servus*, was very early linked to *servare*, to save or set aside. Throughout the Middle Ages and into modern times, popes permitted rulers to enslave their enemies. This permission was granted to Ferdinand and Isabella of Spain when their colonists moved into the New World, except that there the enemy was not the Saracen but the Indian.

With the recrudescence of slavery on a vast scale in the Americas, missioners and theologians, horrified at the ill-treatment of natives, began to re-examine the question, and launched a campaign for the prohibition of enslavement there. Results can perhaps be seen in numerous Spanish royal edicts of the early sixteenth century designed to ensure the liberty and well-being of Indians. Among them is the legislation of the emperor Charles V

(Charles I of Spain) of 4 December 1528 and 2 August 1530 prohibiting, respectively, ill treatment and enslavement of Indians.

The captains of the king, with thousands of miles of jungle, mountain, and ocean between him and them, displayed little readiness to obey. A Dominican friar who confronted Francisco Pizarro over his disregard for these laws and for the well-being of the Indians was told by the future conqueror of Peru that his only interest was gold. Probably with the support of misrepresentations from other ecclesiastics, contrary laws were published, whereupon the Dominican, Fra Bernadino de Minaya, returned to Spain and, begging for food and shelter along the road, walked halfway across the country to confront the cardinal responsible for the new laws. Getting no satisfaction, he walked to Rome to see Pope Paul III. The pope then issued, on 9 June 1537, his momentous bull *Sublimis Deus*, dismissing as inventions of the devil various claims that the Indians were subhuman and incapable of religious belief, and declaring:

". . . the said Indians and all other people who may later be discovered by Christians are by no means to be deprived of their liberty or the possession of their property, even though they be outside the faith of Jesus Christ. . . . "

[18] See, for example, Seneca's *47th Letter*. Cf. Juvenal's savage *Sixth Satire*.

[19] *In aris et focis est res publica*, according to Cicero's maxim. (I quote from memory, because I am unable to find the locus.)

[20] See G. H. Joyce, *Christian Marriage: An Historical and Doctrinal Study*, 2nd ed., (London: Sheed and Ward, 1948), p. 43.

[21] "For who," asks Constantine in justifying his decree, "could bear the separation of children from parents, sisters from brothers, wives from husbands?" (See *Codex Theodosianus*, II, 25.)

It is striking that the very first civil empowerment of bishops was to witness and record the manumission of slaves. (See *Codex Theodosianus*, IV, 7, 1, and *Codex Justinianus*, 1, 13, 2.) This was the work of Constantine. Eventually episcopal courts of arbitration, empowered by the emperor to decide disputes of all kinds, were founded across the Empire. (See *Codex Justinianus*, I, 27, 1.) Thus bishops were positioned to fall heir to full civil authority when the centralized administration of the Western Empire grew weak and finally collapsed, and the uniquely Christian principle of "Render to Caesar" was obscured.

Other Constantinian reforms respecting Christian custom and doctrine included setting aside Sunday as a day of rest, to be strictly enforced even in the army, and "sterilizing" the cult of the emperor so that Christians might take part in it. (See Andrew Alfoldi, *The Conversion of Constantine and Pagan Rome*, trans. Harold Mattingly [Oxford: The Clarendon Press, 1948], pp. 48-49 and p.106 respectively.)

The Constantinian law on the treatment of persons in the custody of courts is found in the *Codex Theodosianus*, IX, 3, 1.

Constantine's edict of 1 October 325 outlawed the very existence of gladiators, and hence the custom of relegating convicts to gladiatorial status and pitting them against one another in the arena (*Codex Theodosianus*, XV, 9, 12).

22 The moral licity of penal servitude is a different question. See reference to the opinion of Scotus in note 17.

23 An overview of economic changes in this period, and the social changes they entrained, is given in Henri Pirenne's *Economic and Social History of Medieval Europe* (New York: Harcourt Brace, n. d.), especially in the introduction and first chapter.

24 An instance is the absence of serfdom on the lands of Cistercian monasteries. Citeaux was a reform branch of Benedictine monasticism.

25 It should be noted at the outset of this section on the two sovereignties that a current of theological thought has held that were it not for man's inability by the unaided power of human nature to attain his end, namely final beatitude after death in the enjoyment of God, then the direction of men to this end would be among the duties of the temporal ruler.

The classic text on this is found in a work of disputed authorship. If attributed to Aquinas it now is customarily entitled *De Regno, ad Regem Cypri* (*On Kingship, to the King of Cyprus*) and the relevant section is found in Book Two, Chapter Three (especially numbers 105 through 109 in the Eschmann/Phelan edition published by the Pontifical Institute of Mediaeval Studies, Toronto, in 1949). If attributed to Aquinas's disciple and friend Tolomeo of Lucca, it is entitled *De Regimine Principum* (*On the Governance of Rulers*), and the relevant section is found in Book One, Chapter Fifteen (especially numbers 5 through 8 in the Blythe translation published by the University of Pennsylvania Press, Philadelphia, in 1997).

In any case, the text bears a master touch.

26 Sophocles' *Antigone*, the classical statement of a citizen's duty to put natural piety above civil decree, was probably produced early in the second half of the fifth century B.C.

27 It is commonly held that we owe the first articulation of natural law to Cicero. In this regard his *Republic*, III, xxii, 33, is most often quoted; he wrote

this masterpiece half a century before the birth of Christ. But a more elaborate if less rhetorically striking presentation is found in his *Laws* I, xii-xiii.

Cicero explicitly traces the natural law back to the mind of God in *Laws* II, iv, 8, where he observes that this has been the view of the most perspicacious. He writes:

"I see therefore that it has been the opinion of the very wisest that law is neither the ingenious excogitation of men, nor some enactment of peoples, but something eternal, ruling the whole world by its wise commands and prohibitions. Hence they used to say that law is the first and final mind of God, whose reason rules all things by compulsion or curb."

[28] See Galatians 3:28.

[29] Most readers may agree with that instinctively. After all, what has traditionally been hailed as the summary of all moral law, namely the Decalogue, not only constituted the stipulations of the Covenant but was also, according to widespread understanding, the basic civil law of Israel, comparable to our own Constitution.

But the matter has revealed itself to be less simple than that. Modern linguistic archeology, particularly in allowing the Hebrew *hamad* a further significance of taking steps to appropriate rather than merely coveting, has shown that the Decalogue can be interpreted as dealing exclusively with outward actions, hence as capable of construal as purely civil law.

Moreover the whole of the moral law cannot logically be deduced from the Decalogue. There is, to take the most patent example, no prohibition of lying as such, only of two species of lying, namely lying under oath and offering false witness; but condemnation of the genus cannot be inferred from condemnation of the species. This leads to the conclusion, perhaps shocking, that the Decalogue cannot be the summary of the moral law.

However it certainly can be seen as a symbol of the entire moral law, and in retrospect that has been its function. St. Thomas makes provision for this by asserting that moral precepts are "added" or "superadded" to the Decalogue (*Summa Theologiae* Ia-IIae, Q.100, Art. 11). While a widely used translation of that article has St. Thomas say that moral precepts "are reduced to" the Decalogue, implying logical reduction, the operative verb *reducuntur* is in this case correctly rendered "are led back to." .

A more detailed treatment of this matter is given in chapters one and two of a forthcoming book of the present author, tentatively titled *Chastity and the Common Good.* For an examination of the complicated question of Yahweh's rule over primeval Israel, and the choice of a king, consult *Summa Theologiae* Ia-IIae, Q. 105, Art. 1, especially the body and the reply to the first objection.

[30] St. Thomas points to the equality of husband and wife in his celebrated observation: "The greatest friendship is seen to stand between husband and wife" (*Summa contra Gentiles*, III, 123). (The Latin can be, and usually is, rendered "seems to stand," but to translate *videtur* as "seems" is a habit that translators of St. Thomas tend to fall into, since he uses that sense of the word countless times in introducing objections to his arguments.)

Traditional teaching that the husband is head of the household has met heavy weather since the rise of feminism in the '60s and early '70s. Pastors, preachers, and marriage counsellors—even those who base their practice on Christian principles—steer clear of it if they can. Such a course may seem only prudent. When the present writer cited St. Paul's injunction that wives (*Ephesians* 5) obey their husbands, a student described its effect on her as "a kick in the stomach." But she added that she would willingly obey a husband who followed the second part of the injunction, loving her as Christ loved the Church, and sacrificing himself for her as Christ did.

The notion that in ancient Jewish society the wife was the husband's property is found even among scholars. For a response, see Isaac Mendelsohn, "The Family in the Ancient Near East," in *The Biblical Archeologist*, XI.2 (May 1948), pp. 28-40 (reprinted in *The Biblical Archeologist Reader* 3 [Garden City: Anchor Books, 1970]). An effective response is also found in the alphabetic poem on the good wife in Proverbs 31.

[31] *First Apology*, XXVII. It should not be overlooked that the civil authorities of Rome had for centuries been preoccupied by a decline in marital honesty, and that emperors from Augustus onward attempted to restore marriage and numerous offspring by a system of punishments and rewards. Moreover the generalized decline in sexual mores constitutes a constant lament of Roman historians. The present writer has attempted an outline of these complaints and endeavors in chapter four of his forthcoming *Chastity and the Common Good*, ut supra.

[32] See Acts 15.

[33] *Contraception and Chastity* (London: The Catholic Truth Society, n.d.), pp. 3 and 4.

[34] See note 21.

[35] See Joseph Vogt, *The Decline of Rome*, trans. Janet Sondheimer (London: Weidenfield and Nicolson, 1967), p. 105. Vogt, ibid., also recalls the legal protection that Constantine extended to the livelihood of farmers; this also was bound to protect farming families from destitution.

[36] Joyce, op. cit., p. v.

[37] Op. cit., p. vi.

[38] Matthew, 19:8.

[39] Op. cit., pp. ix-ii.

[40] Cf. *Nicomachean Ethics*, I, iv: "When ill, he calls it health, when poor, wealth."

[41] Nor, seemingly, did it persuade Destutt to be good. The novelist Henri Beyle, who went by the nom de plume of Stendhal, held that Destutt took advantage of a garden gate between his house and the adjoining house of his best friend to gain access to his best friend's wife. For Stendhal's criticisms of Destutt and his philosophy, see Emmet Kennedy, *Destutt de Tracy and the Origins of 'Ideology'* (Philadelphia: American Philosophical Society, 1978), chap. 8.

[42] Simon's most illustrious predecessor in the defense against Neo-Malthusianism was probably Colin Clark. When Clark, then professor of agricultural economics at Oxford, gave a lecture at the London School of Economics late in 1954, the hall was crowded with students expecting his demolition by the principal demographer of the institution, David Glass. Professor Glass, who had publicly characterized Clark as "a theologian" (Clark was a professed and practicing Catholic), took a prominent seat in the very front of the audience. But Clark, who had already shown his eminence in economics by originating the concept of the Gross National Product, disarmed his audience by accurate and friendly responses even to hostile questions. Before the end of the meeting, the questioners had become earnest seekers, not antagonists. Glass, grim as granite, sat silent throughout.

[43] In his concise account of ideology and its differences from philosophy, Yves Simon cites the remarkable case of John C. Calhoun, who called upon the philosophy of Aristotle to justify slavery. See Simon's *The Tradition of Natural Law* (New York: Fordham University Press, 1965, 1992), pp. 17-18; explicit references to Aristotle are found in note 2.

[44] This could be seen in the nervous antagonism that Marxist literary critics showed Dostoevski, who not only presented solutions that Marxist theory necessarily dismissed but drew attention to problems that Marxist theory claimed could not exist.

[45] *The Nature of Catholic Higher Education, Proceedings from the Eighteenth Convention of the Fellowship of Catholic Scholars*, Minneapolis, Minnesota, 1995, Anthony J. Mastroeni editor (Steubenville: Franciscan University Press, 1996).

[46] *Butler's Lives of the Saints*, eds. H. Thurston and D. Attwater (New York: P.J. Kenedy & Sons, 1956), vol. 3, pp. 132-134, s.v. "The Carmelite

Martyrs of Compiegne." At this writing the most complete account in English not only of the martyrdom and events leading to it but also of the roles of Gertrud von Le Fort, Emmet Lavery, Raymond Bruckberger, Georges Bernanos, and Francis Poulenc to present to the public the drama of the nuns of the Compiegne Carmel is found in *Renascence*, XLVIII, 1 (Fall 1995).

[47] *Renascence*, ut supra, p. 76.

[48] Kennedy, op. cit., p. 37.

[49] *Renascence*, p. 71.

[50] Cf. *The Wall Street Journal*, Oct. 29, 1990, op-ed page: Dr. Joël Segall's reflections on pressures on Bernard Baruch College by the Middle States Commission on Higher Education. Dr. Segall was president of Baruch College during the events he describes in this article. He said "When colleges are called upon to depart from normal academic standards to solve societal problems, they are being asked to do something they are not equipped to do, and are diverted from . . . their main job, the pursuit of academic excellence."

[51] Letter of March 7, 1990.

[52] Middle States withdrew its show-cause demand to Westminster Seminary on June 5, 1991, and asked that Westminster withdraw its complaint to the U.S. Department of Education. Three weeks after a November 21-22 meeting with the Department of Education, the board of Middle States voted not to apply "diversity" as a condition for accreditation.

[53] Wrote the president of the University of Southern California, Steven B. Sample:

> I have been appalled over the years at the amount of real harm that can be done by misguided attempts on the part of accrediting bodies (both regional and professional) to "improve" the institutions or programs under their purview. This problem almost always stems from the misuse of the police powers of the accrediting body (which powers are intended to be used only to curtail fraud) to force all institutions to conform to the particular curricular, political or social agenda that happens to appeal to those in control of the accrediting body at the time (letter of 17 January 1995 to Paul Locatelli, S.J., president of Santa Clara University).

14

A Lutheran Vision of Christian Humanism[1]

Robert Benne

If you have been reading the same literature that our administration has been reading, you, like I, will be feeling a bit uneasy. Peter Drucker foresees higher demands for vocational specialization and lower demands for traditional liberal arts colleges.[2] George Dehne tells of the eroding interest in small colleges.[3] The Pew Policy Perspective Papers pose a most troubling question: Why are liberal arts colleges declining in number?[4] They suggest pricing is a very serious problem. These studies and others seem to offer grim predictions for the futures of colleges like ours. But all say that in order to survive these colleges must have a strong, distinctive, and clear vision that includes serious attention to value-formation.

In this struggle for survival it seems somewhat beside the point to engage in reflection on how a specific religious heritage conceives of higher education.[5] In the rough and tumble of staying afloat institutionally isn't it a luxury to think on these things? I suspect not, because it is precisely that ingredient—our specific religious heritage—that may contribute strongly to the kind of character, soul, or ethos that will have real survivability value. More importantly, we hold the proposition that our religious heritage matters as an item of truth; we do it for its intrinsic merits. At least I have wagered my life's energy on such a proposition.

I. The Relevance of an Impossible Educational Ideal

I have shamelessly stolen the above phrase from Reinhold Niebuhr,[6] though I have altered it by substituting "educational" for "ethical." In that book Niebuhr grapples with the question of how a radical ethical ideal—agape love—is relevant to worldly forms of human relationships which are characterized more by balance of power or reciprocity than by selfless love. Agape love, which was embodied in the life, ministry, and death of Jesus, is the highest principle of Christian ethics. On first glance it seems irrelevant to worldly relationships decisively shaped by sin and finitude. As such, these worldly relationships are recalcitrant and unyielding; they seem to make agape love an irrelevant ideal.

But, Niebuhr argues, that is not the case. A radical ideal is relevant precisely because it transcends whatever is achieved in worldly relationships. It always gives us something to shoot for. Though never triumphant in human history, it is nevertheless very relevant. Without such a demanding ideal, human relationships would decline and lack direction, and perhaps even descend into chaos and confusion. So it is with the educational ideal I will spell out later in this paper. It is nowhere triumphant but wherever there is a memory of it or longing for it the ideal is relevant.

But what forces in our educational worlds make it an impossible ideal? What makes the culture of our modern church-related colleges resistant to the allure of such an ideal? Why is such an educational ideal at most a peripheral concern for so many of our church-related colleges? We could spend the whole of the paper on such questions, of course, but then we would concentrate on the analytical rather than the constructive. We would complain but not propose. But let us indulge our human frailties and spend a few paragraphs on analysis and complaint.

One very practical reason for the educational ideal getting lost in the shuffle is the day-to-day struggle for survival and growth. The practical matter of attracting and keeping students makes us adapt constantly to "market conditions." And the markets don't seem to be saying that parents and students are looking for educations shaped by a Lutheran educational ideal. This is true at least for the mainstream middle class types to which most of our colleges appeal, and for which our recruitment approaches are set up.[7] Too much insistence on "Christian humanism," "Christian atmosphere," or "Christian values" makes colleges sound like—horror of horrors!—a Liberty or Bob Jones University. Christian rhetoric drives customers away, and we are above all interested in customers. Indeed, some of us come close to saying the customer is always right and then in our drive for survival we give up our soul. We become overly "practical" and begin to believe we can live by bread alone.

Certainly the dominance of the so-called "Enlightenment paradigm" is a major factor in making our academic culture resistant to the Christian vision. The Enlightenment held that reason, science, and technology would lead to a world of unending progress.[8] The Heavenly City hoped for by Christians throughout the ages would be brought to earth by human means. Humans would be liberated from the obfuscation of priests and the oppression of kings to follow their own reason, which would guide them in harmonious paths. Traditional religion, the Enlightenment philosophers believed, was not based on universal reason and therefore was parochial and irrational; after all, it had brought on the terrible religious wars. Knowledge and morality derived from religion were not trustworthy. Religious and religiously-based moral beliefs best be kept private, isolated on Sundays and in the intimacy of the human heart. They have little relevance for genuine intellectual and ethical inquiry. Though the early Enlightenment thought it was doing natural theology and ethics through rational means, the later Enlightenment lost theological interest and proceeded on more atheistic paths. That more radical or militant—or some would say, vulgar—Enlightenment slowly gained sway in the elite centers of western culture.

This paradigm has dramatically affected higher education in the western world, particularly graduate education. Many faculty in our church-related institutions have been shaped by its outlook, its methods, and its attitude toward religion and religion-based morality. Its influence has been so strong that the idea that a religious vision ought pervasively to condition our approach to education has become incredible. Put differently, the notion of a public Christian intellectual has at best fallen into misuse and at worst been considered oxymoronic. Indeed, if Christian intellectuals try to be public with their convictions and arguments they are often considered to be dangerous proselytizers without intellectual substance or integrity. This attitude sadly is even present in our church-related colleges.[9]

The postmodern movement has ambiguous effects on campus culture insofar as its hospitality to the Christian vision goes. Its emphasis on particular histories and perspectives, especially those of the "oppressed" and "excluded," has helpfully challenged the

Enlightenment's intellectual claims to be operating from a universal rational viewpoint. We are all "socially located," the postmoderns say, and this makes all the difference in making epistemological claims. The more extreme postmoderns fall into a kind of epistemological tribalism, but the more moderate turn attention to specific historical traditions as the source of knowledge and values.

One would think this movement would open the door to a particular living tradition such as the Lutheran Christian, especially since it is the sponsoring tradition of the college itself. Indeed, postmodernism has opened the door to teaching from a Christian viewpoint at many large prestige universities. After all, if African-Americans, feminists, gays and lesbians, Hispanics, Marxists, Freudians, etc., can teach from their particular point of view, why can't Christians? However, postmodernist impulses don't necessarily work that way at a church-related college. There the Christian tradition, because it is privileged or at least perceived to be privileged, is viewed as hegemonic. Thus, postmodernist impulses can accentuate the suspicions toward that dominant tradition and often work to delegitimate or relativize it.

Another strong factor working against a specifically Lutheran vision of higher education is the hyper-individualism of college faculty. Faculty often decry the lack of community in modern college and university life but they are the first to dissent from any attempt to articulate and uphold shared values. Except for commitment to important shared procedural values, faculty tend to be intellectual libertarians, resisting any consensus on substantive values. Other faculty who themselves are religiously involved in their private lives do not connect those private convictions with their public lives at the college. Sunday does not connect with Monday for them.

These sorts of realities in our modern educational world make it exceedingly difficult to make our "impossible educational ideal" relevant. But here we are at this conference,[10] probing the very issue I am concerned about. Many others who are not here are also concerned. Memory, longing, and hope are not extinguished.

II. Dialectical Christian Humanism

A. The Christian Pole of the Dialectic

The calling of a Lutheran college proceeds at least partially from the way it sees Christ related to culture, or, to put it a bit more adequately, from the way that it construes the Christian vision as a coherent and integrated view of the world (Lutheranly viewed) to be related to the culture and tasks of a liberal arts college.

The Lutheran way of relating Christ to culture has been famously termed "Christ and culture in paradox" by H. Richard Niebuhr.[11] This designation flows from the conviction that God's saving relation to the world is paradoxical. God saves through the cross of Christ. What is ostensibly a great defeat (the crucifixion of God's Son who appears as an obscure Jewish peasant) is at the same time a great victory (the expiation for all human sin). Victorious strength is shown most dramatically in vulnerability and weakness. An event in a particular time and space (neither very auspicious according to the world's reckoning) has universal and eternal significance. God's grace does not cancel out but rather transcends His judgment by taking the wrath meant for a disobedient world into Himself through Christ. Such a message is indeed "foolishness to the Greeks and scandalous to the Jews." And, except that its paradoxical edge has been taken off by thousands of years of common usage, such an assertion is as startling now as it was then. Throughout the ages countless attempts have been made to analyze and extract meaning from this stunning affirmation, which would have been quickly dropped had it not been for its surprising confirmation in the resurrection.

This paradox emerges from the background drama of God's conflict with Satan and with those whom Satan has captured, namely us and the world we have constructed. History is a battlefield between God and the forces against Him. Though we were created in God's image, we have fallen to Satan. All are sacred but none are good. All creation and all human artifacts are distorted by this Fall. We have met the enemy and he\she is us. We make idols of the good things God has given us and our misplaced loyalty to them touches off battles among other worshipers of idols and with God. This conflict between God and Satan, God and us, Christ and our culture will never subside on this side of the eschaton. There is an eternal "no" and "yes" to us and all our works and ways. As Niebuhr puts it, "In the polarity and tension of Christ and culture, life must be lived precariously and sinfully in the hope of a justification which lies beyond history."[12] Followers of Christ live in an unresolvable tension between allegiance to Him and life in the world.

Lutherans, of course, share the same basic Christian vision as other orthodox Christians. The paradoxical view of the Christian life is embedded in a much larger narrative common to all Christians. The narrative includes stories of creation, fall, covenants, commandments, judgment, expectation, the event of Christ, the gift of the Spirit and establishment of the Church.

The Lutheran vision, however, gives these themes a paradoxical twist. Humans are viewed paradoxically, as are human history and culture. God reigns paradoxically in two ways, through the Law and the Gospel. We both have and don't have the truth. Above all, though, the Lutheran vision affirms that we are justified by grace through faith on account of Christ.[13] All our human efforts fail at achieving salvation, even though we inevitably try to save ourselves, not least through mistaken notions that education itself is salvatory.[14] These themes, along with the broader vision, have direct relevance to a philosophy of education, to the calling of a Lutheran college.[15]

B. The Cultural Pole of the Dialectic

In order to see that relevance, however, we must stop for a moment to look at the other pole, the pole of human culture. In this case we are looking at the culture of education. Education is first of all an intellectual endeavor, though we know much education also goes on outside our classrooms.

Education is concerned with transmitting knowledge and wisdom about the natural world in which we live, human history and culture, and the perennial issues of the human condition and its possibilities. Our college has thirteen departments that pretty well summarize our formal educational endeavor: fine arts, education, business adminis-tration and economics, mathematics (including computer science and physics), psychology, religion and philosophy, history, public affairs, sociology, English, chemistry, biology, and foreign languages. We also have an extended general education core.

Each of these has their own perspective on humankind and strives to engage the student with something meaningful and useful about that slice of the human subject. Each has its own methods, focus, and accumulated store of knowledge and wisdom. Specialized fields have emerged and proliferated since the Enlightenment. At times they seem foolishly to demarcate themselves from each other in extreme fashion, even at liberal arts schools.

One of the geniuses of the Lutheran tradition is that it has bestowed a tentative autonomy on these "worldly" ways of knowing.[16] The Lutheran doctrine of the two kingdoms has held that reason and experience are trustworthy epistemological tools in inquiry into the truth of worldly matters. Luther said, "How dare you not know what can be known?" The great German universities—Heidelberg, Marburg, Berlin, Königsberg, Erlangen—were on Lutheran territories that encouraged this unfettered inquiry. Thus, Lutheranism has been more open to secular learning than the less dialectical forms of Christian humanism. It has insisted on intellectual integrity and rigor in this tentatively autonomous realm. This has meant academic excellence in both the European and American expressions of Lutheran higher education.[17]

But Luther and the early Lutherans were operating in a world pregnant with Christian meaning and values. Open inquiry did not at first seem to deny any transcendent source or grounding; it did not close off or deny the truths of the Christian worldview. But as secularization proceeded that very denial occurred. It occurred first at the intellectual level, particularly in the clash between the claims of the natural sciences and the Christian worldview. But even those who gave up the Christian worldview tended to maintain Christian morals. It was much later that both were jettisoned for a more secular approach to things.

In the heyday of the Enlightenment paradigm there was something of a prideful unity and exclusivity claimed for the Enlightenment approach. However, that has broken down with the proliferation of specialization and more recently under the onslaught of postmodern critique, though some of our faculty have not yet heard of that critique. There is a veritable fracturing of method and approach in many fields, particularly in the social sciences and humanities but less so in the natural sciences.

So, our educational culture includes many ways of knowing the world and our place in it. A good deal of the knowledge taught to students in our departments is noncontested. It is "common knowledge." Indeed, many of these disciplinary approaches (economics, for example) do not claim to offer a comprehensive interpretation of human life and action, but they do claim truthful insights into it. Often there are but a few steps (which economists like Gary Becker actually take) to a more comprehensive vision of the world, one which may stand in considerable tension with the Christian vision. Some fields of inquiry can and do make more comprehensive claims. Biology, for example, can adopt certain interpretations of the evolutionary theory as a whole philosophy of life that sets off fiery conflicts with the Christian vision. Some schools of psychology are systematic construals of the human condition.[18] Others are more modest.

In other words, academic culture is a lively and sometimes wild jungle of competing perspectives on the world and the human condition. Its diversity often makes the very designation "university" a sham to those who claim that name. Many specialists can no longer understand each other. For the most part, our liberal arts colleges are characterized by the same kind of diversity and fragmentation of knowledge and interpretation. But perhaps we have a chance to put things together a bit more, or at least set up a conversation that has the promise of making things a bit more coherent.

C. The Dialectic

A Lutheran college is a college where there is an ongoing and unresolved conversation between the two poles of the dialectic, the Christian and the cultural. The Christian vision, Lutheranly construed, is a recognized partner in that ongoing conversation. A conversation, someone has said, is characterized more by questions than by arguments. Each pole—the Christian and the cultural in its many guises—participates in a question and answer dialectic that tries to arrive at more truthful interpretations of our life and world. The Christian pole—the Christian vision—is a comprehensive and coherent vision of life, but is highly general and open to other insights that flesh it out. So it offers insights and raises questions about almost anything of importance. The cultural pole—the many disciplines—also offer insights and raise questions not only with regard to each other but also in relation to the Christian vision itself. The disciplines offer more detailed theories and knowledge that both complement and challenge the Christian vision.

The "fit" between the conversation partners is never perfect, but there is a great chance for mutual critique and enrichment, perhaps even a chance for synthesis. But these syntheses are always fragile; they break down as new knowledge is accumulated and brought to the conversation. The conversation is ongoing and never fully resolved. "Now we see through a glass darkly." Perhaps later we will see how it all fits together, just as the coherence and meaning of our own lives will be fully seen only from the perspective of eternity.[19]

This dialogue, it seems to me, takes place first within professors. Christians across the several disciplines engage in an effort to make their faith intelligible in relation to their own discipline and vice versa. The Christian's faith seeks understanding in science, sociology, psychology, etc. The conversation is first of all intrapersonal before it is interpersonal. The conversation takes place within the professor's own intellectual quest for meaning and coherence. So, for example, before my teacher of Shakespeare at Midland College back in 1958 could point out to me how Shakespeare's plays illustrated his Christian insight into human character, she had to work it out for herself. Then she could tell us about it, something that has stuck with me all these years.

This means that a Lutheran college has to have a significant number of persons who are interested in relating their Christian faith to their intellectual life. Not everyone has to do that. Those that do make such connections need not be Lutheran. In fact, the conversation will be immeasurably enriched by other Christians and sympathizers who strive to make such connections. Some faculty may simply support the process in others. Nor does it mean that we carry on this conversation all the time; we need much time simply to communicate our "common knowledge" to the students, and we need time to keep up in our own fields. But there should be a sympathy on the part of all faculty for this sort of intrapersonal quest in appropriate times and places.

This sympathy can help insure that the conversation is not only intrapersonal, but interpersonal and intracollegiate. A Lutheran college would have enough Christian intellectuals, and others interested in the conversation, to carry on lively dialogues between departments, in retreats and conferences, in convocations and faculty forums.

Such an ongoing conversation gives a special place to the Christian vision, not as an authoritarian arbiter of all truth, but as a honored partner in the dialogue. This kind of public relevance actively commends the Christian vision by taking it seriously in our quest for truth. It is honored as an indispensable voice in the conversation.

D. The Lutheran Difference

This dialectical form of Christian humanism can be distinguished from two temptations in the modern educational world, and from two other forms of Christian humanism that are not as dialectical as the Lutheran. Let us briefly make those distinctions.

The first temptation is to withdraw from all the difficult challenges presented by the culture, i.e., the insights and knowledge that come from the "secular" disciplines. This is the route of Christianity without humanism and leads to fundamentalist approaches to higher education. The insights of modern learning are so threatening to some Christians that they retreat into a world of learning ostensibly governed solely by the Bible. The school ignores modern learning and communicates what it thinks the Bible says about everything important. This is the route of a Bob Jones University, some Bible colleges, and other small fundamentalist institutions. This approach impoverishes the educational offerings of the colleges that adopt it, as well as the intellectual life of the students who attend those colleges. What's more, a serious theological error is involved; God's creation is denied as a source for respectful inquiry. Only revelation is allowed as an avenue of understanding. Creation and redemption are torn apart. Such an approach ignores the biblical advice: "Whatever is true, whatever is honorable, whatever is just, whatever is pure, whatever is lovely, whatever is gracious, if there is any excellence, if there is anything worthy of praise, think about these things" (Philippians 4:8).

Further, the position is impossible. We cannot operate without culture. When we think we are doing so we are unconsciously smuggling culture into the mix without being self-critical about it. The whole approach is self-deceptive. This temptation is not a threatening one in ELCA colleges, though opponents of Christian humanism often claim we are succumbing to that temptation whenever public Christian claims are made. It would be absolutely impossible to move our ELCA colleges in that sectarian direction.

The second temptation is much more relevant to us—humanism without Christianity. This is a tendency very much present within our colleges. In one form this approach operates with a closed-minded secularism. All theological claims are denigrated or ruled out as irrelevant to the intellectual endeavor. This hard-nosed secularism operates among some in the social, psychological, and natural sciences. It is positivist and reductionist. It holds all religious claims, but particularly Christian ones, in contempt. It is a hangover from the vulgar Enlightenment. Persons holding this position generally have little use for the college's connection to a religious tradition. They would like to end the connection or at least sequester the Christian voice to a small corner of the college.

In another form this secular humanism denies the religious tradition any public or integrating role. It then proceeds toward a chaotic pluralism that can find no shared meanings. This is the fate of many public institutions, I believe. There is then a short step from chaotic pluralism to a nihilism where all intellectual claims are simply viewed as cloaks of hegemonic power. (Foucault and Derrida may be the endpoint of a desiccated western humanism.)

But there are two other forms of Christian humanism that are different from the Lutheran form of dialectic humanism. One is represented by the classical Catholic tradition. Classical Catholicism has the admirable impulse toward a complete and settled synthesis of knowledge and morality. St. Thomas attempted such a marvelous synthesis in the high Middle Ages when he fused Christian revelation with Aristotelian philosophy. Twentieth-century Catholics attempt similar syntheses with Marxism (liberation theology) or with integral humanism (the recent popes). While in many ways admirable, this tradition tries to be too neat and tidy; in doing so it closes off too many other sources of truth that do not accord with its favorite philosophical partner.

Reformed humanism takes a different tack. Its biblical/theological vision transforms or converts worldly knowledge. The autonomy of secular inquiry is a momentary thing; human knowledge will in time be converted by theological vision. So, many Reformed Christian humanists can talk of "Christian sociology" or "Christian economics." Such intellectuals press toward a conversion of human knowledge to Christian knowledge. Again, while admirable in many ways, such a tradition can be totalistic and oppressive, both to persons and to intellectual endeavors.

The Lutheran tradition, operating from more paradoxical theological roots, is most promising in holding Christian revelation and cultural knowledge in creative tension, not allowing Christianity to proceed without humanism nor humanism without Christianity. Moreover, among religious traditions, it is most likely to live with an unresolved but lively and fruitful dialogue with culture. Its dialectical tendencies lead to an unsettled Christian humanism. It complements the more settled humanism of its Reformed and Catholic compatriots.

III. The Calling of a Lutheran College

Given all this, then, let me briefly summarize the calling of the Lutheran college. I will be very schematic and terse, trusting that my major argument has already been made.

1. A Lutheran college seeks to be the best liberal arts college it can be. Lutheran ethics have always insisted that one must be competent in one's worldly responsibilities before one can transform them into a Christian calling. Luther said that a Christian cobbler performing his calling first of all makes good shoes, not inferior shoes with crosses on them. The Christian teacher first of all teaches well, then grounds, infuses, and transforms those teaching activities through faith, hope, and love into a genuine calling.[20] Likewise for a college. We first of all have to do education well.

For most of us that means a vigorous commitment to the liberal arts, to the provision of strong majors and to a challenging general education core. It means having faculty committed to and competent in achieving those ends. We also aim at educating the whole person, though we sometimes forget that we must educate whole students with whole faculty. We have to recruit whole faculty to do that kind of education. Those faculty must also be models for the goals and values we want to inculcate in our students. Faculty must do scholarly research and writing, just as we expect that of our students. Faculty must model scholarly conversation among themselves if they want to encourage students to talk about intellectual matters outside of class. Faculty must also model the moral virtues, first in their commitment to the education and well-being of their students, but also in living an honorable life.

There is, of course, much student learning that goes on outside our formal classes. Also, many activities that educate the whole person happen outside our classrooms. I will not address those sorts of things, except to emphasize that they often give specific character and color to our colleges. They are very important. What would a college be without choirs, teams, plays, concerts, recitals, service organizations, social organizations, chapel, conferences, informal friendship, and ethnic traditions?

2. Cultivate a dialectical form of Christian humanism. In order for this to happen one must have a board and administration that understands the Lutheran brand of humanism and is willing to create the conditions for it to happen. Obviously one must have a critical mass of faculty who are willing to nurture the kind of conversation I described above. Enough new faculty sympathetic with this "impossible educational ideal" must be recruited to sustain it. There must be real experts in the Lutheran heritage in order for the conversation to go on at a high level.[21] And all of these parties must talk about it, argue about it, and plan for it.

I have already sketched what I think this amounts to in the realm of formal education, which is the heart of what we are about as colleges. But this ongoing and unresolved conversation between Christ and culture must go on in our curriculum discussions, our faculty forums, our conferences and convocations, and in our own research and writing. Certainly we do not focus only on this conversation—that would be a dreary and tiresome thing—but we do not forget that it has a central place in the ongoing intellectual life of the college.

The Christian vision should also be publicly relevant in shaping the social life of the campus. We should not be reluctant to give an alluring account of Christian ideals with regard to service, civility, respect for authority, and social life (including sexual ethics). We are often tempted to promote only the minimal standards of conduct for our students. Then we fail to legitimate the struggle of many who are already trying to live the Christian life, and we miss the chance to exhort the less committed to a higher and more strenuous ideal. Amid the unraveling of our secular consensus on moral standards, our colleges may have an advantage in their connection to a concrete tradition that has a coherent and challenging vision of a good life.

The Christian vision should obviously be celebrated in the worship life of the college. Chapel should be given a sacrosanct time, it should be publicly encouraged by the administration and faculty, it should be of high quality, and it should be voluntary.

IV. Conclusion

Niebuhr, in his *Interpretation of Christian Ethics*, articulated several important functions of an impossible ethical ideal. It does several important things: 1) As a transcendent ideal it exercises indeterminate judgment on all penultimate achievements; 2) it points to indeterminate possibility; 3) it aids in making determinate decisions; and 4) it leads to contrition and humility because we never come close to achieving the ideal. The Lutheran idea of Christian humanism, as an impossible educational ideal, can play exactly such a role in the emerging definition and mission of Lutheran colleges.

It is clear that taking this ideal seriously will be initiated and sustained by the colleges themselves. The church cannot and will not dictate to the colleges; it can scarcely give any money in direct support . . . and whoever pays the piper calls the tune. The church is now the junior partner in the church's mission in higher education. Being a church-related college means we are primarily related to the intellectual, spiritual, and moral tradition of the church, not predominately to the supporting Synods or to the Evangelical Lutheran Church in America.

The colleges themselves have to elect to make the Lutheran ideal of Christian humanism perennially relevant. And they have to do it freely because it is the right and true thing to do, not because someone makes them do it or because it has always been done that way. But, as with many things of this nature, if they seek first to do the true and right thing, many other things may be added to them, not least of which will be a distinctness, a character, a descriptness or soul that will serve us well in the tough times ahead.

Robert Benne is the Jordan-Trexler Professor and Chair of the Department of Religion and Philosophy, and the Director of the Center for Church and Society, all at Roanoke College.

Bibliography

Becker, Carl. L. *The Heavenly City of the Eighteenth Century Philosophers*. New Haven: Yale University Press, 1932.

Benne, Robert. *Ordinary Saints*. Fortress, 1988.

_____. *The Paradoxical Vision: Toward a Public Theology for the Twenty-first Century*. Minneapolis, MN: Fortress, 1995.

_____. "A Lutheran Vision/Version of Christian Humanism." *Lutheran Forum*, vol. 31, No. 3 (1997), 40-46.

Niebuhr, H. Richard. *Christ and Culture*. New York: Harper and Row, 1956.

Niebuhr, Reinhold. *An Interpretation of Christian Ethics*. New York: Meridian Books, 1956.

Notes

[1] A slightly abridged version of this paper (without all the footnotes) originally appeared in *Lutheran Forum*, vol. 31, No. 3 (1997), 40-46, and is reprinted here (with all footnotes) by kind permission of the author and *Lutheran Forum*.

[2] Drucker, *The Age of Social Transformation*, p. 68.

[3] Dehne, *A Look at the Future of the Private College*, pp. 4-5.

[4] *Policy Perspectives*, pp. 1-3.

[5] One could well argue that a college's strength of connection to its religious heritage is accurately marked by the presence or absence of continuing public discussion about the relevance of the college's religious heritage to its educational enterprise. If the question is never raised it is doubtful that there is much life left in the connection. The college's religious attachments simply do not matter enough to make a difference. Sadly enough, many church-related colleges, particularly those of mainstream Protestantism, fit such a description.

[6] Niebuhr, *An Interpretation of Christian Ethics.*

[7] Rev. Louis Smith (*Lutheran Forum*, May, 1995, p. 16) tells of a visit with his daughter to a Lutheran college for the purpose of exploring the possibility of attending it. The tour guide did not mention anything about the church-related character of the college, so when the pastor asked what difference it made for the college to be related to the ELCA, the guide said, "To tell the truth, I don't know. Maybe if you asked someone in the chapel over there they could tell you."

[8] Cf. Becker, *The Heavenly City of the Eighteenth Century Philosophers.*

[9] At our college we meet this attitude almost daily in the continuing criticism of how the Religion and Philosophy Department teaches a required general education course, "Values and the Responsible Life." Even in its developmental stage, the course was submitted to more scrutiny and monitoring than any other course being developed. Were they going to "impose" religious views on our students, the critics wondered. The course has now been going for four years and suspicions have not abated. In a recent assessment of the Gen Ed curriculum by outside evaluators, a significant cohort of faculty voiced their displeasure with the course. It was "Sunday school," proselytical, intellectually thin, and biased. There continue to be great fears that we are actually teaching normative Christian values in a church-related college! (We are, of course, but without coercion or narrowness, we think. We also teach "secular" moral theories.) Meanwhile, some of the complaining faculty teach from a strong feminist, multiculturalist, anti-religious, or politically liberal or conservative point of view. It seems that the missionaries are fighting over the same prospects—our students! What is hard to take is that many critics are not even aware of their own biases; they think they are teaching unvarnished truth. It can be much worse in public institutions. A friend of mine who teaches English at a nearby state university proposed an elective course with the word "Christian" in it. The house about fell down! It seems that Christianity has nothing to offer intellectual discourse, or what it does offer is very dangerous indeed!

[10] Dr. Benne gave a version of this paper during the inauguration activities for the new president of Concordia University Wisconsin in November 1997.—Ed.

[11] Niebuhr, H. Richard, *Christ and Culture.*

[12] *Ibid.*, 43.

[13] I have elaborated these themes in detail in my book, *The Paradoxical Vision: Toward a Public Theology for the Twenty-first Century* (Fortress, 1995). In that work I try to show how these Lutheran themes provide a

framework for the church's relation to the public world of politics. In many ways this essay is simply an effort to apply the same framework to another public realm, the realm of higher education.

[14] One would think that such inflated views of liberal education would be rare in the confused and chaotic world of college life. After all, most claims for worldly salvation have been imposed with great cost by utopian political movements. But when faith in the God-man (Christ) is lost, faith in the man-God (human achievement) fills the vacuum, even in the realm of church-related college education. In a recent lecture on the importance of the liberal arts given by a professor at our college, the theme was: "You shall know the truth, and the truth shall set you free." And the truth to which the professor was referring was certainly not the Christian Gospel. I fervently believe that a good liberal arts education brings a certain kind of liberation, but not the ultimate kind.

[15] It is important to emphasize that the Christian vision in its Lutheran interpretation is itself under constant critique and discussion from within. As in most religious traditions, there is theological strife. But the Lutheran theological heritage has a good deal of definition and coherence. Many of the themes elaborated above are held in common by serious Lutherans. But there is debate. The Lutheran vision is not one grand monolithic consensus that can be used to dominate other fields of knowledge and modes of inquiry. Humility is called for. But granting that, the Lutheran heritage is part of a living tradition that has brought our colleges into being and continues to claim an important part of their ongoing life. It certainly deserves a hearing.

[16] This autonomy is tentative in several ways. First, the Lutheran tradition honors an epistemological autonomy in the worldly or horizontal level. Reason and experience are generally trustworthy tools of knowing, although they too can become idolatrous and claim too much for themselves. This epistemological autonomy, however, is not an ontological autonomy. Reason and experience, and the world they explore, are creations of God. They do not stand independently of the divine reality. Second, reason and experience are given autonomy solely in the worldly or horizontal sphere. They are not tools of salvation; indeed, when they are used to try to raise us up to God they become idolatrous and dangerous to both our souls and the world. This conviction about the uselessness of reason as a tool of religious salvation lies behind Luther's famous remark that "reason is a whore."

[17] This vaunted Lutheran intellectual excellence was evident in the famed "evangelische Gymnasium" of Budapest, where Jewish families were fond of sending their brightest sons and daughters. Such Jewish luminaries as John

von Neumann, Leo Szilard, and Edward Teller were all students at the same time at that Lutheran high school.

[18] It is noteworthy that faculty from non-theological fields who propose comprehensive theories of life sometimes criticize theologians for partisan proselytizing. But theologians have just as much right to speak *for* their view of life as Darwinists, Marxists, or Freudians. As the theologian T. F. Torrance responded to a caution that theology must be taught "objectively" in a liberal arts school: "When I teach theology, I try to lay out the integrity and coherence of the Christian faith. I cannot guarantee you that no one will believe it." (As quoted by Louis Smith in *Lutheran Forum*, Pentecost, 1995, p. 17.) In truth, there is a wide continuum between coercive imposition, on the one hand, and perfect objectivity (if there is such a thing), on the other. Every teacher ought to be able sympathetically and intelligibly to portray many competing views. But it is certainly legitimate to commend one's own view, providing that one gives adequate reasons for it and that one allows students to opt for other views if they give adequate reasons for theirs. The most dangerous proselytizers are those who think their own partial views of the truth are complete and settled. They actually take points off for "errors."

[19] An exciting example of this kind of conversation emerged in an exchange I had with one of our mathematics professors who happens to be interested in chaos theory. He sent me an article from *The Scientific American*, "The Arithmetics of Mutual Help," June, 1995, pp. 76-81, that reported on a computer experiment by three scientists. The scientists were trying to discern which response-relations among persons and animals had the most survival value. They were using game theory to lay out the options in their inquiry into evolutionary biology. It turns out that the most effective strategy is a "tit-for-tat" response to each other. Pure selfishness or pure altruism did not have much survival value. But "tit-for-tat" had serious problems if the logic of positive relations were interrupted by a nasty act. Then "tit-for-tat" meant eternal recrimination. So "tit-for-tat" had to be supplemented by what the authors called "gracious tit-for-tat," which was able to forgive and forget. This was all very exciting to me as a theological ethicist, because it bears out theological claims which contend that mutuality is the God-given logic of human relationships; it is a part of "natural law." But sin interrupts these mutual relations and they have to be repaired by forgiveness, which assumes a certain kind of grace. The authors ended their article by marveling about this formal logic that seems to govern the process of evolution. Indeed, their last sentence was: "In a sense, cooperation could be older than life itself." This, I suggested to my mathematician friend, certainly suggests the Trinity as an ontological ground for evolution. At any rate, this is the kind of conversation I

find exciting and very appropriate for a church-related liberal arts college. A Lutheran college encourages and is hospitable to such a conversation.

[20] I've sketched out a contemporary version of the Lutheran idea of the calling in a book aptly titled *Ordinary Saints*, Fortress, 1988. Worldly excellence in one's place of responsibility—family, work, citizenship, state—is an essential first step in exercising one's calling.

[21] These Lutheran intellectuals may reside in any number of departments, but it is certainly necessary that a number occupy important positions in the religion or theology department. It is not difficult to find such persons for the religion or theology department, given the propensity for Lutherans to study theology and given the buyers' market on the recruitment side of things. At Roanoke we are involved in endowing a Lutheran chair of studies. Such an endowed chair would insure that a Lutheran intellectual would always have a prominent place in the Religion and Philosophy Department. The religion department need not be exclusively Lutheran or even Christian, but there must be enough competent Lutheran theologians (in the broad sense) in the department in order for it to fulfill its calling as the trustee of the Lutheran voice in the ongoing